# BOOK PUBLISHING 101

## Inside Information to Getting Your First Book or Novel Published

### Martha Maeda

# BOOK PUBLISHING 101: INSIDE INFORMATION TO GETTING YOUR FIRST BOOK OR NOVEL PUBLISHED

Copyright © 2014 Atlantic Publishing Group, Inc.
1405 SW 6th Avenue • Ocala, Florida 34471 • Phone 800-814-1132 • Fax 352-622-1875
Website: www.atlantic-pub.com • Email: sales@atlantic-pub.com
SAN Number: 268-1250

Library of Congress Cataloging-in-Publication Data

Maeda, Martha, 1953-
Book publishing 101 : inside information to getting your first book or novel published / by Martha Maeda.
pages cm
Includes bibliographical references and index.
ISBN 978-1-60138-564-2 -- ISBN 1-60138-564-1 1. Authorship. 2. Authorship--Marketing. 3. Authors and publishers. 4. Publishers and publishing. I. Title.
PN151.M273 2012
808.02--dc23

2011046663

INTERIOR LAYOUT: Antoinette D'Amore • addesign@videotron.ca
JACKET DESIGN: Jackie Miller • sullmill@charter.net

Printed on Recycled Paper

Printed in the United States

A few years back we lost our beloved pet dog Bear, who was not only our best and dearest friend but also the "Vice President of Sunshine" here at Atlantic Publishing. He did not receive a salary but worked tirelessly 24 hours a day to please his parents.

Bear was a rescue dog who turned around and showered myself, my wife, Sherri, his grandparents Jean, Bob, and Nancy, and every person and animal he met (well, maybe not rabbits) with friendship and love. He made a lot of people smile every day.

We wanted you to know a portion of the profits of this book will be donated in Bear's memory to local animal shelters, parks, conservation organizations, and other individuals and nonprofit organizations in need of assistance.

*– Douglas & Sherri Brown*

PS: We have since adopted two more rescue dogs: first Scout, and the following year, Ginger. They were both mixed golden retrievers who needed a home.

Want to help animals and the world? Here are a dozen easy suggestions you and your family can implement today:

- *Adopt and rescue a pet from a local shelter.*
- *Support local and no-kill animal shelters.*
- *Plant a tree to honor someone you love.*
- *Be a developer — put up some birdhouses.*
- *Buy live, potted Christmas trees and replant them.*
- *Make sure you spend time with your animals each day.*
- *Save natural resources by recycling and buying recycled products.*
- *Drink tap water, or filter your own water at home.*
- *Whenever possible, limit your use of or do not use pesticides.*
- *If you eat seafood, make sustainable choices.*
- *Support your local farmers market.*
- *Get outside. Visit a park, volunteer, walk your dog, or ride your bike.*

Five years ago, Atlantic Publishing signed the Green Press Initiative. These guidelines promote environmentally friendly practices, such as using recycled stock and vegetable-based inks, avoiding waste, choosing energy-efficient resources, and promoting a no-pulping policy. We now use 100-percent recycled stock on all our books. The results: in one year, switching to post-consumer recycled stock saved 24 mature trees, 5,000 gallons of water, the equivalent of the total energy used for one home in a year, and the equivalent of the greenhouse gases from one car driven for a year.

# Dedication

*Dedicated to all the writers and future writers
who enrich our lives and constantly expand our horizons
by sharing their knowledge, thoughts, and ideas in printed words.*

# Table of Contents

**Introduction**.................................................................................. **13**

**Chapter 1: The Business of Publishing**.................................................. **17**

The Process of Publishing ........................................................................18

A Brief History of Modern Book Publishing............................................19

*The paperback revolution* ...................................................................*21*

*The emergence of blockbusters*...........................................................*23*

*The impact of digital and the Internet* ..............................................*24*

Companies, Divisions, Houses, and Imprints .........................................26

*The Big Five* ......................................................................................*27*

Midsized Publishers, Small Presses, and University Presses .....................34

Some Facts About Book Sales ..................................................................35

**Chapter 2: What Are Your Options?** ..................................................... **39**

Conventional Publishing .........................................................................40

*Trade publishers*..................................................................................*40*

*Small and independent presses*...........................................................*41*

*Mass market* ......................................................................................*41*

Self-Publishing .......................................................................................45

Subsidy, Co-op, and Vanity Presses.........................................................46

*Vanity presses in disguise* ...................................................................*47*

*Choosing a publishing option for your book*........................................*48*

**Chapter 3: Creating a Book That Will Sell** ........................................... **51**

Assessing Your Market ............................................................................52

*How large is the potential audience for your book?*......................53
*Does a nearly identical book already exist?* ................................53
*How will you communicate with your market?*............................53
*Popular trends*..................................................................................54
*Timeliness and relevance*..............................................................54
*Seasonal publishing*......................................................................55
Case Study: Writing a Book That Will Sell .................................56
Understanding Your Genre.............................................................57
*Literary fiction*...............................................................................58
*Genre fiction*..................................................................................59
*Nonfiction* ......................................................................................63
*Narrative nonfiction*.....................................................................66
The Quality of Your Writing..........................................................71
*Beta readers and critique partners* .............................................72
*Editing and proofreading*.............................................................74
Case Study: What an Editor Can Do for You .............................76
*Story checklist for fiction books* ...................................................78
*Checklist for nonfiction books* .....................................................79
*Finding and working with a ghostwriter*......................................80

**Chapter 4: Traditional Publishing** .................................**83**
How Traditional Publishing Works.............................................83
Finding a Publishing House .........................................................85
*Get organized* ................................................................................87
Publishing Nonfiction ..................................................................88
*Your platform* ................................................................................89
*Securing rights* ..............................................................................90
Publishing Fiction .........................................................................92
*Dealing with rejection* .................................................................92
What to Expect When You Get a Book Deal...............................95

**Chapter 5: Writing a Good Query, Proposal,
and Cover Letter Traditional Publishing** ................**97**
The Four Elements of a Query Letter .........................................98
Email and Snail Mail.....................................................................100
Case Study: How I Write a Synopsis...........................................101
Email and Query Etiquette...........................................................102

Book Proposals and Manuscript Submissions ............................................105
  *Nonfiction book proposal* ................................................................*105*
  *Fiction proposal* ...............................................................................*109*
Formatting Your Fiction Manuscript .......................................................111
  *Packaging your manuscript for submission by mail* .......................*114*
Children's Books..........................................................................................114
  *Storyboards*........................................................................................*115*
  *Dummy books*.....................................................................................*116*
If You Have Already Self-Published Your Book .......................................118
Your Manuscript on the Other Side..........................................................119

**Chapter 6: Working with a Literary Agent**...................................... **121**
Do You Need an Agent? .............................................................................122
How to Find Reputable Agents..................................................................125
Case Study: How I Acquired My Agent....................................................126
Agent Queries and Pitch Packages ...........................................................130
Your Pitch Package .....................................................................................132
Simultaneous Submissions.........................................................................135
Exclusive Reads ...........................................................................................135
  *When an agent requests revisions* ..................................................*136*
  *The author-agent agreement*............................................................*136*
  *How to protect yourself*....................................................................*138*
Case Study: Expert Advice From Literary Agent ....................................139
Selling the Book .........................................................................................141
Developing a Good Working Relationship with Your Agent....................144
  *When and how to end a relationship with an agent*.......................*145*

**Chapter 7: How to Read a Publishing Contract**.................................**147**
Grant of Rights ...........................................................................................149
  *Term*....................................................................................................*149*
  *Representations and warranties* .....................................................*150*
  *Manuscript delivery and acceptance* ..............................................*150*
  *Indexing*..............................................................................................*151*
  *Publication*..........................................................................................*151*
  *Editing and proofreading* ................................................................*152*
  *Copyright* ............................................................................................*152*

*Royalties* ........................................................................................ *152*

The Advance ...................................................................................... 153

Statements, Payments, and Accounting ................................................ 155

Subsidiary Rights ............................................................................... 155

Revisions and Updated Editions .......................................................... 157

Author Copies .................................................................................... 158

Additional Books and Options ............................................................ 158

Copyright Infringement ..................................................................... 159

Noncompete Clause ........................................................................... 160

Termination of Contract and Reversion of Rights ............................... 160

Bankruptcy ........................................................................................ 160

Miscellaneous .................................................................................... 161

Collaborations and Co-authors ........................................................... 162

**Chapter 8: Self-Publishing** .......................................................... **165**

Why Self-Publishing? ........................................................................ 166

Why Not Self-Publish? ....................................................................... 167

Producing Your Book ......................................................................... 169

Case Study: Advice from a Print-On-Demand Company ...................... 171

Finding a Printer ................................................................................ 173

*Types of printing services* ................................................................. *173*

Deciding How Many Books to Order ................................................... 176

Getting Quotes .................................................................................. 177

Trim Size and Number of Pages .......................................................... 178

Book Covers ...................................................................................... 179

Determining the Price of Your Book .................................................... 179

ISBNs and Bar Codes ......................................................................... 180

Case Study: Office Manager at a Book Publishing Company ................ 181

Publisher Filings ................................................................................ 183

*Library of Congress Control Numbers (LCCN and PCN)* .................... *183*

*Cataloging in Publication Record (CIP data)* .................................... *184*

*Standard Address Number (SAN)* ..................................................... *184*

*Advance Book Information (ABI)* ...................................................... *185*

Distribution ...................................................................................... 185

*Distribution outlets* ......................................................................... *185*

Case Study: The Logistics of Distribution at a Publishing House .............187

*Shipping and order fulfillment* ...............................................................*189*

**Chapter 9: Designing Your Book** ...........................................................**191**

Case Study: Book Design ......................................................................192

Design Your Book from the Beginning......................................................194

Formatting Your Book............................................................................195

Formatting a Book in Microsoft° Word......................................................197

*Photos and illustrations* ........................................................................*198*

*Converting a document to a PDF file* ......................................................*199*

Book Interior........................................................................................199

*Front matter* ......................................................................................*199*

*Back matter* .......................................................................................*200*

Cover ..................................................................................................201

**Chapter 10: Building Your Platform**......................................................**205**

Social Media.........................................................................................206

*Blogs* ................................................................................................*211*

Writing Articles for Newspapers and Magazines .......................................213

Author Profile Pages ............................................................................214

Participate in an Author's Group ............................................................214

Monitoring Your Online Presence ...........................................................215

Your Author Website .............................................................................216

*Planning your website* .........................................................................*218*

**Chapter 11: Marketing and Publicity** ...................................................**225**

Create a Media Portfolio and a Promotions File.........................................226

Set a Publication Date ...........................................................................227

Book Reviews ......................................................................................227

Paid Book Reviews ...............................................................................229

Directory Listings..................................................................................230

Press Releases ......................................................................................231

Radio and Television Interviews...............................................................234

Advertising ..........................................................................................236

Business Cards and Email Signatures........................................................236

Book Publicists.....................................................................................237

Book Signings ............................................................................237

Book Tours ................................................................................238

**Chapter 12: E-Books** ....................................................... **241**

Case Study: Cozy-Mystery Writer Successful in Kindle Publishing ..............242

How to Sell Your Book as an E-Book .........................................243

E-Book Cover Images ..................................................................245

ISBN Numbers ..........................................................................245

Formatting Your E-Book .............................................................246

Electronically Publishing Through Amazon* ................................247

Selecting a Price ........................................................................248

*Promotion tips* ........................................................................*248*

Case Study: Indie Writer Goes the Way of the ePublisher ...........249

**Chapter 13: Copyright Law and Plagiarism** ..................... **253**

Copyright Notice .......................................................................253

Duration of Copyright ...............................................................254

Copyright Registration ...............................................................254

Filing an Original Claim to Copyright with the U.S. Copyright Office ........255

*Online registration* ..................................................................*256*

*Registration with fill-in Form CO* ............................................*256*

*Registration with paper forms* ..................................................*257*

Copyright Infringement and Plagiarism .....................................257

*Public domain* .........................................................................*258*

*Music and song lyrics* ...............................................................*259*

*Images* ....................................................................................*259*

**Chapter 14: Business and Taxes** ..................................... **261**

Hobby or Business? ....................................................................261

Recordkeeping ...........................................................................263

Establishing Your Business ..........................................................264

*Choosing a business name* ........................................................*265*

Business Registration ..................................................................266

Get a Post Office Box .................................................................267

Standard and Itemized Tax Deductions ......................................267

Business Expenses ......................................................................268

*What you cannot deduct* ...................................................................*268*

Business Use of Your Home ...........................................................269

*Figuring the deduction* ............................................................*271*

*Making the most of your home office deductions* ....................*272*

Self-employment Tax .....................................................................273

*How to pay self-employment tax* ............................................*273*

*Calculating your net earnings* ...............................................*274*

Quarterly Estimated Tax Payments ............................................274

Sales Tax .........................................................................................276

*How to collect and record sales tax* .......................................*277*

**Conclusion: The Future of Publishing** ......................................... **279**

**Appendix A: Further Reading** ...................................................... **283**

Associations ....................................................................................283

Big Six Publishers ..........................................................................284

Blog Sites and Author Groups .....................................................285

*Blog tracking* ...........................................................................*285*

Book Design ...................................................................................285

Bookkeeping ..................................................................................286

Business and Taxes ........................................................................286

Cell Phone Novels .........................................................................287

Copyright and Public Domain ....................................................287

Data Storage ..................................................................................287

Directories ......................................................................................287

E-books ...........................................................................................288

Editing ............................................................................................288

Forums and Communities ...........................................................288

Freelancers .....................................................................................288

History ............................................................................................289

Images and Graphics ....................................................................289

Legal Documents and Contracts .................................................289

Legal Information ..........................................................................289

Literary Agents ..............................................................................290

Logo Design ...................................................................................290

News and Blogs.................................................................291

POD .................................................................................291

Poetry.............................................................................291

Printers ..........................................................................291

Publishers.......................................................................292

Research and Education ...................................................292

Sales Tax.........................................................................293

Self-Employment Tax .....................................................293

Social Media ...................................................................293

Website ...........................................................................293

Writing a Synopsis ..........................................................294

**Appendix B: Sample Documents............................. 295**

Sample Query Letter .......................................................295

Sample Cover Letter — When You Are Unpublished ......297

Sample Cover Letter — When You Are Published ...........298

Sample Proposal ..............................................................299

Sample Overview.............................................................300

Sample Author Flier ........................................................301

Sample Book Flier ...........................................................302

Sample Review Query ......................................................303

Sample Review Slip .........................................................304

Sample Press Release........................................................305

Sample Author-Agent Contract.......................................307

Sample Consent Form......................................................314

**Appendix C: Glossary........................................... 315**

**Appendix D: Genre Definitions.............................. 319**

**Bibliography ...................................................... 327**

**Author Biography .............................................. 331**

**Index................................................................. 333**

# Introduction

D o you fall asleep every night composing the opening lines of your next chapter? Do you believe you have a unique story that would captivate millions of readers if you could just find a publisher? Whether you aspire to become the next J. K. Rowling, James Patterson, or Stephen King, selling millions of copies of your books and spinning off movie scripts and merchandise franchises, or you want to share your memoirs with a few family members, this book will help you get started.

Publishing is more than getting a book into print. It is a business model that turns the creative work of an author into a marketable product and sells it to as many readers as possible to make a profit. Experienced writers know that to succeed, they must think of the readers who are going to buy their books even before they begin to write and work hard to draw attention to their books. First-time authors often have unrealistic expectations and romantic notions about what happens when a book is published. This book will strip away some of the mystery and give you a whirlwind tour of the publishing industry. It will explain how the publishing industry operates and what your options are, and it will take you through each step of producing, publishing, and marketing your book. The reality is, in many ways, more exciting than the myths and certainly far more challenging.

There are as many reasons for writing a book as there are for reading one. Most people think books are written to showcase an author's creativity and literary genius, but if you consider the last five books you picked up, chances are that four of them were not literature, but textbooks, self-help guides, cookbooks, instructional manuals, or factual accounts of political or historical events. We read not only to entertain ourselves but also to inform ourselves. Some writers produce enduring literary works, but many want to pass on practical knowledge, educate the public about current issues, or share thoughts and ideas. A writer believes what he or she has to say is important to somebody, somewhere. This book will show you how to select subject matter that is sure to attract readers and how to plan a writing career that will extend far beyond your first book.

Learn how to copyright your work and protect your intellectual property, how to write a query and prepare a manuscript for submission to a publisher, how to produce and publish your own book, and how to market and sell your book once it is in print. Determine whether you need a literary agent or an editor and how to find one that is both reliable and affordable. Set up your website and create an online personality to help promote and sell your book. Use Twitter', Facebook', blogs, and social networking to build an audience.

New technology has brought about unprecedented changes in conventional publishing during the last decade. Although the traditional publishing industry is still going strong, computer technology and the Internet have changed self-publishing forever with affordable on-demand printing that allows copies of books to be printed only when they are ordered. As a result, the number of new titles appearing on the market each year has exploded since 2007. Many traditional publishers have opened their own self-publishing branches. Self-published books, once scorned by bookstores and book reviewers, are now respected as a source of new talent and new ideas. During the last decade, new opportunities have emerged for would-be authors to publish and sell their own books online, bypassing traditional publishers altogether.

In 2010, Amazon reported, for the first time in history, that it had sold more electronic books than printed books. The Kindle˚, the Nook˚, and the iPad have revolutionized not only the way people read books, but the way they buy them. New developments are occurring so fast, it is hard to keep up. Your book idea might be a candidate for electronic publishing as an e-book or even an iPhone application. New forms of writing, such as blogging and text messaging, are a potential arena for authors who want to sell themselves or write for specialized audiences. The last chapters of this book review the latest developments in the publishing industry and show how flexibility and innovation can help you stay on top of a rapidly changing business model.

Every aspect of publishing cannot be covered in detail in one book. Each chapter of this book tells you where you can find additional information on topics that might be of special interest to you. Appendix A, Further Reading, lists books and websites where you can learn more about the topics introduced in each chapter.

Every book is unique, and no one publishing model will succeed for every author. You must develop your own strategy for getting your book published, and for selling it. When you reach the end of this book, you will be well on your way to becoming a published author.

## Chapter 1

# The Business of Publishing

Writing is a creative art — publishing is a business. A first-time author and a publisher perceive the same book very differently. The author seeks public recognition and an income, while a publisher sees the book primarily as a business investment. No matter how brilliant and interesting a manuscript may be, the publisher will not want to invest in it unless there is a strong possibility of making a profit. The publisher considers a number of factors besides literary merit when evaluating a manuscript's potential. Is there a large audience for this book? Is the author already in the public eye or actively working to promote and sell the book? Is the topic of the book attracting current interest in the media? Are similar books already on the market? Is this book a good fit for the publisher? Will this book advance the publisher's reputation in a particular genre?

Many novice writers do not realize how much time and effort has to be invested in marketing a book. Authors must involve themselves actively in promoting their books and be willing to take advice and direction from the publisher. When you understand what publishers and readers expect from you, you automatically will write in a way that fulfills those expectations.

Even as you read this book, the publishing industry is undergoing a transformation. In just a few years, the Internet dramatically has altered business models that remained relatively unchanged for more than 200 years. The activities of writers are evolving along with the ways in which people access information and read books. A historical and practical understanding of the role of writers in today's society will help you keep up with these changes. Always be open to ideas, be aware of the new technologies being adapted by your readers, and be alert for trends as they emerge. Flexible and innovative authors can succeed by learning to express themselves using new forms of media and by being sensitive to the needs and interests of their readers.

Whether you are seeking a publisher for your book or planning to self-publish, your chances of success are greater if you understand the publishing industry well. Immerse yourself in your genre and learn as much as you can about the publishers who specialize in it. Visit bookstores and libraries to see how books are displayed, marketed, and read. Pick up books similar to yours, and find out what company published them, how they are designed and formatted, and what features are attractive. Visit the publishers' websites, study their new releases and events calendars, and read book reviews and interviews with authors and industry professionals. *Appendix A, Further Reading, lists many helpful websites and resources.*

## The Process of Publishing

A writer creates original material; a publisher turns that material into a money-making proposition by mass-producing it in a form that will appeal to the public and bringing it to market. A publisher orchestrates a number of processes, some of which may be performed by third parties. The writer's original manuscript is polished and perfected by one or more editors. Artists and designers create a cover

for the book and decide how the finished book should look, including its size and the type of paper to be used. A graphic designer makes a layout of the text so that it is visually appealing and meets the requirements of the printer. The layout goes to a printer who produces multiple copies of the book. Then a logistics specialist organizes the storage and delivery of the finished books to distribution outlets and buyers. The book will not sell if its target audience does not see it, so the publisher plans and executes an aggressive marketing campaign, in which the writer often collaborates, to promote the book.

The process does not end there. Unsold books returned by bookstores and retail outlets must be processed and/or disposed of. A legal team negotiates contracts, protects copyrights, and defends against legal challenges. A successful book may generate a sequel, a movie, TV show, or comic book series. In today's digital world, the book also will be published as an e-book, an audio book, and might have interactive tie-ins with blogs, online games, Facebook, or Twitter. A successful author must continue to develop his or her public image, engage with readers, and produce new material of similar or better quality.

Large publishing companies perform many of these functions in-house and maintain large staffs of experienced specialists. Medium and small-sized publishers contract much of the work of producing books to third-party service providers and focus on author development and marketing. A self-published author typically works with a publishing company that provides printing and distribution services and might hire independent contractors to do the editing, book design, layout, and, sometimes, the marketing.

# A Brief History of Modern Book Publishing

The development of the modern publishing industry was fueled by technology that allowed mass production of printed books and the rise of literate classes demanding information and entertainment. Until around 1439, when Johannes Gutenberg invented a printing press using a winepress and movable type, books were copied by hand and were owned by churches, monasteries, and wealthy families. Most books were copied on animal vellum (usually treated calfskin). The concept of paper, a much more suitable material for mechanical printing presses, was imported from Asia, where books were printed using hand-carved wood blocks. By 1500, 1,000 printing shops in Europe had produced 35,000 titles and 20 million copies. The Frankfurt Book Fair, today the world's largest trade fair for books, originated during the 1400s as a medieval fair where booksellers and printers could display their wares and buy the supplies they needed for their print shops.

The growth of cities and expansion of international trade led to the emergence of a prosperous merchant class that sought education and bought books. Printed books had a powerful impact on European thought and culture, challenging the authority of the Roman Catholic Church, facilitating the development and spread of scientific theories, and rapidly re-introducing ideas from early Greek and Roman manuscripts. Books on science, medicine, and philosophy replaced the religious subject matter of medieval books, and the public began to read prose for entertainment.

Until the 19th century, multiple pages of a book were printed on one side of a large sheet of paper, a configuration called an "imposition." The large paper then was folded in half (folio), fourths (quarto) or eighths (octavo). The right page was called "recto" and the left page, "verso." Each folded unit was called a "signature." Customers would buy a book as a packaged stack of signatures and take it to a bookbinder to be stitched, bound, and covered according to the buyer's personal preferences. Early in the 19th century, large publishing houses and commercial bookbinders began to replace individual printer/booksellers. In the U.S., publishing firms such as Cummings & Hilliard in Boston, J. & J. Harpers in New York, and Mathew Carey and Son in Philadelphia were established, as the spread of literacy increased the demand for books. These larger publishers sought a cheaper, faster alternative to the tedious process of hand-binding books in leather covers. A radical development took place in 1825, when British publisher William Pickering used cloth bindings on a production run of his Diamond Classic series. Pressed cloth book covers came into use in the U.S. in 1831. At first covers were designed by the craftsmen who produced them, but by the end of the century, professional designers such as Sarah Whitman and Margaret Armstrong created elegant, easily reproduced designs, and publishing houses developed distinct trademarks and cover styles.

The invention of the linotype by Ottmar Mergenthaler in 1886 transformed the printing industry by enabling one machine operator to do the work of ten hand typesetters, inputting with a keyboard to set complete lines of type. In 1952, *The Wonderful World of Insects* was the first book to be printed using phototypesetting. Photosensitive paper was exposed to light to create lines of black text that were then cut apart and "pasted up," after which a large film negative was shot of each page to produce a printing plate. Phototypesetting soon replaced continuous casting machines but was rendered obsolete 20 years later by fully digital systems that can render an entire page as a single high-resolution digital image, through a process known as imagesetting. Technology introduced during the 1960s also began to empower individuals to reproduce their own printed materials. The first Xerox machine appeared in 1961, to be followed by photocopiers, fax machines, and personal computers. Desktop publishing software became available in the 1980s, along with word processing software that automated the inclusion of features such as footnotes and a table of contents in a document.

# The paperback revolution

Another revolution in modern publishing was the paperback book, which went through several evolutions before becoming the versions that fill bookstore shelves today. The first "paperbacks" in the U.S. were sold by mail order to settlers in rural and backwoods areas. These were printed in newspaper format to circumvent the higher postage rates for books. Books by European authors such as Dickens were printed because publishers did not have to pay royalties on foreign works, but American authors including Washington Irving, Nathaniel Hawthorne, Fenimore Cooper, and Edgar Allan Poe also got public exposure through these "paperback books."

The availability of cheap paper, along with the opening of railway lines to the West, triggered a proliferation of "railroad literature," inexpensive disposable paper books that were sold on newsstands, in train stations, and general stores. In 1860, Beadle Books began churning out "dime novels" written by teams of hack writers. The onset of the Civil War created a new market for cheap books among soldiers, and competition flourished. During the 1870s, newspapers and traditional publishers began producing paperbound versions of better literature. Nearly a third of the 4,500 titles published in America in 1885 were paperbacks.

The paperback business in the U.S. floundered in 1891, when Frank Munsey, publisher of the youth magazine *Argosy*, began publishing pulp fiction magazines using a newly invented, very cheap pulp paper. These magazines sold for five cents — half the price of a paperback novel — and contained not only full-length novels but also short stories and other features. At the same time, traditional publishing houses began publishing inexpensive hardcover books using the same cheap paper, which the reading public seemed to prefer to paperbacks.

## Paperback Wars

The first paperback books to come on the market were looked down on by traditional publishing houses, which regarded them as being for the uncultured and poorly educated. Nevertheless, their popularity soon posed a threat to publishers of hardcover books. On more than one occasion, the large publishing houses appealed to the U.S. Congress to put a stop to the paperback revolution.

In 1843, regular book publishers allied with preachers and citizens concerned about the racy content of paperbound books and appealed for legislation to outlaw them. As a result, Congress increased postal rates for all publications with book inserts and for paperbound books. The mail-order paperback book businesses disappeared within a year.

In 1891, Congress passed the International Copyright Law requiring publishers to pay royalties to foreign authors. Paperback publishers were unable to pay royalties and still keep the price of their books under five cents, and many went out of business.

In 1952, E. C. Gathings convened hearings by a special committee of the House of Representatives, the Select Committee on Current Pornographic Materials to investigate charges that "immoral, obscene and otherwise offensive" publications, including gory comic books and pulp novels with sexually suggestive cover art violated pornography laws. The committee deliberated for a week, reached no conclusions, and recommended no legislation, but they did charge that comic books inspired juvenile crime. The Committee concluded that "... pocket-size books, which originally started out as cheap reprints of standard works, have largely degenerated into media for the dissemination of artful appeals to sensuality, immorality, filth, perversion, and degeneracy."

In 1931, German entrepreneur Kurt Enoch bought out the publisher Tachnitz, which had been publishing limited runs of paperbound literary classics since 1845, and established Albatross Books, whose dignified paperback books were a success in London. Allan Lane, president of Bodley Head Publishing House in the U.K., observed the success of Albatross and established Penguin Books. He arranged with the retailer F.W. Woolworth to place ten literature titles in its department stores. The first run sold out in two days. In the U.S., Robert Fair deGraff noted Penguin's success and approached Simon & Schuster with the idea of a paperback line to be called "Pocket Books." To lower the price, he cut the size of the book to 6.5 x 4.5 and used a newly invented glue instead of stitching for the binding. His first press run, ten times larger than Penguin's, sold out in 24 hours in Macy's and Liggett's Department Stores. American Penguin and Bantam Books soon followed, as pulp magazines rapidly switched over to paperback novels.

World War II ensured a permanent market for paperback books. Sixteen million soldiers had an insatiable appetite for books that they could carry in their pockets and read during moments of leisure. Friends and relatives were able to mail a paperback book to a serviceman or servicewoman anywhere in the U.S. by putting a 3-cent stamp on it and dropping it in a mailbox. For soldiers, sailors and marines deployed on active duty, Armed Services Editions printed 1,322 numbered editions, which were distributed free, including some anthologies that it compiled from poetry and war stories serialized in newspapers and magazines.

Today, about 80 percent of the books purchased in the U.S. are paperbacks, which are sold in more than 80,000 outlets. Fiction typically is released first as a hardcover book, supported by massive advertising, because the publisher makes more profit from the sale of a hardcover book. Six months to a year later, when hardcover sales have dwindled, the book is released as a trade paperback for readers who do not want to pay the higher price of a hardcover book. After that, it is released again as a cheaper mass-market paperback. Mass-market books and books on quickly outdated topics, such as technology, science, politics, and health, often are released entirely in paperback.

## The emergence of blockbusters

During the 1980s, media corporations expanded by buying up both established publishing houses and smaller presses. The managers of the new conglomerates, seeking ways to increase publishing's relatively low profit margins, began marketing mass-market fiction as more expensive hardbacks. At the same time, the bookstore chains that were taking over the market from independent booksellers used their leverage to demand wholesale discounts and charge fees for favorable placement on their shelves. Stores such as Costco and Walmart began selling large quantities of books by a few selected authors at deeply discounted prices. Under all these financial pressures, publishers became less willing to take chances on unknown authors. They began investing most of their resources in promoting sales of books by a few established authors, paying for massive publicity campaigns and prime placement in the front of large chain bookstores. With all the attention they received, these books sold in unprecedented

numbers and became blockbusters. While these books achieved commercial success, many other new releases languished unnoticed on bookstore shelves.

## The impact of digital and the Internet

In addition to fast and accurate typesetting, digital technology brought about another revolution in printing, the print-on-demand (POD) industry, in which books can be printed in small quantities as they are ordered. POD allows small runs to be printed economically, eliminates the need to keep large inventories in stock, and avoids sinking money into large press runs of books that might not sell. POD companies serve traditional publishers as well as individual authors who want to self-publish and promote their own books. *Learn more about POD in Chapter 8.*

During the 1990s, the Internet began to change the way in which books were sold. Instead of browsing the shelves in bookstores such as Borders, Waldenbooks, and B. Dalton, readers began browsing the catalogs of online book retailers such as Amazon (**www.amazon.com**) and Alibris" (**www.alibris.com**) and ordering books by mail order. Online booksellers were able to offer a wider selection of books and service the entire country from a few central warehouses. Readers were able to see all the books on a particular topic or by a favorite author at a glance. In addition, online booksellers made it possible for individuals and used book dealers to sell their used books in competition with new books, creating a secondary market. Even recently published books are sold as used books at much lower prices side-by-side with their new counterparts, and students and readers are no longer forced to pay high list prices for the books they need. Readers searching for out-of-print books can find them easily and purchase them directly from their owners. Amazon led the way in attempting to capture the experience of shopping in a "bricks and mortar" bookstore online by allowing prospective buyers to "look inside" a book and read sample pages, and by suggesting other books based on the buyer's preferences. Traditional bookstores were forced to adapt their business models and strive to create an enhanced shopping experience by adding coffee bars, cultural events, and listening rooms to draw customers into their stores. While mall bookstores Borders, Waldenbooks, and B. Dalton did not survive, Barnes & Noble, creator of the Nook, is largest book retailer in the U.S.

E-books first appeared in the 1970s as PDF files of printed manuscripts or simple word documents that could be downloaded and printed, or opened and read online. In 1998, libraries began to offer access to e-books through NetLibrary (now OCLC'). In 2001, major publishers and booksellers began to develop business models for selling e-books and partnered with electronics companies to produce high-quality e-book readers. By 2010, sales of e-books had exploded and completely digital publishing houses were emerging. The concept of books that do not have to be printed or shipped opened new possibilities for authors and readers. *See Chapter 12 for information about e-book publishing.*

## James Patterson: Publishing Superstar

James Patterson's first thriller, *The Thomas Berryman Number* (1976) was rejected 26 times before it was published by Little, Brown and Company (now a unit of Hachette Book Group). The book sold 10,000 copies and received the Edgar Award for Best First Novel in 1977. In 2009, *Forbes* magazine estimated his net worth as $150 million, and in 2010, he published 20 best-sellers. According to Nielsen BookScan, in recent years, Patterson has sold more books than Stephen King, John Grisham, and Dan Brown combined. Since 2006, Patterson has been the author of one out of every 17 novels bought in the United States. He holds the Guinness World Record™ for the author with the most *New York Times* best-sellers, 51, with 35 reaching No. 1.

Patterson's success has served as a catalyst to transform the publishing industry. Until the 1990s, the concept of mass-marketing authors and publishing mass-market books in hardback was alien to most publishing houses. At that time, bookstores actively promoted books that were already best-sellers. For the release of his breakthrough novel, *Along Came a Spider*, in 1993, Patterson, then working as an advertising executive at J. Walter Thompson, wanted to run a TV commercial promoting the book. When Little, Brown balked, he produced the commercial himself. After viewing it, Little, Brown agreed to pay to run it in several key markets. When the book hit the stores, it went immediately to No. 9 on the *New York Times* hardback best-seller list, ensuring it prime placement in bookstores and further increasing sales until it reached No. 2.

Patterson focuses on a product that will sell to large numbers of people. He turned the main character of *Along Came a Spider* into a franchise, with catchy titles and a uniform jacket style. He invested in advertising and book tours in the cities where his books were selling best. To attract West Coast readers, he began a new series set in San Francisco, "The Women's Murder Club." Publishers thought that authors releasing more than one book in a year would hurt their own sales; Patterson releases more than nine hardcover books a year and all of them do well. Each book is published several times, first as a hardback, then as a traditional paperback and finally as a mass-market paperback. Most of his books are written with cowriters who contribute their own expertise; Patterson outlines the book and the cowriters flesh out the chapters.

Patterson is committed to motivating people to read. When he observed his own son's reluctance to read, he entered the young adult fiction genre to write books that are fun and easy to read. His first young adult title, *Maximum Ride: The Angel Experiment*, published in 2005, made its debut at No. 1 on the *New York Times* best-seller list for children's chapter books. His website, **ReadKiddoRead.com**, helps parents choose books their children will enjoy.

According to Forbes magazine, Patterson earned Hachette about $500 million in 2008 and 2009. In addition to two editors, three Hachette employees and their assistants work full-time on producing and selling Patterson's books. Patterson himself takes an active role in the publication and marketing of his books. Hachette Group now hosts several successful publishing franchises modeled on Patterson's, including novelists Nicholas Sparks and Stephenie Meyer (author of the *Twilight* vampire series), and best-selling authors such as Sandra Brown and Nelson DeMille.

## Companies, Divisions, Houses, and Imprints

The largest publishing companies in the U.S. are concentrated in New York City, though publishing businesses of various sizes, from corporations to small family-operated presses, are scattered all over the country. During the last three decades, as in other media industries, publishing houses have undergone acquisitions and mergers with larger companies to form megapublishers (see *The Big Six* below).

*A press operator examines a newly made book while the presses run behind him. Photo courtesy of Rose Printing Company*

Larger publishers have what are known as "imprints." An imprint is a specialized subdivision of a publishing house that focuses on a specific market and often carries a unique brand. An imprint is sometimes named after a well-established editor (such as Joanna Cotler Books at HarperCollins), employs editorial staff, and sometimes marketing personnel, who are particular to that imprint. Many imprints retain the names of smaller companies that were acquired by the larger company over the years. The *Writer's Market* lists imprints by publisher. You can find an extensive list of imprints on the website of the AccessTextNetwork, a joint venture with the American Publishers Association (**www.publisherlookup.org**).

A division is a group of imprints in a publishing house that form a department, such as adult fiction, inspirational books, technical manuals, or children's books. For example, Macmillan's education division comprises four imprints and publishing lines, including Worth Publishers, W.H. Freeman & Company, Bedford/St. Martin's, and BFW High School. Worth Publishers publishes college textbooks for the social sciences. Bedford/St. Martin's publishes texts and media for students on English, history, communication, music, and college success. W.H. Freeman publishes academic books in the sciences.

A line is part of an imprint and might include a series of books by the same author or with a similar purpose or theme. Books in a series are issued as new titles once a month or several times per year. A line can comprise several series, and several lines can fall under one imprint. Simon & Schuster's Aladdin Paperbacks is aimed at readers aged 4 to 12 and is primarily a reprint list from other (hardcover) imprints. The Little Simon imprint specializes in books for young children including classic titles such as *Cloudy with a Chance of Meatballs* and *Orange, Pear, Apple, Bear.*

## The Big Five

The largest North American publishing houses referred to as "the Big Six" officially became the Big Five with the July 2013 merger of Penguin Books and Random House. The Big Five are megacorporations that collectively control approximately two thirds of the consumer book market publishing in the U.S. according to the ALA website. and a large portion of international publishing through their branches and affiliates. Each of the Big Five publishing houses has offices in New York City. Through their distribution networks, these publishing houses control much of what you see in the "new release" sections of bookstores.

The Big Five accept manuscripts for review only from acknowledged literary agents. If your book is accepted for publishing by one of the Big Five imprints, you can be assured that the finished product will meet the highest standards of quality. Books are selected for publication only if the publishers believe they can sell thousands of copies. Large publishing houses have the staff and the resources to launch massive promotional campaigns and distribution networks that land a new release in retail outlets all over the country on the same day.

Each of the Big Five is an amalgamation of smaller publishing houses that have been acquired over the years and is owned in turn by an even larger media corporation. Many of your favorite books are published by a Big Five imprint.

## Hachette Book Group (HBG)

Hachette Book Group (HBG) (**www.hachettebookgroup.com**) was created when Hachette Livre, the second-largest publishing company in the world, acquired Time Warner Book Group from Time Warner in 2006. Lagardère, a French multinational media conglomerate, owns Hachette Livre. HBG's earliest imprint is Little, Brown and Company, founded in 1837 by Charles Coffin Little and James Brown. In 1968, that company was acquired by Time Inc., which merged with Warner Communications to form Time Warner in 1989. Macdonald & Co. was bought in 1992 to become part of the Time Warner Book Group UK. In 1996, the various branches merged to become Time Warner Trade Publishing, later Time Warner Book Group. In 2013, Hachette began releasing e-book editions to libraries simultaneously with print editions with unlimited single-user at a time circulation.

## HarperCollins

News Corporation owns HarperCollins Publishers (**www.harpercollins.com**). It began as J. and J. Harper, founded in New York City in 1817 by James and John Harper. Later named Harper & Brothers, it was Harper & Row in 1987 when News Corporation bought it. In 1990, News Corporation acquired the British publisher William Collins & Sons (founded 1819), the home of H.G. Wells, Agatha Christie, J.R.R. Tolkien, and C.S. Lewis. HarperCollins has publishing groups in the United States, Canada, the United Kingdom, Australia/New Zealand, and India. HarperCollins was the first publisher to digitize its content and create its own global digital warehouse. Its e-book titles sent to vendors are able to circulate only26 times before the license expires.

## Macmillan

Two brothers Daniel and Alexander Macmillan founded Macmillan (**http://us.macmillan.com**) in England in 1843 to publish literary works. The company later produced educational materials and textbooks. When Harold Macmillan retired as prime minister of England and became chairman in the late 1960s, the company expanded into reference works, college textbooks, and educational and scientific journals. In 1995, the German media giant Verlagsgruppe Georg von Holtzbrinck GmbH purchased a 70 percent share in the company and completed its acquisition in 1999. Macmillan has offices in more than 70 countries on six continents. Macmillan began offering limited e-book titles to libraries in 2013 with a license of two years or 52 lends, whichever comes first.

## Penguin Random House

Penguin Group (USA) Inc. and Random House, Inc. merged in 2013 to become Penguin Random House (**www.penguinrandomhouse.com**), the first global trade book publishing company. Penguin Random House now has publishing companies in U.S., the U.K., Canada, Australia, New Zealand, Ireland, India, Spain, Mexico, Argentina, Uruguay, Colombia, Chile, South Africa, and China.

Penguin Group (USA) (**www.us.penguingroup.com**) is the U.S. affiliate of the Penguin Random House. Penguin Group (USA) Inc. was formed in 1996 when Penguin Books USA merged with The Putnam Berkley Group. *See The Paperback Revolution for the history of Penguin Group.*

Random House, Inc. (**www.randomhouse.com**) was founded in 1925, when Bennett Cerf and Donald Klopfer purchased The Modern Library, reprints of classic works of literature, from publisher Horace Liveright. Two years later, they renamed the company Random House. After changing hands several times and acquiring a range of imprints, Random House was acquired by Bertelsmann AG, a German multinational media corporation in 1998 and merged with the former Bantam Doubleday Dell. Random House adult publishing groups include Crown Publishing Group, the Knopf Doubleday Publishing Group, and the Random House Publishing Group. The Random House Children's Books division is the world's largest publisher of books for young readers. Random House has produced more Pulitzer Prize winners than any other publisher, including four in 2013.

## Simon & Schuster

Richard L. Simon and M. Lincoln Schuster founded Simon & Schuster (**www.simonandschuster.com**) in 1924. Its first release, a crossword puzzle book, launched a new fad. In 1939, Simon & Schuster partnered with Robert Fair de Graff to found Pocket Books, launching the paperback revolution. Simon & Schuster, owned by CBS, publishes 1,800 titles annually. In 2000, it became the first publisher to issue a book by major author exclusively in electronic form with the publication of Stephen King's eBook *Riding the Bullet.*

# The "Big Five" Publishing Firms

| Publisher | Owned by | | Major Imprints | Well-known Authors |
|---|---|---|---|---|
| Hachette Book Group | Lagardère | 800+ adult books (including 50-100 digital-only titles), 200+ books for young readers, and 300 audio book titles (including both physical and downloadable-only titles) | Center Street, FaithWords (Jericho Books), Grand Central Publishing (Business Plus, Forever, Forever Yours, Grand Central Life & Style, Twelve, Vision, 5 Spot), Hachette Audio, Hyperion Books, Little, Brown and Company (Back Bay Books, Mulholland Books), Little, Brown and Company Books for Young Readers (Poppy, LB Kids), Orbit (Redhook), Yen Press | Sherman Alexie, Julie Andrews and Emma Walton Hamilton, David Baldacci, Julianna Baggott, James Bradley, Marc Brown, Sandra Brown, Christopher Buckley, Jimmy Buffett, Clayborne Carson, Lincoln Child, Stephen Colbert, Michael Connelly, Jeffery Deaver, Ted Dekker, Nelson DeMille, Emily Dickinson, Judy Finnigan, Malcolm Gladwell, Chelsea Handler, Lisi Harrison, Christopher Hitchens, Mary Ann Hoberman, David Jeremiah, Robert Kiyosaki, Elizabeth Kostova, Nelson Mandela, Steve Martin, John Maxwell, Patrick McDonnell, Brad Meltzer, Joyce Meyer, Stephenie Meyer, Joel Osteen, Todd Parr, James Patterson, Douglas Preston, Ian Rankin, Keith Richards, JK Rowling, J.D. Salinger, Amy Sedaris, David Sedaris, Anita Shreve, Anne Rivers Siddons, Nicholas Sparks, Jon Stewart, Trenton Lee Stewart, Scott Turow, David Foster Wallace, Brent Weeks, Cecily von Ziegesar |

| Publisher | Owned by | | Major Imprints | Well-known Authors |
|---|---|---|---|---|
| **Harper Collins** | News Corporation | 194 adult titles on the *New York Times* best-seller list in 2013 with 10 titles hitting number one; 53 children's books on the *New York Times* best-seller list including eight that reached the number one position | Amistad, Avon, Avon Impulse, Avon Inspire, Avon Red, Bourbon Street Books, Broadside Books, Ecco Books, Harper Books, HarperBusiness, Harper Design, Harper Luxe, Harper Paperbacks, Harper Perennial, Harper Voyager, HarperAudio, HarperCollins 360, HarperOne, Igniter, It Books, Newmarket Press, William Morrow. William Morrow Cookbooks, William Morrow Paperbacks, Witness | Mark Twain, Brontë sisters, Charles Dickens, John F. Kennedy, Martin Luther King Jr., Cecelia Ahern, Adele Ashworth, David Attenborough, J.G. Ballard, Margaret Wise Brown, Michael Burleigh, Kathryn Casey, Paulo Coelho, Bernard Cornwell, Jamie Lee Curtis, Neil Gaiman, Tony Hillerman, Erin Hunter, Wally Lamb, Derek Landy, Elmore Leonard, C.S. Lewis, Johanna Lindsey, Pittacus Lore, Peter Mandelson, Sarah Palin, Terry Pratchett, Lisa Marie Rice, Maurice Sendak, Sara Shepard, Shel Silverstein, Lemony Snicket, J.R.R. Tolkien, Rebecca Wells |
| **Macmillan** | Verlagsgruppe Georg von Holtzbrinck | | Farrar, Straus and Giroux; Henry Holt and Company; Picador; St. Martin's Press; Tor/Forge; Macmillan Audio; and Macmillan Children's Publishing Group | Alfred Lord Tennyson, Lewis Carroll, Henry James, Thomas Hardy, Rudyard Kipling, William Butler Yeats, Charles Kingsley, Thomas Hughes, Francis Turner Palgrave, Christina Rossetti, Matthew Arnold, Rabindranath Tagore, Sean O'Casey, John Maynard Keynes, Charles Morgan, Hugh Walpole, Margaret Mitchell, C. P. Snow, Rumer Godden, Ram Sharan Sharma |

| Publisher | Owned by | Major Imprints | Well-known Authors |
|---|---|---|---|
| **Penguin Random House** | Bertelsmann AG | Ace Books, Alpha Books, Amy Einhorn Books/Putnam, Avery, Berkley Books, Blue Rider Press, C.A. Press, Current, Dial Books for Young Readers, Dutton, Dutton Children's Books, Firebird, Frederick Warne, Gotham Books, G.P. Putnam's Sons, G.P. Putnam's Sons Books for Young Readers, Grosset & Dunlap, HP Books, Hudson Street Press, Jove Books, Kathy Dawson Books, Nancy Paulsen Books, NAL, Pamela Dorman Books, Penguin, The Penguin Press, Perigee Books, Philomel Books, Plume, Portfolio, Prentice Hall Press, Price Stern Sloan, Puffin Books, Razorbill, Riverhead, Sentinel, Speak, Tarcher,, The Viking Press, and Viking Children's Books<br><br>Crown Trade Group, Knopf Doubleday Publishing Group, Random House Publishing Group, RH Audio Publishing Group, Random House Children's Books, RH Information Group, RH International, RH Large Print | Nevada Barr, Saul Bellow, A. Scott Berg, Judy Blume, Lilian Jackson Braun, Dan Brown, Julia Cameron, Deepak Chopra, Tom Clancy, Patricia Cornwell, Clive Cussler, Roald Dahl, His Holiness the Dalai Lama, Fran Drescher, Ken Follett, Dick Francis, Al Franken, John Lewis Gaddis, Sue Grafton, John Grisham, Jack Higgins, Clark Howard. Jan Karon, Garrison Keillor, Stephen King, Ursula K. Le Guin, Leonard Maltin, Nora Roberts, Salman Rushdie, Ruta Sepetys, William Shatner, Amy Tan, Betty White |

| Publisher | Owned by | | Major Imprints | Well-known Authors |
|---|---|---|---|---|
| **Simon & Schuster, Inc.** | CBS Corporation | In 2012, Simon & Schuster placed 317 titles on the *New York Times* bestseller list, including 35 No. 1 best-sellers. Simon & Schuster titles have received 55 Pulitzer Prizes, 16 National Book Awards, 14 Caldecott, and 19 Newbery Medals. | Aladdin, Atheneum, Atria, Beach Lane Books, Folger Shakespeare Library, Free Press, Howard Books, Little Simon, Margaret K. McElderry Books, Paula Wiseman Books, Pimsleur, Pocket, Scribner, Simon & Schuster, Simon & Schuster Audio, Simon & Schuster BFYR, Simon Pulse, Simon Spotlight, Threshold, Touchstone/Fireside | Stephen E. Ambrose, Glenn Beck, Holly Black, Sandra Brown, James Lee Burke, A.S. Byatt, Jimmy Carter, Cassandra Clare, Mary Higgins Clark, Hillary Clinton, Kressley Cole, Jackie Collins, Jesse Duplantis, Hilary Duff, Bob Dylan, Janet Evanovich, Becca Fitzpatrick, Mark Gatiss, Doris Kearns Goodwin, Al Gore, Ursula K. Le Guin, Walter Isaacson, Audrey Niffenegger, David McCullough, Malalai Joya, Richard Madeley, Pervez Musharraf, Joel Osteen, Mark Radcliffe, Richard Rhodes, Rachel Renee Russell, R.L. Stine, Brad Thor, Lauren Weisberger, Bob Woodward, Taboo |

# Mid-sized Publishers, Small Presses, and University Presses

In addition to the Big Five, there are between 300 and 400 mid-sized publishers in the U.S., 100 university presses (such as Stanford University Press), and 85,000 small and self-publishing companies (for instance, Archipelago Books: **http:// archipelagobooks.org** and Dog Ear Publishing Press: **http://dogearpublishing. net**).

Small publishing houses come and go; between 8,000 and 11,000 are established every year, most of which are self-publishing companies.

Mid-sized publishers are more likely than the megapublishers to be open to first-time authors. While the megapublishers are looking for commercial successes with potential to sell 100,000 copies or more, mid-sized publishers are satisfied with books that sell reasonably well and make a profit. Like the largest publishing houses, most mid-sized publishers accept manuscript submissions only from agents. Mid-sized publishers offer royalty rates similar to those of the large publishers but are less likely to give advances.

Most small presses do not require authors to have agents and, therefore, are easier to approach. Small presses often cater to a niche market or a specialized genre. Typically, they do not offer advances. The average first run is 5,000 but could be as few as 1,000 books. Small presses bring out approximately 78 percent of new titles. They are estimated to make between $13 billion and $17 billion a year compared to trade publishers (publishers who produce books specifically for the bookstore trade) that represent approximately $26 billion in annual sales. Publishing with a small press is a good way for a novice writer to gain experience and a reputation. Larger publishing houses review the catalogs of the smaller presses to find candidates for their own lists.

University presses publish work of scholarly, intellectual, or creative merit, often for a specialized audience or a regional community. They are extensions of their parent universities and complement research libraries and scholarly associations in preserving and disseminating knowledge. Because they serve a public purpose, they are granted nonprofit status by the U.S. government. Though most of their books are scholarly and academic works, they also publish works of general interest, such as narrative history, poetry, translations of literature from other languages, and books of local or regional interest that are not attractive to large commercial publishing houses. University presses pay royalties (but not advances) and prefer to work directly with authors rather than agents. Before approaching a university press, confirm that it handles your genre and your type of book.

## Some Facts About Book Sales

Bowker (**www.bowker.com**) assigns ISBNs (International Standard Book Numbers) and maintains Bowker's Books In Print*, the industry's largest bibliographic database with information on more than 7.5 million U.S. book, audio book, and video titles, as well as 12 million international titles. Since 2001, Nielsen BookScan, owned by Nielsen Company, has collected and compiled cash register data from a number of major booksellers. Nielsen BookScan's U.S. Consumer Market Panel currently covers approximately 75 percent of retail sales; it does not track sales from Walmart/Sam's Club or BJ's and excludes sales of books to students who are required to buy them for classes. While the *New York Times* and *USA Today* base their best-seller lists on surveys of bookstores and wholesalers, Nielsen BookScan analyzes raw sales figures and captures information about books that are in the public domain or available from multiple imprints. Both Bowker and Nielsen regularly release reports on the publishing industry and sell their data to publishers, booksellers, and libraries. The Association of American Publishers (AAP) reports provide a snapshot of what is occurring in the publishing industry as a whole. The AAP notes that in 2012 trade publishing (general-interest fiction and non-fiction for adults, children and young adults and religion) experienced significant growth over 2011 and e-books grew 45 percent and constituting 20 percent of the trade market and playing an integral role in 2012 trade revenue.

Bowker's magazine *Publishers Weekly* annually surveys 40,000 U.S. book-buying men, women, and teens and reported that, "Online book retail, including ebooks, accounted for 44 percent of all spending by consumers on books in the U.S. in 2012" up from 39 percent in 2011, which was the first year when online retail eclipsed physical retail as the No. 1 place U.S. consumers buy books.

An AAP report from August 2013 indicated that:

- The AAP reported that the book market as a whole was up nearly 6 percent in August 2013 ($633.5 million from $598.4 million), and it was also down 4.8 percent for the January to August period ($4.26 billion from $4.47 billion).

- The combined digital sales (audiobook and e-book) for the first eight months of 2013 totaled $882.8 million, down 3.5 percent from $915 million during that period last year. In the adult segment, downloadable audiobooks were up 14.4 percent in the first eight months of 2013 while e-books increased by 4.8 percent. Religious e-books were up 2.6 percent, while kid's e-books dropped by 40 percent.

- Digital sales (e-book plus audiobook) for August 2013 totaled $144.4 million, down 1.7 percent

- Adult audiobooks, on the other hand, were up 18.3 percent ($11.4 million from $9.6 million). Along with religious ebooks, this was one of only two digital segments that increased in August.

- Categories of print books that increased their sales in 2010 included educational books (up 7.8 percent), university press paperbacks (up 1.3 percent), and professional books (up 5 percent).

These statistics help to put book publishing in perspective:

- A report published by statista.com indicated that 19 percent of American adults read 21 or more books per year. The same number read between three to ten books per year in 2012.

- Women buy more, representing 60 percent of book buyers and spend more on books. According to a Bowkers report, women accounted for 58 percent of book spending in 2012, up over 55 percent in 2011.

- Total book sales in the U.S. for 2012: $6.533 billion (including e-book sales of $1.251 billion).

- Number of new titles in 2011: 1,608,751

Number of new titles in 2010: 4,152,906
Number of new titles in 2009: 1,335,475
Number of new titles in 2005: 282,500

- According to the U.S. Census Bureau Annual Retail Trade Report, bookstore sales in the U.S. peaked in 2007 at $17.18 million. The economic recession together with the rise of online booksellers and e-books has resulted in bookstore closures and bankruptcies. Sales at major bookstores declined 12 percent between 2007 and 2009.

- Traditionally, nonfiction sales outnumber fiction sales two to one. According to Nielsen BookScan, only 282 million adult nonfiction books were sold in 2009 in the U.S. Average sales for U.S. nonfiction books are now fewer than 250 copies per year and fewer than 3,000 copies total. Meanwhile, 20 percent more fiction books are published today than in the past, via the Internet and POD. From 100 to more than 1,000 titles are competing for each available space on a bookstore shelf. Bookstores are steadily reducing the amount of shelf space dedicated to books and increasing space devoted to music, audiobooks, DVDs, games, gifts, and bargain books. They also are displaying more books "face out" (with their front covers showing instead of their spines), which further reduces available shelf space. The number of inches devoted to book review columns in newspapers has decreased 20 to 50 percent.

- At any given moment, there are 1.5 million books in print in the U.S., but including out-of-print books and digital formats, more than seven million books are available for sale.

- Fifty-two percent of all books are not sold in bookstores; instead, they are sold by mail order, online, through book clubs, or in warehouse stores.

- On average, a bookstore browser spends eight seconds looking at the front cover and 15 seconds scanning the back cover. Most customers do not read past page 18 in a book after they buy it.

- It is becoming increasingly harder to sell books. Many niche markets are saturated with multiple titles. Libraries now make e-books available to their members, so that they can locate and download them easily from home. Potential readers are increasingly distracted by other forms of entertainment, such as television and video games, and by other forms of writing such as blogs and Facebook pages.

- In 2004, of the 1.2 million titles tracked by Nielsen Bookscan:
    950,000 sold fewer than 99 copies
    200,000 sold fewer than 1,000 copies
    25,000 sold more than 5,000 copies

## Chapter 2

# What Are Your Options?

U ntil the last decade, a would-be author had two basic options for publishing a book: Get the book accepted for publication by a conventional publishing company, or pay thousands of dollars in printing costs and sell the book directly to bookstores and wholesalers, through mail-order ads, or at public events. The advent of POD technology (see below), digital publishing, and the Internet has created a range of new options for publishing and selling books, including low-cost self publishing, paperless e-books, and even cell phone apps (applications). The Internet offers a new arena for marketing books directly to readers, as well as to special-interest communities, but it also has created massive competition. Today, there are still two basic options, but they are much more complex: Get the book accepted by a conventional publishing company that might promote the book for you or require you to pay for and execute your own marketing campaign; or pay from a few hundred to several thousand dollars to print your book, doing everything yourself or contracting various services and organizing and paying for your own distribution, marketing, and publicity.

Depending on the route you choose, a world of new experiences lies ahead. If you want to land a contract with a conventional publisher, your first challenge is to sell yourself to an agent or an independent publisher. Once over that hurdle, you will begin to learn firsthand about the publishing business. If you decide to self-publish, be prepared to acquire many new skills or pay someone else to do the work for you. You soon will be immersed in a world of desktop publishing software, layout design, graphics, search engine optimization, social media, blog-ging, ad-buying, accounting, book contests, press releases and book reviews. Your teachers are everywhere — agents and publishers, editors, fellow writers, websites and blogs, the people you hire to help you, and books like this one.

# Conventional Publishing

Under the conventional publishing business model, a publisher signs a contract to publish an author's book. The publisher agrees to pay the author a royalty for each book sold and often pays an established writer an advance on future royalties. The publisher pays the costs of printing and distributing the book. In the past, publishers also paid the costs of marketing and promoting the book, but recently, publishers have begun requiring authors to pay all or some of these costs. The publisher's editorial and design staffs ensure that the book meets high standards and maintains the publisher's brand. The publisher distributes the book through its network of wholesalers and booksellers and collaborates with the author in publicizing and marketing the book.

# Trade publishers

Books produced for general readership are referred to as "trade books" because they are sold to the "trade" — booksellers and wholesalers. Limited editions, textbooks, and mass-market paperbacks are not trade books. Trade publishing houses range from megacorporations to small, independent presses. Trade publishers produce high-quality, more expensive books, often with hard covers, which they sell to bookstores and libraries. Trade paperback books are of better quality than mass-market paperbacks. Trade publishers typically have the largest staffs and budgets. They commonly offer royalties and advances to authors and seek quality and origi-nality in the manuscripts they review. The subdivisions, or imprints, of trade pub-lishing houses are managed independently of each other and have different edito-rial staffs. Trade publications tend to receive the most and highest-profile reviews.

A publishing house is considered "large" when annual sales exceed $50 million. Large publishing houses publish and promote more than 500 books per year, and their authors receive the highest industry standard of marketing, publicity, and promotion. They review a large volume of manuscripts and typically require manu-scripts to be submitted by an acknowledged agent.

Mid-sized publishing houses typically bring in between $10 million and $50 million in annual sales and publish more than 100 books every year. These publishers are not corporate giants like the large houses; their sizes and structures vary widely and range from newspaper chains to private businesses managed by a family or an individual.

## Small and independent presses

Small presses, small publishers, and independents sell through mail order and sometimes directly or indirectly to the same outlets as large and mid-sized trade publishers. Although their budgets are smaller than those of larger houses, with annual sales under $10 million, they offer several benefits. Small presses often market to specialized audiences, such as readers of poetry, for example, and will keep a title in print longer than a larger house might. Small publishers might offer royalties and advances, might give royalties with no advance, or might pay in contributor copies (the author is provided copies of his or her books in lieu of monetary payment).

Small and independent presses are attractive to authors whose work may fall into a niche market or specialty category. Small presses also tend to be somewhat more approachable than larger houses and more likely to accept unsolicited and unagented manuscripts. These houses frequently provide a breakthrough into the market for first-time authors and illustrators and allow them to establish new careers.

*Pages coming out of a press stacker.*
*Photo courtesy of Rose Printing Company*

## Mass market

Mass-market publications are less expensive paperback books literally marketed to the masses. They often host syndicated and well-known characters, spin-off characters, series books, and popular media tie-ins, such as books based on movies, television shows, and websites. They also can be cheaper versions of successful trade books. Though available at large chain bookstores, mass-market paperbacks commonly are found in supermarkets, budget retail stores, hospital gift shops, newsstands, and airport shops. They often reach these markets via independent distributors, rather than the distribution channels that supply bookstores.

These books are sized to fit into standard display racks with their front covers facing out. The covers usually carry dramatic illustrations to attract readers. They are made of cheaper paper and priced low enough to be bought on impulse.

Mass-market publishers sometimes hire ghostwriters or freelance writers to produce series books and illustrators to reproduce images of pre-existing characters, such as those from popular movies and television shows. Mass-market books are not as widely reviewed as trade publications but can achieve widespread levels of distribution. Examples of mass-market books are the *Camel Club* series by David Baldacci and the *Shelter Bay* series by Joann Ross.

## E-publishers

E-publishers are often small presses publishing in both traditional print and online formats or in electronic format only. They produce previously unpublished work or reproduce in digital format works that are currently in print or that have fallen out of print. Some e-publishers offer print-on-demand (POD) options, so readers can print a hard-copy version. Due to the wide variety of e-publishers and low production costs, manuscripts are accepted more readily for e-publication. E-publishers expect you to submit edited work, ready for publication. E-publication does not bring with it the same sales figures, marketing initiatives, and prestige as traditional publication. Use caution when considering e-publishers because they acquire the rights to your work when you sign their contracts just as print publishers do. Beware of subsidy or vanity publishers who market themselves as e-publishers (See below). You can find a directory of e-publishers on eBook Crossroads.com (**www.ebookcrossroads.com/epublishers.html**).

The number and popularity of e-publishers reflects the changes taking place in the publishing industry. As handheld electronic reading devices (e-readers) such as Amazon.com's Kindle and Barnes & Noble's Nook proliferate, sales of e-books are increasing. Massive advertising campaigns by manufacturers of e-readers have helped speed readers' adoption of them, and they are now becoming standard equipment in classrooms and libraries. E-readers have video and audio features that make them suitable for audiobooks, animated illustrations, and other enrichments to printed text.

## Educational Publishers

Educational publishers are part of what is known as the institutional market, which sells its product to libraries, schools, and educational distributors. Educational publishers produce encyclopedias, nonfiction, general textbooks, homeschool materials, and other academic publications, such as ancillary materials (workbooks, teacher's textbook editions, flashcards, preparatory testing materials, study guides, CDs and tapes, maps, and software).

Institutional publishers also produce books in a series more commonly than trade publishers. Authors seeking to publish work in the educational market must be familiar with the educational curriculum for the targeted age group. Educational publishers typically offer a flat fee or royalties with little to no advance. Large publishers such as Houghton Mifflin and Macmillan/McGraw-Hill publish textbooks and ancillary materials, as do smaller houses specializing in educational publications.

## Religious publishers

Publishers of religious books and materials focus on one or more religions, topics, or themes and sell their product to specialized markets, such as religious bookstores and churches, or to bookstores with religious and inspirational sections. Similar to educational publishers, religious publishers usually provide a flat fee or royalties with little to no advance to their authors. These publishers are highly specialized and typically offer books of prayer or traditional verse geared toward a particular religious belief system, as well as fiction, nonfiction, and poetry concerning specific mores and values.

## Book packagers

Somewhere between publishers and writers, there are book packagers. Book packagers bring publishers' ideas and projects to life and sometimes bring their own ideas and projects to publishers. Packagers handle writing, editing, illustration, and book design for a single book or a series. The publisher then receives the package and sends it off for printing and distribution. Book packagers contract with illustrators and writers for their content and always are seeking talent. Some authors and illustrators find this type of work a good way to break into the industry, hone their skills, and learn how to work with editors and other publishing professionals. Writers and illustrators for book packagers are subcontracted under work-for-hire contracts, in which they receive a flat fee and limited or no royalties.

The writer's name often appears under a pseudonym, and the author is considered a ghostwriter. Book packagers produce many children's and young adult series books, such as romance and adventure books.

## Print-on-Demand (POD)

Print-on-demand (POD) is technology that prints a single copy of a book, as it is needed. POD publishers keep in-print, out-of-print, and self-published titles without having to maintain stock in a warehouse or worry about unsold copies. The cost per book is higher for POD than for a conventional press run, but because of the low setup costs, small quantities can be printed at affordable prices. POD allows libraries and readers to obtain copies of books no longer available through traditional means. Publishers of academic books, specialty books, and books for niche markets find POD useful.

POD has revolutionized self-publishing by making it possible for authors to print small quantities of their books conveniently and economically. It also allows authors to experiment with books and make alterations when a book is already in print.

Modern versions of the vanity press package POD with layout and cover design templates and sell add-ons such as professional editing, layout, cover design, and marketing services.

Traditional presses also have adopted POD technology to cut costs and maintain lines of specialty books that are printed only when orders come in. They use POD to supply books when a print run has sold out and the next run has not yet been printed and to keep their older titles in print when the demand for them does not justify a full print run. POD goes hand-in-hand with online book sales — instead of putting physical copies of books on the shelves of retail stores at multiple locations, the publisher lists them in catalogs that can be browsed on the Internet. POD also is used to manage risk for "surge" titles such as celebrity biographies that are expected to experience large sales for only a short time. To avoid piling up excess inventory, the publisher produces a smaller conventional print run and uses POD to supply extra copies only if they are needed.

# Self-Publishing

In self-publishing, the author becomes the publisher. The author pays all the costs of editing, designing, printing, and distributing his or her book, as well as organizing and paying for marketing and promotion. All profit from sales of the book goes to the author. Until the advent of POD, a self-published author had to pay for an entire print run, including setup costs, and ended up with boxes of books to peddle. Today's technology has reduced the cost of self-publishing greatly. Though conventional printing costs less per book, many self-published authors prefer to use POD and avoid sinking money into books they cannot sell. POD providers often offer printing and distribution services in exchange for a percentage of the price of each book sold.

As a self-published author, you do not have the support of a massive distribution network and a large marketing budget managed by seasoned professionals, but you have flexibility, freedom, and creative control. You do not have to sell thousands of books to make a profit because the financial investment is relatively small. Self-publishing allows you to bypass the painful process of selling yourself to agents and publishing houses and devote your time and energy to selling yourself to the public instead. When a large publisher accepts a manuscript for publication, it may be years before the book appears on the market. You can self-publish a book on a topic of current interest within a few weeks. Many self-published authors sell to specialized communities or niche markets too small to interest publishers of trade books. Successful self-publishing can be a way to catch the attention of large publishers, which are always on the lookout for books that sell.

Digital books, such as those available from Amazon.com as Kindle books or e-books sold as downloadable PDF files from an author's website or an e-book publisher, require no investment in printing or distribution. However, digital books sell far fewer copies than print books; on average, a self-published digital book sells fewer than 200 copies, while a traditionally published book sells an average of 10,000 copies.

Many companies offer POD and other services for self-publishing. You retain the rights to your work. Fees range from nothing to several thousand dollars for professional editing and layout. Essentially, you are sold printed copies of your own book. These companies often combine elements of traditional publishing with POD services; They pay you royalties for books sold through their online distribution networks and format books for sale as e-books. They also may sell you additional services such as editing, design, and marketing packages. As a publisher, it is your responsibility to determine whether you need these services and to find a pricing model that will allow you to make a reasonable profit on sales of your book. *See Chapter 8 for more information on self-publishing.*

# Subsidy, Co-op, and Vanity Presses

These companies publish your work, or anyone's work, for a fee paid by you, the author. Be careful not to confuse subsidy, co-op, or vanity publishers with self-publishing. They are also known as author-investment publishers and author-subsidized publishers. Some subsidy publishers currently offer POD technology or e-book publishing services for a smaller fee than they would demand for print copies; this is essentially self-publishing.

A subsidy or co-op publisher contributes a portion of the cost of printing the book and/or provides editing, distribution, warehousing, and marketing services. You pay the rest. Subsidy publishers select the manuscripts they print and maintain the standards of their brands. In return for its contribution, a subsidy publisher claims at least some rights to your book. The printed books are the property of the publisher, which owns the ISBN, and the publisher keeps them until they are sold. The writer is paid a royalty.

Vanity presses are so named because their success depends on the vanity of writers who want to see their names in print. While the target market for conventional publishing companies is the reading public, the target market for vanity presses is the author. The author pays for the entire publishing process, plus a substantial markup. Most would-be writers never recoup their investment on books published through these outlets. Vanity presses may print products of questionable quality, and they do not normally promote, market, distribute, or edit your work. When they do offer these services, it is often for additional fees and without any guarantee of quality or success. They are recognizable through slogans such as "Get Your Book Published" or "Seeking Children's Authors" that pepper their ads online and in the backs of magazines.

Avoid vanity presses — they have earned a reputation for draining authors' wallets and damaging credibility. Authors who publish through vanity presses have a difficult time having their work taken seriously and will be hard-pressed to eke out a review from a reputable source. Be honest with yourself about your work. If you and a few good peer editors feel your manuscript does not yet have the quality to be submitted to a trade publisher, it is not ready for publication. Instead, bring it back into the workshop, and find ways to make it the best book it can be.

## Vanity presses were an early form of self-publishing

Self-publishing with a vanity press did not always have the negative connotations it has today. During the 19th and early 20th century, legitimate writers often paid to publish their own books. By doing so, they retained creative control of their work and made more money if the book was successful. Lewis Carroll paid for publishing *Alice's Adventures in Wonderland* and most of his subsequent work. Mark Twain, Zane Grey, Upton Sinclair, Carl Sandburg, Edgar Rice Burroughs, George Bernard Shaw, Edgar Allan Poe, Rudyard Kipling, Henry David Thoreau, Walt Whitman, and Anais Nin self-published some or all of their works.

## Vanity presses in disguise

Any "publisher" that turns you into a customer is not going to make an effort to sell or promote your book because it is making its profit from selling its services to you. Some vanity presses masquerade as legitimate publishers by disguising their fees as some other type of expense or make money by charging exorbitantly for incidental services. You will find many vanity presses advertising themselves in magazines and on the Internet as though they are conventional publishers.

Writer Beware*, a project of the Science Fiction and Fantasy Writers of America's Committee on Writing Scams (**www.sfwa.org/for-authors/writer-beware**) and the Mystery Writers of America, warn authors to be wary of:

- **A setup fee or deposit.** A publisher may ask you to pay a "setup fee" of several hundred dollars to "help with the cost" of preparing your book for printing, or as an "investment" in your own success. The "setup fee" more than covers the expenses of the POD technology used by these publishers and guarantees them a profit.

- **A fee for some aspect of the publication process other than printing/ binding.** You might be required to pay for editing, artwork, liability insurance, or a publicity campaign. These services may cost thousands of dollars and are often minimal and not of professional quality.

- **A claim that your fee is only part of the cost, and the publisher will spend as much or more than you do on the book.** Most vanity presses today use the same distribution channels as POD self-publishing services, and do little or no editing. Your fee pays the whole cost, with some left over as profit for the company.

- **A prepurchase requirement.** Some contracts require you to buy a specific quantity of finished books, often at little or no discount. This can cost you more than straightforward vanity publishing.

- **A presale requirement.** You may be required to presell a certain number of books before publication, or to "guarantee" a minimum number of sales. If you do not, the publishing deal is cancelled.

- **A sales guarantee.** If your book does not sell X number of copies within X amount of time, you must agree to buy the remaining copies. Because vanity publishers do little or no marketing and distribution, you will almost surely end up paying for your own books. Some companies get even more money out of you by pressuring you, just after the book is printed, to buy books to sell yourself, but they do not include those numbers when calculating the final number of books sold.

- **Withheld royalties.** You get no royalty income until the cost of production has been recouped.

- **Pressure to buy your book yourself.** The contract might not require you to purchase your own book, but you will be pressured heavily to buy your books for resale, with special discounts for large quantities and frequent phone solicitations.

## Choosing a publishing option for your book

A book's success is defined by your expectations for it. You may be aiming for a best-selling novel and a writing career, a book to sell as a sideline to your business, or a memoir for your family members. Success is measured differently in each circumstance. A blockbuster is a success when it sells a million copies. A book intended for the public is a success when it sells more than 2,000 copies. A book created to support your business is successful if it sells 200 copies, establishes your reputation, and attracts new clients. A personal memoir or family history is successful if 30 family members buy a copy. The first step in deciding what to do with your new, well-written manuscript or your nonfiction book proposal is determining what you want to accomplish with it, and who will buy your book.

If you are confident that your book will appeal to the public and has the potential to sell tens of thousands of copies, aim for traditional publishing with a large publishing house. If you write poetry, short story collections, academic books, or specialized nonfiction, or if your writing focuses on a specific area, such as bed and breakfast inns of Maine, approach small publishers directly. If you wish to retain complete control of your project and develop your own channels for selling it, your best option is self-publishing.

## Chapter 3

# Creating a Book That Will Sell

A book is a business proposition. Whether you choose the route of traditional publishing or decide to self-publish, your book will not sell if it is poorly written, full of errors, obscure, trite, dull, out-of-date, or just like a hundred other books out there. Even worse, it might establish your reputation as a poor writer. Before you begin the process of contacting publishers or literary agents, take a good look at your manuscript or nonfiction book proposal. Do you have a high-quality product to sell? Try to see it through the eyes of a publisher, an editor, an agent, and a reader. Imagine yourself picking up your book in a bookstore or library. Would you want to read it? Would you buy it?

Visit bookstores and libraries, and study books similar to the one you want to publish. What do you like or dislike about them? How are they laid out? Do they have special features that appeal to you? How can you improve on them? Study the listings of Internet booksellers to see what books have been published recently in your genre. Click on individual books and look at the other titles recommended by the bookseller. You soon will understand whether your book is ready for market or needs a serious makeover. You are about to invest time, energy, and money in this project. It makes sense to do ev-

erything possible to ensure your success. Do not sabotage yourself by trying to sell a mediocre manuscript or book idea when you could be marketing a winner. Perhaps you can seize on a unique approach that will make your book stand out. By rearranging the content, including photos or illustrations, or adding more detail, you may be able to turn a lackluster book into a gem.

Literary agents often say they accept only one percent of the manuscripts submitted to them. The other 99 percent of submissions are rejected either because they are poorly written or because the agent does not think he or she can sell them to a publisher:

- 87 percent are considered amateurish and unpublishable.
- 4 percent are considered quality material but lack a target market.
- 4 percent are considered good writing, but the market for it is already saturated.
- 3 percent have a potential market but are poorly written or researched.
- 1 percent are considered potentially good material if the writing is revised and polished.
- 1 percent are considered well written, promising, and ready to be presented to a publisher.

## Assessing Your Market

How much do you know about the target audience for your book? Large publishers continually analyze sales figures, survey bookstore customers to see how they react to new releases, and monitor industry news and statistics. Each new release is accompanied by a carefully orchestrated advertising campaign designed to motivate as many people as possible to buy the book. When that publicity dies down, publishers strategize to continue sales by promoting the book through book clubs, talk shows, media interviews, and eventually, price discounts. You should be equally aware of the market for your book — who is likely to buy it, where and how they buy books, and what kind of media they enjoy. You will need to present this information to agents or publishers when you approach them about your book.

If you write nonfiction and can identify a large, specific group of potential readers who want or need what you plan to write about, you will increase your chances of snagging a book deal. If you write fiction in a genre that sells particularly well, an agent has more opportunities to sell your book. When the market is already saturated with young adult novels about teen vampires or nonfiction books on the next best diet, an agent or publisher will pass up your book unless you can prove your manuscript is unique and that you have an established network of potential readers.

## How large is the potential audience for your book?

Who will buy your book? If your topic is interesting only to members of your family or to a small, highly specialized community, your book will not be attractive to a publisher or agent. Browse the sales ranks of similar books on the market and review the best-seller lists in your genre to get an idea of how many potential readers exist for your book. *Publishers Weekly* magazine online (**www.publisher-sweekly.com**) provides best-seller lists and columns on "Retail Sales" and "Trends and Topics" that you may find helpful. *The New York Times'* book review section (**www.nytimes.com/pages/books**) also lists best-sellers by category. The website Titlez (**www.titlez.com**) allows you to track Amazon.com sales rank history by keyword, title, or author and compare similar books by genre or title.

## Does a nearly identical book already exist?

If a book already exists that is almost identical to your concept, you will have trouble selling yours to an agent or publisher. You must be able to demonstrate how your book will be better than those already on the market. The fact that the other book exists demonstrates the public's interest in your subject matter, but you must come up with a new approach.

## How will you communicate with your market?

How are you going to let your audience know about your new book and encourage them to buy it? If a conventional publisher publishes your book, it will be advertised through the publisher's publicity and distribution network. The publisher will expect you to be active in promoting your book through public appearances and book signings, and your contract may require you to produce a marketing plan. Some self-publishing companies place you in a distribution network as part of the publishing package, but you are still responsible for publicizing your book. You may be planning to sell your book as part of your business — for example, you might be a public speaker on the topic or have a company that sells products associated with your book. E-books can be sold entirely online, through author websites, blogs, Internet ads, and social media.

## Publishing Trends and Seasons

If you attend writer's conferences, read writing magazines, or subscribe to industry newsletters or blogs, you will hear opinions from the "experts" that *this* type of writing is in and *that* type of book is out. "Chick-lit is dead, and memoirs do not sell." "No one reads western novels anymore." "Gothic romance is the next big thing." Such pronouncements should not interfere with your primary goal, which is to write an exceptional manuscript or book proposal and sell your book. Know the market, but do not worry about the market.

# Popular trends

Whenever a book becomes a best-seller, publishers and readers look for more of the same. When *Marley and Me* by John Grogan became a hit, publishers released similar books about dogs and their owners, and readers devoured them — for a while. Eventually, the market becomes saturated, and readers grow tired of reading the same story or subject matter.

Publishing trends come and go. A popular topic today will be different a year from now. For that reason, it is best to be aware of trends but not to let them influence your writing unduly. Focus your writing on what you love. You must be invested in and passionate about your subject. Otherwise, you will not be able to convey enthusiasm to an agent, publisher, or reader.

# Timeliness and relevance

Your book has a better chance of selling if its contents are timely and relevant. Do not attempt to follow a current "popular trend," but be aware of lifestyle shifts and readers' changing interests. Think about ways your book might tie in with current events and book sales. The economic downturn that began in 2007, concern for the environment, depletion of natural resources, and an aging generation of baby-boomers are four major influences on readers' lifestyles during the first two decades of the 21st century. As baby boomers age, they must plan for their parents' medical and caretaker needs and focus on staying healthy and fit. People who lost their jobs and savings during the financial crisis that began in 2007 are looking for unique ways to find employment, repair their credit, clear their debts, avoid foreclosure, and generate new streams of revenue. The result: an increase in entrepreneurship and a need for books on running and marketing small businesses. Many readers are looking for ways to save money by doing their own repairs and home improvements, which stimulates sales of do-it-yourself-books; or by vacationing close to home, increasing sales of regional and local travel books. Concern about environmental degradation has created a market for "green" books.

Some books are tied to the calendar. Milestones like the 50th anniversary in 2013 of President John F. Kennedy's assassination created reader interest in a specific subject. In 2009, readers saw the release of a plethora of historical books commemorating the bicentennial of Abraham Lincoln's birth.

# Seasonal publishing

Publishers study their readers carefully and time the release certain types of books for specific times of the year.

## January

Readers are planning for the year and focusing on their New Year's resolutions. Publishers release books on fitness, health, dieting, parenting, weddings, tax preparation, relationships, starting a business, home improvements, daily planners/calendars, budgeting, travel, how-to, and self-help.

## February

February is the month for romance novels, relationship self-help books, and books celebrating Black History Month.

## March, April, and May

Easter, Passover, and Mother's Day books are released, and books for dads, graduates, and sports fans are published.

## June, July, and August

Summer brings books for beach reading, travel getaways, and Father's Day.

## September and October

Books by bestselling authors often are launched this time of year, along with rereleases of standards and classics that may be required high school or university reading. Halloween books, gothic romance, thrillers, and horror are also popular genres.

## November and December

Gift books, holiday books, cookbooks, craft books, books by bestselling authors, and calendars are big sellers during the holiday season.

```
CASE STUDY:
WRITING A BOOK THAT WILL
SELL
```

*Douglas R. Brown, president and founder of Atlantic Publishing Group, Inc., an award-winning author who writes primarily about the food service industry, has written or cowritten 16 books. His bestselling book, The Restaurant Managers Handbook, originally self-published in 1982, is now in its fourth edition and continues to sell thousands of copies every year. The book has won numerous awards, including the prestigious Benjamin Franklin Award for excellence in independent publishing. His extensive background and years of experience in the food service industry provided practical insight into the highly volatile industry.*

*In 1989, Doug and his wife Sherri founded Atlantic Publishing to publish and distribute titles about the food service industry. Today, Atlantic Publishing serves virtually every area of the nonfiction how-to market, with books on topics as diverse as raising goats and pigs, brewing your own beer, and buying your first home. Atlantic Publishing book categories include real estate careers, real estate investing, investments, career planning, personal finance, Internet, education, legal, home ownership, photography, study guides and educational resources, advice and practical guides on how to start a new business, eBay, retirement, employee programs, parenting, home maintenance and improvements, self help, energy efficiency and green homes, elder law, legal resources, nonprofit resources, employee management, marketing, business, photography, reference books, and food service. We have a book for that™.*

*The first and foremost element of a good book in the field that we publish is that it must compel the reader to continue reading. I do not know how many times I have not finished a book because it is just so boring, or the* author talks down to the reader or tries to impress the reader with his or her extensive vocabulary. The main problem I see with many "how-to" books is that the author wants to tell you how he or she did something; for example, "How I made a million dollars in real estate." This type of book rarely will teach you anything. We take a more journalistic approach by teaching the readers all sides of the subject in a nonjudgmental manner. Then, we fill our books with "case studies," numerous examples of real world stories from people who work in the field we are writing about. I hope that when a reader finishes one of our books, he or she will have been entertained, will have learned an unbiased view of all sides of the subject matter, and will have been inspired by the real-life stories.

Evaluating the marketplace today is easy — simply look up other similar books on Amazon.com and see how they are selling. There are numerous software tools available as well; one good tool that is currently free is Title-Z (**www.titlez.com**).

# Understanding Your Genre

Genre is a set of criteria for a category of composition. A book's genre helps inform a potential reader what to expect emotionally, structurally, and intellectually. Genre creates a set of expectations, and your job as the writer is to know what those expectations are and deliver them to the reader. Bookstores categorize books by genre so that readers easily can find the type of books they enjoy. Understanding your genre also assists you in marketing your manuscript or book idea effectively to agents, publishers, and readers. For example, books of each genre are a specific size; if your book is too short or too long for its genre, publishers will not be interested. *Appendix D includes definitions for all genres and subgenres listed here.*

It is important to categorize your genre accurately. If you label your novel as romance, but it is actually a thriller that incorporates a romance, you risk losing the interest of a potential agent because you pitched it incorrectly. Readers searching for thrillers in online catalogs will miss your book because it is listed under "romance." Your genre defines your marketing strategy — book signings, promotional appearances, and online advertising should target readers who have demonstrated an interest in books similar to yours. Knowing your genre well also helps you decide on a publishing strategy and select the right agents or publishers to pitch your book to.

## Literary fiction

The writing style or voice of the author, in-depth exploration of characters, and a profound use of symbolism, imagery, and theme distinguish literary fiction from mainstream or genre fiction. Literary fiction may fall into any of the categories of fiction genre but appeals to a smaller audience than genre fiction. It is considered to be of greater artistic and cultural value. Examples of literary fiction are *Cold Mountain* by Charles Frazier, *To Kill A Mockingbird* by Harper Lee, and Ian McEwan's *Atonement*.

### Classic novels outsell best-sellers

In 2001, when Nielsen Bookscan began tracking book sales at bookstore cash registers, some surprising figures emerged. Until then, bookstores had been reporting only sales of new releases and top sellers. Sales figures from cash registers showed that literary classics like Jane Austen's *Pride and Prejudice* continue to perform steadily, year after year, while sales of current best-sellers dwindle after a few months, never to rise again. In 2003, BookScan reported that *Pride and Prejudice* sold 110,000 copies while *The Runaway Jury* by John Grisham, the No. 1 best-seller in 1996, sold 73,337 copies. Leo Tolstoy's *War and Peace* sold 33,000 copies in 2003, while Tom Clancy's Russian spy novel, *The Cardinal of the Kremlin*, 1988's No. 1 best-selling book, sold 35,000 copies — only 2,000 more. Although sales of literary classics cannot compete with sales of new releases, over time they surpass them by far. Nielsen Bookscan excludes academic sales, so the sales figures do not include books students are required to buy as texts.

Many literary classics already have been in the public domain for a long time, and they are available from multiple imprints. Newer literary fiction does not achieve the same consistent sales as the classics.

# Genre fiction

Genre fiction, also called popular fiction, mainstream fiction, or commercial fiction, is plot-driven and attracts a wider audience than literary fiction. Each category and subgenre has specific conventions and formulas to meet readers' expectations. You will find many of the subcategories overlap.

## Romance

According to the Romance Writers of America, the main plot of a romance novel must center on the hero and the heroine as they develop romantic love for each other. Romance novels provide an emotionally satisfying and optimistic ending.

Popular books and authors include *Dark Witch* by Nora Roberts, *The Duchess* by Jude Deveraux, and *Blindsided* by Fern Michaels.

Subgenres include chick-lit, Christian, contemporary, fantasy, erotica, glitz/glamour, historical, multicultural, paranormal, romantic comedy, romantic suspense, sensual, spicy, sweet, and young adult.

## Horror

According to the Horror Writers Association, horror novels are primarily about emotion. It is writing that delves deep inside and forces readers to confront who they are, to examine what they are afraid of, and to wonder what lies ahead down the road of life.

Popular books and authors include *Carrie* by Stephen King, *Mister B. Gone* by Clive Barker, *Relentless* by Dean Koontz, *Interview with the Vampire* by Anne Rice, and *The Pit and the Pendulum* by Edgar Allan Poe.

Subgenres include child in peril, comic horror, creepy kids, dark fantasy, dark mystery/noir, erotic vampire, fabulist, Gothic, hauntings, historical, magical realism, psychological, quiet horror, religious, science-fiction horror, splatter/splatterpunk, supernatural menace, technology, weird tales, young adult, and zombie.

## Thriller / suspense

According to the International Thriller Writers Association, Inc., thriller stories center on a complex plot and present ordinary people caught in extraordinary circumstances; they are typified by the protagonist running for his or her life before turning to face and ultimately triumph over the danger.

Popular books and authors include *The Scarpetta Factor* by Patricia Cornwell, *Presumed Innocent* by Scott Turow, *A Time to Kill* by John Grisham, *Clear and Present Danger* by Tom Clancy, *Cross My Heart* by James Patterson, and *The Traitor* by Stephen Coonts.

Subgenres include action, comic, conspiracy, crime, disaster, eco-thriller, erotic, espionage, forensic, historical, horror, legal, medical, military, police procedural, political intrigue, psychological, romantic, supernatural, and technological.

## Science fiction / fantasy

Science fiction novels center on the imagined impact of science on society, while fantasy novels include fantastic elements, such as magic and supernatural forms, inspired from mythology and folklore to convey the story, plot, and theme.

Popular books and authors include *Lord of the Rings* by J.R.R. Tolkien, *I, Robot* by Isaac Asimov, *Fahrenheit 451* by Ray Bradbury, *War of the Worlds* by H.G. Wells, and *2001: A Space Odyssey* by Arthur Clarke.

Subgenres include Arthurian fantasy, Bangsian fantasy, biopunk, children's fantasy, comic, cyberpunk, dark fantasy, dystopian, erotic, game-related fantasy, hard science fiction, heroic fantasy, high/epic fantasy, historical, mundane science fiction, military science fiction, mystery science fiction, mythic fiction, new age, post-apocalyptic, romance, religious, science fantasy, social science fiction, soft science fiction, space opera, spy-fi, steampunk, superheroes, sword and sorcery, thriller science fiction, time-travel, urban fantasy, vampire, wuxia, and young adult.

## Mystery / crime

Mystery novels revolve around a crime that needs to be solved. Characteristics of crime fiction include intrigue, victims, clues, suspects, and an investigation.

Popular books and authors include *W Is for Wasted* by Sue Grafton, *L.A. Confidential* by James Ellroy, *Bad Monkey* by Carl Hiaasen, *The Maltese Falcon* by Dashiell Hammett, *Feast Day of Fools* by James Lee Burke, *The Fifth Witness* by Michael Connelly, and *The Big Sleep* by Raymond Chandler.

Subgenres include amateur detective, child in peril, classic whodunit, comic (bumbling detective), cozy, courtroom drama, dark thriller, espionage, forensic, heists and capers, historical, inverted, locked room, medical, police procedural, private detective, psychological suspense, romantic, technothriller, thriller, woman in jeopardy, and young adult.

## Westerns

Western novels, also referred to as "novels of the West," often convey themes of honor, inequality, and sacrifice and are set primarily in the western part of the United States, Mexico, South America, Western Canada, and Australia. Though most westerns are set during the late 1800s, modern writers are not restricted to a specific period.

Popular books and authors include *Riders of the Purple Sage* by Zane Grey, *Under the Sweetwater Rim* by Louis L'Amour, *Open Range* by Lauran Paine, *Night Passage* by Robert B. Parker, and *3:10 to Yuma* by Elmore Leonard.

Subgenres include frontier and pioneer.

## Religious / inspirational

Religious or inspirational novels deal with religious themes (for example Christian themes, such as God, sin, salvation, sacrifice, redemption, and service to others) and incorporate a religious worldview.

Popular books and authors include *The Shack* by William P. Young, *A Christmas to Die For* by Marta Perry, and *The Reckoning* by Beverly Lewis.

Subgenres include Biblical, Christian, historical, mystery, romance, science fiction/fantasy, and visionary.

## Action–adventure

Action-adventure novels are characterized by gritty, fast-paced physical and violent action with an emphasis on danger. They are set in exotic locales and offer little character development.

Popular books and authors include *Mirage* by Clive Cussler, *Live or Let Die* by Ian Fleming, and *Designated Targets* by John Birmingham.

Subgenres include disaster adventure, espionage adventure, industrial/financial, medical, male-action adventure, political intrigue, military and naval, soft adventure, survival adventure, thriller adventure, and western adventure.

## Historical

Historical novels dramatize past events and characters; they present believable and plausible representations of history.

Popular books and authors include *The White Queen* by Phillipa Gregory, *Centennial* by James Michener, *Lady of Hay* by Barbara Erksine, and *The Pagan Lord* by Bernard Cornwell.

Subgenres include alternate histories, pseudo-histories, time-slip novels, historical fantasies, romance, and multiple-time novels.

## Young adult

Young adult novels are written specifically for adolescents, ages 12 to 18. The protagonist of the story is a young adult, and the plot revolves around his or her point of view. YA stories span the entire spectrum of fiction genres and focus on the challenges of adolescence and coming of age.

Popular books and authors include *Harry Potter and the Sorcerer's Stone* by J.K. Rowling, the *Twilight* series by Stephanie Meyers, and *Forever* by Judy Blume.

## Women's fiction

Women's fiction focuses on women's issues and their relationships with their families and friends. They revolve around a theme of female empowerment. These novels include strong female protagonists and portray women triumphing over adversity. These stories conclude with a life-affirming message. Both male and female writers author women's fiction.

Popular books and authors include *I'll Take Manhattan* by Judith Krantz, *Someone* by Alice McDermott, *The Accidental Tourist* by Anne Tyler, *The Storyteller* by Jodi Picoult, and *Sex and the City* by Candace Bushnell.

Subgenres include chick lit, domestic dramas, erotic thrillers, family sagas, historical romances, kitchen fiction, lipstick fiction, mom novel, and single women.

| Fiction Genre | Average Word Count |
|---|---|
| Action-adventure | 75,000 to 85,000 |
| Historical | 85,000 to 110,000 |
| Horror | 75,000 to 85,000 |
| Literary fiction | 85,000 to 110,000 |
| Mystery / crime | 75,000 to 90,000 |
| Religious / inspirational | 80,000 to 90,000 |
| Romance | 75,000 to 100,000 |
| Science fiction / fantasy | 80,000 to 115,000 |
| Thriller / suspense | 85,000 to 100,000 |
| Western | 55,000 to 80,000 |
| Women's fiction | 80,000 to 100,000 |
| Young adult | 50,000 to 75,000 |

# Nonfiction

Nonfiction books stand or fall on the delivery of the promise to help the reader. Regardless of your genre, as a nonfiction writer, you either:

1. Help the reader fix a problem. Examples are self-help, how-to, reference, inspirational, travel guides, and cookbooks.

2. Provide information to expand a reader's knowledge and worldview. This is the intent of most narrative nonfiction works including memoirs, biographies, autobiographies, historical accounts, and books on current events.

The most effective way to understand nonfiction genre is to peruse complementary, as well as competitive, books in the same genre as your book idea. Analyze the books in your niche and note:

- The layout — Do most contain sidebars, case studies, anecdotes, photos, or charts?

- The structure — How many chapters and sections do they contain, and what is the overall book length?

- The delivery — Is the style casual or formal? Is the tone fun and motivational or sincere and cautionary?

- The content — Is the manuscript packed with hard-hitting information, statistical/technical overload, complex theories, or detailed historical accounts? Or does it contain simple step-by-step instructions, homespun advice, basic processes, or easily understood philosophy?

- The purpose — Is it to educate, motivate, expose, entertain, convince, inspire, or connect and share the human experience?

## How-to

How-to books outsell every other nonfiction genre. Within the how-to niche, the best-selling categories are: business/leadership/career, parenting, sex, money/finances, dieting/weight loss, and health/fitness. How-to books are filled with instructions, valuable information, tips, suggestions, examples, and illustrations. Information is presented sequentially with each chapter supporting the overall concept. These books conclude with the reader achieving the "goal."

Books: *Starting on a Shoestring: Building a Business without a Bankroll* by Arnold S. Goldstein, *Scrapbook Basics* by Michele Gebrandt, and *Meditation for Beginners* by Jack Kornfield.

## Self-help

Self-help books encompass the realm of psychology. The most popular category is relationships. Self-help books have more examples than how-to books. The author's style is casual, as if conversing with an old friend across the table.

Books: *Surviving the Breakup* by Judith S. Wallerstein and Joan B. Kelly, *From Panic to Power* by Lucinda Bassett, and *Overcoming Depression* by Demetri Papolos.

## Travel guides

Travel guidebooks are always in demand, especially if they cover a location that has not been saturated or take a fresh spin on a topic, such as *The Top 100 Romantic Places to Kiss*. Travel guides require detailed research and must provide all the necessary information and tips to help the reader successfully plan a trip to the destination.

Books: *Michelin the Green Guide Paris* by Michelin Travel Publications, *Hiking Yosemite National Park* by Suzanne Swedo, and *Frommer's Best RV and Tent Campgrounds in the U.S.A.* by David Hoekstra.

## Cooking and food

Hundreds of new cookbooks are published each year. To succeed in this competitive genre you need a distinctive theme that captures the reader's attention. Cookbooks incorporate vibrant photos, systematic detailed instructions, and a casual "you-can-do-it" style.

Books: *Mastering the Art of French Cooking* by Julia Child , *The Joy of Cooking* by Irma S. Rombauer, and *Vegetarian Cooking for Everyone* by Deborah Madison .

## Inspirational / religious / spiritual / metaphysical

Religious, inspirational, and spiritual books share themes of a particular belief system and provide wisdom, motivation, and advice to guide readers to live a full life in harmony with specific concepts. Metaphysical books investigate principles of reality that transcend science, such as astrology, numerology, and psychic ability. These books uplift readers' spirits and require an author who is closely attuned to the readership: who the readers are, what they assume, and their "language." The writer must have a full understanding of the history of the subject.

Books: *The Purpose-Driven Life* by Rick Warren, *Conversations with God* by Neale Donald Walsch, and *The Case for Faith* by Lee Strobel.

## Reference

A reference book contains authoritative facts. Successful reference books never go out of date. Authors can update the content every five to eight years. Popular reference categories include computer and Internet books as well as directories. "Coffee table" books also fall under this genre, and architecture, art, and photography are popular subgenres.

Books: *The Quotable Star Wars* by Stephen J. Sansweet, *60,001+ Best Baby Names* by Diane Stafford, and *The Concise 21st Century Crossword Puzzle Dictionary* by Kevin McCann and Mark Diehl.

## Humor

Humor books are filled with witty and entertaining content. They usually are given as gifts. They are short and funny, and they have an identifiable audience, such as cat owners, golfers, or parents.

Books: *If Dogs Could Talk* by Joel Zadak, *Egghead: Or, You Can't Survive on Ideas Alone* by Bo Burnham, and *Stupid American History: Tales of Stupidity, Strangeness, and Mythconceptions* by Leland Gregory.

## Medical and science

Medical and science books enlighten and educate readers about medical and scientific fields. They can be successful sellers. They require extensive research, interviewing, and fact checking. They incorporate charts, graphs, illustrations, and a thorough glossary.

Books: *A Brief History of Time* by Stephen Hawking and *The Physics of Star Trek* by Lawrence M. Krauss.

# Narrative nonfiction

Narrative nonfiction, also referred to as creative nonfiction, is truthful writing that reads like a novel. It straddles the line between nonfiction and fiction, incorporating storytelling techniques such as plot, conflict, and dialogue. Narrative nonfiction requires:

1. Factual subject matter
2. Exhaustive research
3. Compelling narrative or a literary prose style

## History

History books have a scholarly tone and often are written by experts — not necessarily a professional historian, but at least someone who has studied the subject extensively. Historical stories are compelling to readers when they evoke a sense of place by maintaining the customs, culture, and knowledge of the period, as well as providing relevance to our lives today or revealing something new about a well-known, or little-known, event. Military books are considered a subgenre of history.

Popular books and authors: *The Bully Pulpit: Theodore Roosevelt, William Howard Taft, and the Golden Age of Journalism* by Doris Kearns Goodwin, *Band of Brothers* by Stephen E. Ambrose, *1776* by David McCullough, *The Guns at Last Light: The War in Western Europe, 1944-1945* by Rick Atkinson, and *Seabiscuit* by Laura Hillenbrand.

## Adventure

Adventure books consist of a man-against-nature story. They have an extreme and dramatic quality and are set in an exotic location.

Popular books and authors: *Into the Wild* and *Into Thin Air* by Jon Krakauer and *The Perfect Storm* by Sebastian Junger.

## Travelogues

Travelogues incorporate the author's travel experience and may include travel guide details about the destination.

Popular books and authors: *A Walk in the Woods* and *In a Sunburned Country* by Bill Bryson, *A Year in Provence* by Peter Mayle, and *Under The Tuscan Sun* by Frances Mayes.

## Biography

Along with extensive research and minute fact verification, biographies require the author to be devoted to the subject matter but objective enough to go wherever the truth may lead in order to create an accurate portrayal. Biographies come with their own set of challenges, such as:

- Will the subject (if alive) or the family cooperate with the telling of his or her story?

- How will "fans" of the subject respond to negative revelations?

- Has the subject been covered thoroughly, or do you have a new perspective or theory to present to readers?

- Does the subject warrant cradle-to-grave coverage, or is there one inspirational event or portion of your subject's life worthy of exploration?

Popular books and authors: *John Adams* by David McCullough, *JFK* by James W. Douglass, and *The Snowball: Warren Buffett and the Business of Life* by Alice Schroeder.

## Memoir

The challenge of memoir is to write a personal account, whether tragic or inspiring, that has a universal connection. Memoir must transcend the personal and become a shared experience for readers.

Popular books and authors: *Angela's Ashes* by Frank McCourt, *Running with Scissors* by Augusten Burroughs, and *Dreams of My Father* by Barack Obama.

## True crime

True crime accounts incorporate the art of the newspaper reporter. It requires investigative, analytical attention to detail and some understanding of police and forensic procedures. The author must present an in-depth study of the cast of characters, the victim's family, the detectives, the lawyers, and the perpetrator, and effectively capture and convey what is identifiable and intriguing.

Popular books and authors: *In Cold Blood* by Truman Capote, *When the Mob Ran Vegas* by Steve Fischer, *The Stranger Beside Me* by Ann Rule, *TA Captain's Duty: Somali Pirates, Navy SEALs, and Dangerous Days at Sea* by Richard Phillips, with Stephan Talty, *Echoes in the Darkness* by Joseph Wambaugh, and *The Executioner's Song* by Norman Mailer.

The chart below, excerpted from Bowker's *New Book Titles and Editions, 2002-2011*, shows the number of new books published each year by subject matter. It shows the rapid growth in the number of new nonfiction books about practical subjects such as philosophy/psychology, religion, and the arts. It also shows the explosive growth brought about by POD publishing, under the "non-traditional" category.

## New Book Titles 2002-2011

| Subject | 2002 | 2010 | 2011 Projected | % change 2010 - 2011 | % change 2002 - 2011 |
|---------|------|------|----------------|----------------------|----------------------|
| Agriculture | 1,418 | 1,886 | 1,861 | -1% | 31% |
| Arts | 6,574 | 11,242 | 11,812 | 5% | 80% |

| Subject | 2002 | 2010 | 2011 Projected | % change 2010 - 2011 | % change 2002 - 2011 |
|---|---|---|---|---|---|
| Biography | 6,873 | 12,885 | 14,319 | 11% | 108% |
| Business | 6,918 | 11,058 | 12,263 | 11% | 77% |
| Computers | 7,564 | 7,793 | 7,615 | -2% | 1% |
| Cookery | 1,956 | 3,416 | 3,697 | 8% | 89% |
| Education | 6,829 | 10,916 | 13,070 | 20% | 91% |
| Fiction | 25,102 | 53,139 | 60,075 | 13% | 139% |
| General works | 2,085 | 3,106 | 3,079 | -1% | 48% |
| History | 11,362 | 15,003 | 14,022 | -7% | 23% |
| Home economics | 1,434 | 2,021 | 2,152 | 6% | 50% |
| Juveniles | 30,504 | 32,372 | 36,027 | 11% | 18% |
| Language | 5,924 | 5,253 | 5,243 | 0% | -11% |
| Law | 4,432 | 6,239 | 6,585 | 6% | 49% |
| Literature | 6,261 | 9,384 | 8,608 | -8% | 37% |
| Medicine | 9,495 | 13,599 | 14,332 | 5% | 51% |
| Music | 3,376 | 4,059 | 4,645 | 14% | 38% |
| Personal finance | 473 | 725 | 792 | 9% | 67% |
| Philosophy, psychology | 8,894 | 16,207 | 18,481 | 14% | 108% |
| Poetry, drama | 5,742 | 12,890 | 12,676 | -2% | 121% |
| Religion | 12,253 | 20,642 | 23,219 | 12% | 89% |
| Science | 11,688 | 21,205 | 18,499 | -13% | 58% |
| Sociology, economics | 20,969 | 29,497 | 31,633 | 7% | 51% |
| Sports, recreation | 5,800 | 7,425 | 7,624 | 3% | 31% |
| Technology | 6,896 | 11,590 | 10,360 | -11% | 50% |
| Travel | 4,316 | 4,707 | 4,490 | -5% | 4% |
| **Subtotal** | 215,138 | 328,259 | 347,178 | 6% | 61% |

| Subject | 2002 | 2010 | 2011 Projected | % change 2010 - 2011 | % change 2002 - 2011 |
|---|---|---|---|---|---|
| Non-traditional (reprints, often public domain, and other titles printed on-demand, plus records received too late to receive subject classification) | 32,639 | 3,806,260 | 1,185,445 | -69% | 3532% |
| Total | 247,777 | 4,134,519 | 1,532,623 | -63% | 519% |

Source: New Book Titles and Editions, 2002-2011. Bowker. (*http://www.bowker.com/assets/down-loads/products/isbn_output_2002-2011.pdf*)

## Romance fiction is the top-selling genre

The Romance Writers Association confirmed that romance fiction consistently commands the largest share of the consumer market (16.7 percent), surpassing other market categories such as mystery, science fiction/fantasy, and religion/inspirational. (Source: Business of Consumer Book Publishing 2013)

According to R.R. Bowker's *Books In Print*, 9,089 of the 832,253 new titles published in 2009 were romance titles.

Romance fiction titles dominated the best-seller lists during 2009, with 375 editions of 357 titles by 167 authors under 51 imprints on the *New York Times*, *Publishers Weekly*, and *USA Today* lists. Romance fiction ranked only behind movie tie-in books on the best-seller lists. The top performing romance subgenres included history, suspense, fantasy, and horror titles. One reason romance outperforms other genres is that women in the U.S. buy more books than men, and women make up 90.5 percent of the romance readership.

**Romance Fiction Sales** (source: Simba Information, 2010)
- 2005: $1.4 billion
- 2006: $1.37 billion
- 2007: $1.375 billion
- 2008: $1.37 billion
- 2009: $1.36 billion
- 2010: $1.36 billion

**2012 Romance Fiction Sales Compared to Other Genres**
(source: Simba Information)
- Romance: $1.438 billion
- Religion/inspirational: $$717.9 million
- Mystery: $728.2 million
- Science fiction/fantasy: $590.2 million
- Classic literary fiction: $470.5 million

# The Quality of Your Writing

If you are serious about selling your book, you must be serious about the quality of your writing. Good writing brings together many elements: imagination and creativity, a consistent point of view, knowledge of the subject matter, clever plot structure, appropriate vocabulary, and correct grammar and sentence construction.

A well-written work of fiction is characterized by:
- A powerful, distinctive "voice"
- Unique storyline
- Original, compelling, well-crafted sentences
- Interesting characters
- Dialogue that reveals character and subtext
- Narrative that evokes images
- An intriguing and immediate opening hook that contains action, conflict, and crisis

A good nonfiction work has these qualities:
- A strong narrative element
- A structure that flows logically and leads the reader to a specific goal
- Writing that delivers help to solve a problem or make one's life better

Good writing skills are not acquired overnight, and some people never master the technical aspects of grammar and sentence structure. Perhaps you have a captivating story to tell but lack a rich vocabulary and the ability to write well-crafted sentences. You might have a good idea and excellent writing skills but lack the knowledge and authority to produce a marketable manuscript. Do not let obstacles like these stand in your way. Do whatever is necessary to remedy the situation. Participate in a writing workshop or creative writing classes. Hire a professional editor to rework your manuscript, or find a cowriter or a ghostwriter to help you.

(See below.) Many celebrities use ghostwriters to write their memoirs and commentaries — they provide the name recognition, and the ghostwriters provide interesting, readable books. The extra expense of hiring someone to perfect your book will pay off when your well-written manuscript becomes a top seller.

## Beta readers and critique partners

"Beta readers" are people who read your manuscript and give you feedback while you are still working on it. Beta readers look out for typos and grammatical loose ends, passages that need to be clarified, and flaws and weaknesses in your manuscript. A beta reader can be anyone who is willing to read your book, including friends and family members. You also can find volunteer readers by joining writers' groups and participating in online writers' communities such as Absolute Write (**http://absolutewrite.com**) and Writers Beat (**www.writersbeat.com**) or virtual reader communities such as Library Thing (**www.librarything.com**) and Good Reads (**www.goodreads.com**). Most family members and friends will praise your work, whether it is good or not. Get at least one objective opinion from a person who has professional knowledge of writing and publishing, and take his or her advice seriously.

Most people who volunteer to be beta readers enjoy reading books of a particular genre and encouraging emerging authors. Beta reading is most effective when you tell your reader exactly what kind of feedback you want — a general opinion, proofreading, or a line-by-line critique — and give the reader a schedule or deadline. Do not hand your work-in-progress (WIP) over to a complete stranger without first learning something about him or her. A beta reader is someone who wants to support you in achieving your goals, and your relationship should be one of trust and mutual respect. It is unlikely that a beta reader would steal your work because it is copyrighted as soon as you write it, but if

you feel uneasy, give him or her only one or two chapters to start with. Hold back on sending the rest of your manuscript until you are certain you can trust the person.

A critique partner is a fellow writer who comments on your work in exchange for your feedback on his or her writing. The ideal critique partner is someone who writes in a similar genre to yours, agrees with you on fundamental issues, and has the same or a higher level of experience writing professionally. Search for someone who has the qualities you need in a critique partner by joining local writers' groups and associations, networking at conferences, reading blogs and forums, and posting notices. Do not be shy about approaching fellow writers — the worst they can do is say "no." As with beta reading, critiquing works best when each partner clearly understands what is expected. Some critique partners sign informal contracts specifying how they will communicate (email, face-to-face meetings), how often they will exchange manuscript pages, and policies about turnaround time, deleting/returning material, and sharing emails with others. Try out a potential critique partner by exchanging some trial pages before you commit yourself. The relationship between critique partners can be delicate because criticism is being exchanged, and not all comments are positive. A successful critique partnership often develops into a deeper professional relationship or a personal friendship.

## More about critique partners

You can read more about finding and working with critique partners on these websites:

- Stiefvater, Maggie. "2011 Critique Partner Love Connection." April 7, 2011. (**http://maggiestiefvater.blogspot.com/2011/04/2011-critique-partner-love-connection.html**)

- Absolute Write (**http://absolutewrite.com/forums/forumdisplay.php?f=30**)

- Anderson, Jessica. "How to Find the Perfect Critique Partner." The Knight Agency. Thursday, June 12, 2008. (**http://knightagency.blogspot.com/2008/06/how-to-find-perfect-critique-partner.html**)

- Gwyn, Kelly. "Romance Writers on the Journey." (**http://romancewritersonthejourney.wordpress.com/critique-partnerships-tips-and-techniques**)

Writer critique groups are composed of authors with an understanding of the writing craft. The goal of a writers' group is to help everyone involved become a better writer, so each member participates in offering critiques of other members' manuscripts. You can find writers' groups in your community by inquiring at your local library and independent bookstores. You also can locate writers' groups online by using a search engine or exploring writing forums. For Writers (**www. forwriters.com**) offers a listing of writers' groups around the country.

## Editing and proofreading

Many first-time authors are so eager to get their books into print that they submit unpolished and imperfect manuscripts to agents and publishers. You may have only one opportunity to make a good impression on a publisher, agent, or if you are self-publishing, your readers. Do not waste this opportunity by being in too much of a hurry. Read over your manuscript again and again. Ask friends and colleagues to read it and make suggestions. Make sure the quality of your writ-

ing is consistent throughout the book. When you detect a weak area, try to rearrange or rewrite it. Compare your book to similar books and make improvements until your book surpasses them. Let your manuscript "rest" for a few days, and look at it again with a fresh perspective. If your book is worth writing, it deserves the extra time and attention to make it perfect.

Editing and proofreading entails carefully checking your manuscript for typographical errors, spelling, spacing, punctuation, capitalization, sentence structure, syntax, word choice, tense, arrangement, and overall clarity and flow. Techniques you may wish to use to proofread your manuscript include:

- Printing a copy of the manuscript and tracing each word with your finger, so you do not overlook any errors.

- Reviewing your manuscript from back to front, so you are proofing the content rather than reading it.

- Reading the manuscript aloud to catch missing or misspelled words and lapses in clarity.

Professional freelance editors and proofreaders are available to assist you with editing and proofreading. The Editorial Freelancers Association (**www.the-efa.org**) provides a free directory of qualified editors and proofreaders and a standard rate chart. There are different levels of editing and types of editors:

- A **proofreader** is someone who reviews the manuscript for spelling or grammatical errors. Proofreaders' fees average between $25 and $35 per hour.

- **Copy editors** and **line editors** read the text word for word and correct any grammatical mistakes or spelling errors. They also provide comments regarding content. The line editor also will make changes to the manuscript to improve readability, evaluate the text for consistency, and research and check the accuracy of facts. Basic copyediting costs $25 to $40 per hour, and line editors charge an average of $40 to $65 per hour.

- A **developmental editor** provides notes on story structure, character development, plot points, and dialogue. He or she may rewrite sections of the manuscript and rearrange content for better flow and logic. Developmental editors' fees range from $50 to $80 per hour.

# CASE STUDY: WHAT AN EDITOR CAN DO FOR YOU

Gretchen Pressley

*Gretchen Pressley is currently an editor for a book publishing company in Florida. She edits nonfiction books on subjects that range from parenting to farming to self-help. She has been editing or proofreading in some form for more than five years and worked at newspapers and magazines before getting started in the book publishing industry.*

Having an editor for your book is absolutely a necessity, no matter what publishing route you choose to take. The role of an editor, in its most basic form, is to help the author create the best book possible. We editors can be many things for an author: a sounding board for ideas, a safety net for catching typos and errors, and an authority about what the target audience is looking for.

A book is a collaboration between author and editor. We can ensure all your sentences sound brilliant, we fact-check the details, so you do not get caught spreading misinformation, and we can help you brainstorm ideas or suggestions for anything from the organization of the book to the coherency of your statements. If nothing else, we take care of the little details of the book — correcting grammar and spelling mistakes, fixing awkward sentences, rewriting conflicting pieces of information — which leaves you free to concentrate on the important part: the story or the information presented to the reader.

Especially for new writers, an editor can be an invaluable source of information on what readers are looking for in your genre. Most editors specialize in types of books or genres, so they know what is common, what your audience expects from your writing, and what has been done a million times before.

Every good book has a few things in common. First, it is expertly written and offers something — information, a storyline, or a twist — that no reader has seen before. Second, it should benefit the reader in some way. A novel should entertain and move the reader; a nonfiction book should inform the reader. Good books are easy to follow and are organized in the most reader-friendly format possible. And do not forget the visuals. Nonfiction how-to books should have lots of images and graphics to help explain concepts to readers.

It is imperative to be a good writer, no matter what type of book you are trying to publish. If you are planning to make your living writing, you cannot wait for the mood to strike you. Instead of staring at your blank screen when the words are not flowing, start writing. It can be complete nonsense at first, but eventually, you will look at your screen and realize you are writing beautiful, compelling sentences. Then, you can go back and take out any of the beginning paragraphs that are not as perfect as you would like. Also — and this will seem obvious — a writer must write. Try to schedule a time to write something, anything, every day. Write a blog, keep a journal, write your friends letters, anything to keep your brain working and your writing skills sharp.

So, you have perfected your writing skills. You are working diligently on your manuscript, and you have a secured yourself an editor. Here are a few tips for making your editor love you:

- Reread what you write. A typo here and there is expected, but half-formed sentences, repetitive statements, and constant mis-spellings are enough to make any editor throw in the towel — and your manuscript into the trash.

- Do your research, and double-check your facts. Yes, most editors are happy to fact-check details for you, and we expect information to change. But if every date is wrong, common historical events are inaccurate, and your basic math is off, we are going to start feeling like teachers grading particularly troublesome tests. And you might end up failing the course.

- Meet your deadlines. Believe it or not, you are not the only author working with your editor. We have queues of manuscripts behind yours, and if you cannot get your assignment in on time, you run the risk of missing your editing window.

- Be receptive to changes and criticism. We know your book is your baby, and any changes, however small, might not fit in with your vision. But a good editor will never change your words or your ideas without a good reason. We really do just want your book to be the best it can be. And if you have a good reason for leaving a sentence, fact, or idea the way it is, perhaps it can be negotiated to everyone's satisfaction.

## Story checklist for fiction books

Story checklists are helpful for self-diagnosing problem areas of your fiction manuscript. Many checklist books exist solely on this topic, such as Elizabeth Lyons' *Manuscript Makeover: Revision Techniques No Fiction Writer Can Afford To Ignore* and *Self-Editing for Fiction Writers* by Renni Browne and Dave King. Below is a story checklist to help you pinpoint weak areas and revise your manuscript for submission.

√   Rewrite sentences that begin with the words "there" or "it."
√   Revise sentences written in passive voice.
√   Check that the tone is consistent for your story and genre.
√   Ensure that all dialogue and speeches advance the story and reveal plot and character.
√   Make sure your prose is fluent and varied in rhythm.

### Questions to ask when reviewing your manuscript:

- Does each of my characters have a distinctive voice?
- Is the antagonist as complex as the protagonist?
- Is the main character's opponent as strong or stronger?
- Do I open the story as late as possible?
- Does the opening grab the reader and compel him or her to continue reading?
- Is there enough conflict flowing through the entire book to hold a reader's attention?
- Is there a compelling reason for readers to connect with the hero and follow him on his journey?
- Does the plot unfold naturally?
- Have I crafted a key relationship for the protagonist that readers can relate to and root for?
- Is the theme consistent throughout the narrative?

- Does the writing evoke an emotional response for the reader?
- Do I have too much exposition delivered in one section?
- Does each chapter end with a cliffhanger?
- Does each scene contain conflict or tension?
- Have I successfully conveyed the main character's transformation?
- Are my descriptions vibrant and detailed?
- Does the ending pack a punch and leave the reader satisfied?

## The top five reasons a fiction manuscript is rejected

1. The writing is too predictable — there are no surprises or twists.
2. The author does too much "telling" and not enough "showing," stating how a character feels instead of showing it through action.
3. The characters are not interesting or worth caring about — there is nothing compelling to engage the reader.
4. The protagonist does not undergo a transformation — the main character is the same person at the end of the story as he or she was at the beginning of the story.
5. The author does not have a distinct voice — the style and diction of the narrative that is filtered through the author that creates a sense of uniqueness.

# Checklist for nonfiction books

When going over your nonfiction book, review the purpose for which the book was written. Confirm that the manuscript fulfills that purpose and meets the expectations aroused by the book title, introduction, and book copy on the back cover.

√ Rewrite sentences that begin with the words "there" or "it."

√ Revise sentences written in passive voice.

√ Check that the tone is consistent throughout the book.

√ Make sure your prose is fluent and varied in rhythm.

√ Remove unnecessary words and phrases that are not essential to the meaning of a sentence.

√ Avoid using superlatives (such as "great," "huge," "extremely," "terrific") or clichés ("and more"), unless you have a very good reason.

√ Make sure your verbs agree with the subject of the sentence (one … is, some … are) and that pronouns agree with the nouns they refer to. ("company … its," "people … their").

## Questions to ask when reviewing your manuscript

- Is the introduction compelling? Does it explain how the reader will benefit from my book and entice the reader to delve further into the book?
- Is the book well organized, with an outline and a clear progression from one topic to the next?
- Are headings, sidebars, numbering, chapter introductions, and title headings consistent throughout the book?
- Are there short, choppy sentences that could be combined to make a smoother, longer sentence?
- Are there long, awkward sentences that could be broken up into shorter segments and recombined?
- Is the meaning of each sentence clear?
- Does each paragraph have a topic sentence that is then developed further in the rest of the paragraph?
- Does the text flow smoothly from one idea to the next?
- Are all quotations properly cited?
- Have you checked all your facts with reliable sources?
- Does your book accomplish its purpose?
- Does the conclusion recap the book with an inspiring message? (Some readers will look at the conclusion before buying your book.)

# Finding and working with a ghostwriter

A ghostwriter writes your book or article but does not take credit for it. A ghostwriter also can edit or rework your manuscript, do research, or work side-by-side coaching you as you write your book. If you already have an agent or a publishing deal, your publisher or agent may find a ghostwriter for you. You can find your own ghostwriter through the Internet by typing "ghostwriter" in a search engine to get a list of ghostwriting professionals and agencies. Read the classified ads of publications such as *Writer's Digest* and *Writers' Journal* and writer forums with message boards where ghostwriters advertise their services. You also can post ads on freelance sites like Monster.com, Elance.com, and Guru.com, but you will need to screen responses carefully. Look on blogs for writers that you like, and post messages that you are looking for a ghostwriter. Ask for recommendations from agents, other writers, or anyone who may have worked with a ghostwriter.

Network with local writers' associations. Look at the acknowledgments in books of your genre — a ghostwriter may be named there as a contributor.

Contact potential candidates, give them a synopsis of your project, and see how they react. Approach at least three ghostwriters so that you can get a good sense of their styles of work and their personalities. Ask for references and writing samples; a writer's style might not suit your needs. Interview the references about their experiences with the writer:

- Was the ghostwriter easy to communicate with?
- Was the work done on time and according to budget?
- Were there any surprises? What was the person like to work with?
- Did the finished book sell?

Meet the ghostwriter in person to establish a relationship and make sure you are comfortable collaborating with each other. Does the ghostwriter listen to you, and will he or she be able to accept your suggestions?

Explain exactly what you want the ghostwriter to do. Ask how long the project will take and get an estimate of the cost. Ghostwriters are paid either a project fee (the national average is $15,000 to $25,000), an hourly rate ($25 to

$85 per hour), or by the page ($100 to $175 per page). You might pay a larger fee or a share of the royalties if the writer is given credit as a co-author or if the ghostwriter must do research. An inexperienced ghostwriter will charge less, but the result might not be as professional. There is a risk that an inexperienced ghostwriter will underestimate the amount of work involved and run out of steam before the project is finished. You can ask the ghostwriter to prepare a table of contents and a few sample pages — most ghostwriters who are interested in a project will do this for a small fee.

Once you have selected a ghostwriter:

- Include a timeline and a payment schedule in the contract, as well as a cancellation clause stating what will happen if either of you fails to uphold the agreement. Make your expectations clear. State whether you want to claim sole authorship of the finished book to avoid misunderstandings later. Expenses such as travel and postage are your responsibility. Have a lawyer or publisher look over the contract before you sign it.

- Respect your own timeline — give your ghostwriter the materials and interviews he or she needs, and be quick to read and return chapters sent for your approval.

- Keep in contact with your ghostwriter and follow up on your timeline, so your project is given priority over his or her other projects.

- Give your ghostwriter constructive feedback; tell him or her why you do not like something and how you want it changed.

- If you discover after starting the project that the ghostwriter is not going to work out, cancel the contract, and find a new writer. Do not waste time and money waiting for the situation to improve.

## Chapter 4

# Traditional Publishing

✳

T he biggest hurdle for a first-time author who wants his or her book published by a conventional publisher is getting a publisher or literary agent to accept it. Competition is stiff. Agents and publishers are deluged with submissions every day. Many authors testify that they got their first break through some lucky encounter or chance circumstance that attracted a publisher's or agent's attention. It may take months or even years to find a publisher for your first book. Surviving that process takes patience and determination. You only have to find one publisher interested in publishing your book, but until that happens, you and your manuscript are unknown and unacknowledged. You might become discouraged as one rejection follows another. In the end, only perseverance brings success. If you believe strongly enough in the value of your book, you will keep trying, using different tactics and approaching more and more editors until you finally find a way to get published.

## How Traditional Publishing Works

For fiction books or narrative nonfiction work, your complete manuscript is submitted to an acquisitions editor for consideration. For nonfiction books, the acquisitions editor is provided with a book proposal and sample chapters. If the editor likes your book, he or she will prepare a presentation for an editorial committee, including information about the target market and the book's sales potential. The manuscript or book proposal is analyzed by the editorial review committee, which may consist of editors, production staff, sales representatives, in-house publicists, and even the publisher or owner herself. If the review committee decides your manuscript is compelling or your idea is viable, the publishing company will offer you a contract, and often, an advance against future book sales.

Approximately 80 percent of all published books fail to earn back the advance given to the authors, and with the cost to produce an average hardcover book escalating upward of $50,000, publishers consider several factors before committing to produce a book:

- The quality of your writing
- If your idea or novel is marketable
- Your ability to promote and publicize the book
- If the book will be timely when published
- How large the audience is for the book
- If the book has other sales potential, such as film rights
- If your book could be a series or produce spin-offs
- If you can acquire cover quotes and a foreword
- Potential distribution channels
- How many similar books are on the market?
- If major bookstores will stock it

## Fast facts

- 85 percent of new titles published each year are nonfiction.

- 15 percent of new titles published each year are fiction.

- First-time authors write 75 percent of the new nonfiction books published each year.

- According to the Association of American Publishers, the publishing industry reported $11.67 billion in book sales in 2010.

- As much as 85 percent of a publisher's sales have come from Barnes & Noble, Amazon.com, Borders, and Ingram.

- According to *Bowker's Books In Print*, 4,134,519 new book titles and editions were published in 2011, an increase of 132 percent from 2009. Ninety-two percent of the new titles published in 2010 were "nontraditional" — self-published books, e-books, and some that were submitted too late to be classified.

- According to the Author's Guild, a successful fiction book sells 5,000 copies and a successful nonfiction book sells 7,500 copies.

# Finding a Publishing House

When your manuscript or book proposal is complete, you are ready to send query letters to acquisition editors at prospective publishing houses. A well-written query letter is crucial because it is probably the only exposure your book will have to the editor. *Chapter 5 explains the basics of writing a good query letter.* An editor who is interested in your query then will contact you and ask you to submit your proposal, manuscript, or synopsis for further review.

Sending your query letter to the wrong publisher is a waste of time and energy. No matter how well written your query is, a publisher that does not handle your type of book will not be interested. If you have researched your genre thoroughly, as suggested in Chapter 3, you probably already know the names of a few publishers that might be interested in your book. Another good source of recommendations is fellow writers. Join online communities of writers in your genre, and read testimonies and articles by published authors. When you find authors of books similar to yours, look them up on Amazon.com, or look at their websites to see whom their publishers are.

The best resource for finding a publisher for your work is *Writer's Market*, a directory containing 3,500 listings of book publishers, literary agents, and consumer magazines published annually by Writer's Digest Books. The online directory is updated daily. It lists publishers by genre, with the names of their acquisition editors, royalty rates, submission guidelines, and number of books published every year. A $19.96 annual membership to *Writer's Digest* (**www.writersdigest.com**) gives you 12 months of online access to *Writer's Market*. The printed version retails for around $30 on Amazon and includes a year of online access. You can read it free in your local library. Another good resource is *Jeff Herman's Guide to Book Publishers, Editors, and Literary Agents* (**www.jeffherman.com**). These specialized directories also might be helpful:

- *2014 Novel And Short Story Writer's Market*
- *2014 Children's Writer's and Illustrator's Market*
- *Christian Writers' Market Guide 2013*

Make a list of publishers who are good candidates for your book. Look up each publisher's website, and read the submission guidelines and mission statement. Most publishers make their policies clear. Many do not accept unsolicited manuscripts for review. Larger publishers accept submissions only from their acknowledged agents, and their websites often warn that packages from unfamiliar sources will be thrown into the mailroom trashcan. This might sound harsh, but it is their way of managing the hundreds of submissions that come their way every day. They do not have time to sort through stacks of unread manuscripts; instead, they rely on agents to screen authors and send only the best candidates on to the publisher. Unless you have a friend or relative on the staff of a publishing house, the best way to have your manuscript taken seriously is to follow the publisher's instructions exactly. If your targeted publishers want to be approached through an agent, the best thing to do is find one to represent you. *See Chapter 6 for more information on finding and securing a literary agent.*

## Get organized

Pitching your book to a series of publishers or literary agents is a sales and marketing operation. As in any type of sales, the more people you approach, the more likely you are to find a buyer for your product. Plan to contact 40 or 50 publishers or agents.

You will be most successful if you organize your contacts, keep accurate records of your interactions with them, set goals and priorities, create a timeline, and regularly review your files to see what you need to do next. There are times when a publisher might contact you after several months; it will be much easier to respond if you have all the contact information at your fingertips.

**Create a publisher database.** Take your list of publishers who might be interested in your work and create a chart or spreadsheet with important information such as telephone numbers, names of acquisition editors, email addresses, and notes about submission guidelines. Look through each publisher's website and find the name of the specific acquisitions editor to whom you will address your query letter, as well as information about the publishing company's newest releases in your genre. Call the publishing company's customer service number and confirm that you have the correct spelling of the editor's name and his or her correct title. The publishing industry is known for its high job turnover, and there is always a chance that the editor you want has been replaced with someone new. Leave space to make notes about each company. Rank each publisher according to importance — those most likely to accept your book, or whom you are most interested in, should get the highest scores. Divide the list of publishers into groups of six or so, with the highest-ranking publishers in the first group and the least important publishers in the last. It will take time and effort to contact each publisher, so you want to focus on the best possibilities first.

**Create a file for each publisher.** This can be a paper file, a folder on your computer, or both. Save a copy of everything you send to the publisher and every communication you receive. Also, keep a record of all your interactions with the publisher, including the date, the name of the person, email address or phone number, the outcome, and any follow-up activities with deadlines.

**Set up a calendar.** Mark it with target dates for sending out query letters and/ or submissions and any appointments you might make. Record the dates when you send out queries and make phone calls and tentative dates for following up if you receive no response. When you have finished contacting the first group of publishers, start on the next.

Keeping records and setting timelines will help you track your progress and change your strategy when needed. For example, you might notice that one type of publisher responds more positively than another and expresses interest in your future work. After you publish your first book, the information in your files will be ready to use for your next project. Files and records serve another purpose — if you ever are selected for an income tax audit, they are evidence that you are conducting a legitimate business as a writer.

## TIP: Always keep a backup of your files and records

All of your information, including manuscripts and query letters, could be lost in a few seconds if your computer hard drive crashes without warning or your home office is destroyed in a fire. You can find instructions for setting up regular backups of your computer system and data files on your computer manufacturer's website. An automatic backup saves copies of your files on a CD, DVD, flash drive, an external hard drive, and/or online. A number of companies such as Just Cloud (**www.justcloud.com**), ZipCloud (**www.zipcloud.com**), CrashPlan (**www.crashplan.com**), Carbonite™ (**www.carbonite.com**), Mozy (**www.mozy.com**), and My PC Backup (**www.mypcbackup.com**) charge a monthly fee as low as $2.95 to back up your files on their servers in what is known as cloud storage. If you do not use an online backup, regularly make copies of your files and documents on flash drives or external hard drives, and store them at another physical location. Do not forget to save backup copies of your websites, emails, photos, graphics, and any other files you might need. In an emergency, such as a sudden storm, save your latest documents by quickly emailing them to yourself.

If you do not know enough about computers, a computer repair shop or the computer center in an electronics store can assist you in setting up virus protection and an appropriate backup system.

## Publishing Nonfiction

Most publishers of nonfiction books want an author to submit a book proposal rather than a completed manuscript, so they can have input during the writing process. Even if you have already written the book, prepare the query letter and book proposal as though you are submitting an idea to the publisher for consideration. An agent or publisher who likes your concept can advise you on how to give your book a unique angle that sets it apart from other books on similar topics.

For nonfiction, it is particularly important to define your genre. Picture a bookstore, with shelves labeled "history," "biography," "travel," and "spiritual and religious." Which shelf does your book belong on? For a bookstore to sell a non-fiction book, it must be categorized so that customers interested in a particular subject can find it. Nonfiction books that belong to more than one genre, known as "hybrids," are difficult to categorize. Examples of hybrids might be a travel book combined with a collection of local recipes, or a personal memoir combined with advice on managing personal finances. Publishers of nonfiction books specialize in specific genres and types of books. When you are compiling your list of publishers to contact, research each one carefully, and eliminate those that do not publish books similar to yours.

## Your platform

Publishers of nonfiction books are looking primarily for two things: a good idea and an author with a strong "platform." Your platform is your résumé: all the characteristics that qualify you to write this book and sell it, including expertise, professional and academic certifi-  cations, first-hand experience, celebrity status, previously published books and articles, media exposure, name recognition, and public reputation. For example, a pediatrician has a good platform for a book about children's health. A pediatrician who has previously published two popular books on the subject has an excellent platform. A pediatrician who treats the children of Hollywood movie stars and regularly appears on national talk shows has a superlative platform.

To sell a nonfiction book, an author needs visibility — articles in magazines and newspapers, speaking engagements, workshops where books can be advertised and sold at a table near the entrance, and radio and TV interviews.

*Chapter 10 discusses how any author can build a platform by establishing an identity in the media, the publishing industry, and on the Internet through websites, blogs, and social media.*

# Securing rights

If you are writing a biography, history, expose, or true crime story, you might need to obtain written permission to use quotations, song lyrics, or excerpts from letters.

Get written permission to use someone else's work in the form of a signed consent form. *A sample consent form can be found in Appendix B.*

## Life story rights

Obtaining the rights to a compelling life story or the biography of a person who recently has been in the media can get you a publishing contract even if you have no other "platform."

Technically, under the First Amendment you are free to write about anyone without his (or her) permission, as long as you do not invade his privacy, harm his reputation, or infringe on his right of publicity. However, when you write about someone without permission, you take the risk that your subject will sue you for damages or block publication of your book on one of these grounds. Once the subject of a life story is deceased, the rights of defamation and invasion of privacy no longer apply, but any living person mentioned in your book could sue you for infringing on his or her rights.

The right of publicity gives an individual the exclusive right to license the use of his or her identity for commercial promotion and prevents the unauthorized commercial use of his or her name, likeness, or other public image. In the U.S., the right of publicity is protected under state laws, but only about half of the states have clearly defined rights of publicity. Often, it is incorporated in a right of privacy law. Privacy laws identify four types of invasion of privacy: intrusion, appropriation of name or likeness, unreasonable publicity, and false light. In some cases, such as when a celebrity's name has been trademarked, commercial rights to the name pass on to a deceased person's heirs.

You are safe as long as anything you write can be verified independently and you say only positive things about living people. If you say something unflattering, make sure it can be supported by at least two credible sources.

Securing the rights to someone's life story typically gets you a signed release protecting you from a lawsuit based on defamation, invasion of privacy, or infringement of right of publicity. Sometimes, it also gives you access to confidential documents and information and exclusive interviews with your subject. Templates for a Letter of Agreement granting rights to a personal story can be downloaded from the Internet and customized (see an example at **www.absolutewrite.com/ screenwriting/life_rights.htm**) or purchased as a legal form, or you can have an attorney draft one for you. If your subject's input is essential for writing the book, or if you need input from several key people, you can make an arrangement to share a portion of the proceeds of the book, as well as a portion of any other deals such as the sale of e-books, audiobooks, movies or foreign rights, with them. In some cases, the person may share the cost of promoting the book and agree to appear at book signings and promotional events.

## TIP: Paying for interviews undermines the credibility of your book

Other than an agreement to share the proceeds of your book with your principal subject(s), never pay for an interview. There is a very thin line between paying for information and bribery. Paying for interviews will cast doubts on the truth of your story  because a paid informant has little motivation to be honest. Sometimes legitimate sources think they should be compensated for an interview. Explain that you cannot compromise your credibility as an author and that you are giving him or her a chance to become part of a historical record.

If the subject of your book does not want to give you permission to write about him or her, you have several options. You can fictionalize the story completely by changing characters' names and physical descriptions. You can write the book using only information from public records, such as court records and newspaper articles. Another strategy is to use peripheral sources and tell the story from the point of view of someone other than the main character, someone who has agreed to work with you.

# Publishing Fiction

The query letter you send to an agent or publisher is especially important for selling a fiction book. If the query letter sparks enough interest, a publisher or agent will ask you to send a synopsis and sample chapters, or even the entire manuscript, to be reviewed.

A good work of fiction has many elements — character development, storyline, subplots, language, background, and atmosphere, which are woven together throughout the book. The last few pages of some novels are what make them great. For this reason, an agent or publisher needs to see the polished manuscript in its entirety to determine whether the book is good enough to publish. Before you submit a manuscript for review, perfect it by going over it again and again, asking other people to proof it for you, and getting feedback from beta readers and critique partners.

Your platform is not as important for a fiction book because the quality of the manuscript speaks for itself. However, the agent and publisher still will want to know if you have published books or articles previously or appeared in the media — anything that will demonstrate your professionalism and help sell the book.

As with nonfiction, research your list of potential agents or editors carefully to be sure they publish your genre before you begin sending out query letters.

# Dealing with rejection

After you submit your query or manuscript sample, you might receive a polite letter telling you the editor or agent is not interested in your book. Rejection is part of any author's life. You will be rejected over and over again, but one day you could receive a letter, email, or phone call with good news. It is important for your own peace of mind and for your professional success as an author to maintain a positive attitude and persevere until you land a book deal. A rejection by a publisher or an agent is not a personal attack on you. The publisher receives hundreds of submissions and can only accept a small number of them. There are many reasons why a publisher might not choose your book for publication. The rejection notice is not necessarily a reflection on the quality or merit of your book.

## Famous rejections

To encourage other authors, Ray Bradbury, who received 700 rejections before any of his work was published, compiled a list of famous books that were rejected by publishers multiple times. Among them:

*A Time to Kill* by John Grisham — 45 times
*A Wrinkle in Time* by Madeleine L'Engle — 30 times
*And to Think That I Saw It on Mulberry Street*, by Dr. Seuss — 27 times
*Carrie*, Stephen King's first novel — 30 times
*Diary of a Young Girl*, by Anne Frank (posthumous) — 15 times
*Dubliners*, by James Joyce — 22 times
*Dune*, by Frank Herbert — 13 times
*Gone With the Wind* by Margaret Mitchell — 38 times
*Harry Potter and the Philosopher's Stone*, by J.K. Rowling — 14 times
*Jonathan Livingston Seagull* by Richard Bach — 140 times
*Lolita*, by Vladimir Nabokov — 7 times
*M*A*S*H*, by Richard Hooker — 17 times
*Peyton Place*, Grace Metalious — 14 times
*The Lost Get-Back Boogie* by James Lee Burke — 111 times
*The Mysterious Affair at Styles*, by Agatha Christie — more than 20 times
*The Peter Principle*, by Laurence Peter — 16 times
*The Princess Diaries*, by Meg Cabot — 17 times
*The Thomas Berryman Number* by James Patterson — 26 times
*Watership Down*, by Richard Adams — 26 times
*Zen and the Art of Motorcycle Maintenance*, by Robert W. Pirsig — 121 times

E. E. Cummings eventually self-published his first work, *The Enormous Room*, and dedicated it to the 15 publishers who rejected it.

No one enjoys being rejected, but there is no reason to give way to anger, frustration, resentment, and disappointment. File the rejection notice away; make a note in your file; gather your forces; and contact the next round of publishers. Think of the rejection notice as confirming that particular publisher is not "the one" for your book and opening the way for you to seek out the right one.

The most common type of rejection is a form rejection letter — a standard form sent out when a publisher or an agent chooses not to accept a manuscript. Even though a form rejection letter seems impersonal and does not provide specific advice to help with your rewrite, it is a definite response, which releases you from waiting limbo and allows you to pitch other publishers — and move closer to your goal of becoming a published author.

Occasionally, you may receive some notes or comments on your manuscript suggesting how it can be improved. Take that as a good sign — the publisher thought your manuscript had merit but needs more work. Occasionally, you might get sarcastic or extremely derogatory comments. Ignore them. The person who wrote them was probably having a bad day, and your manuscript just happened to be in the way.

If you consistently receive large numbers of rejection form letters, consider that there might be a reason. Re-examine your query letter — does it contain errors or sound amateurish? Ask a friend or fellow writer to critique your query for you. Are you sending your queries to the right publishers and agents? Could it be that the market for your type of book is already saturated? Perhaps you could reinvent your book idea with a new angle to give it more appeal. If you are determined to publish your book, you might have to alter it several times to achieve your goal.

## How to face rejection

Jack Canfield and Mark Victor were motivational speakers in 1991 when they set out to sell their book, *Chicken Soup for the Soul®*. First, they flew to New York with their agent to pitch their book to major publishers, all of whom said they were not interested. They mailed the manuscript to another 20 publishers who rejected it, and their agent told them he could not sell it for them. Next, they printed an order form and collected more than 20,000 pre-orders, mostly from the audiences at their motivational seminars. They took their stack of pre-orders to the American Booksellers Convention and went from booth to booth, being turned away by one company after another. At the end of the second day, the presidents of Health Communications, Inc., a publisher of addiction-and-recovery books, agreed to take the first few chapters of the book and read them. One of them, Gary Seidler, loved the book. After being rejected 144 times, *Chicken Soup for the Soul* sold 8 million copies. A series of 80 best-selling books based on the concept have been translated into 39 languages.

# What to Expect When You Get a Book Deal

After a traditional publishing company has purchased the rights to your book, it will:

- **Take editorial control of the content**
  An editor works with the author to prepare the book for publication. Substantive editing is done to ensure the content is arranged appropriately for clarity and flow. Copyediting is performed to correct any errors in formatting, punctuation, spelling, grammar, word tense and usage, and syntax. The text also is checked for copyrights, trademarks, permissions, citations, and libel. The editor also will register the copyright and obtain an ISBN (International Standard Book Number) and Library of Congress Control Number.

- **Design the book cover and sales copy**
  The graphic department will prepare the artwork; lay out the cover elements; and select the typefaces. The marketing department writes the sales copy and selects testimonials and review quotes for inclusion on the back cover and dust-jacket flaps.

- **Prepare the book for printing**
  The art department designs the interior layout, typesets the text, and creates the necessary graphics, such as charts, maps, and illustrations. A galley is prepared for final review and proofing.

- **Print the book**
  This process involves selecting and ordering the paper, scheduling the press, making the plates, folding and trimming the printed press sheets, and sewing or gluing them into the book's spine.

- **Prepare promotional material**
  The publisher's marketing staff designs and distributes sales aids such as posters, signs, fliers, and bookmarks. They also write cover letters to book reviewers and create advertising copy.

- **Market the book**
  Copies of the book are sent to reviewers, advertising space is secured in magazines and online, book tours and media interviews may be organized, and catalogs are created to presell the book to book dealers.

- **Handle distribution**
  Fulfill orders to major dealers, stores, and libraries

- **Store returns**
  An average of 20 to 30 percent of books shipped to dealers are returned to publishers who then store the books in warehouses. Returned books usually are sold at a discount at bookstore outlets and through online booksellers.

## Chapter 5

# Writing a Good Query, Proposal, and Cover Letter Traditional Publishing

Y ou have written, rewritten, and polished your fiction manuscript or nonfiction book proposal until you are sure an editor would be delighted with it. Now it is time to start pitching your book to prospective buyers. This is done through a query — a one-page letter sent to an agent or publisher that contains vital information about your book and explains why it will sell and why you are the person most qualified to write it. Your query letter is your only opportunity to grab the attention of an editor or agent and motivate him or her to request a copy of your manuscript or proposal. It must be written with as much care and deliberation as your book.

The essence of your book must be distilled into a few paragraphs. Those paragraphs also reflect your professionalism and your ability to write. You cannot afford to misspell words or make grammatical errors. Thousands of query letters arrive at large agencies and publishing houses every day, where junior employees or interns screen them. A sloppy, amateurish, error-filled query letter will be discarded before it ever reaches an agent's or editor's desk.

Take your time writing a good query. You have spent months perfecting your manuscript; you can afford to spend a few days working on the query. Ask friends or fellow writers to read your query letter and suggest improvements. Check and recheck your spelling and your sentence structures. Do not be shy about promoting yourself and your work, but do not make exaggerated claims about the sales potential of your book or about your experience and qualifications. Agents and editors appreciate straightforward letters that allow them to make a realistic appraisal of your book.

Writing good queries is an art. If copywriting is not your strength, ask a fellow writer to help you or hire a professional publicist or ghostwriter to write queries (and press releases) for you. Entire books and websites are devoted to writing queries, including Query Shark˚ (**www.queryshark.com**).

Before you begin sending out your query letters, have your manuscript or book proposal ready to go. It may be up to a month before you receive a response to your query, but if the agent or editor should contact you right away and ask for additional materials, do not delay in sending them. You do not want to appear unprofessional or disorganized. Agents and acquisitions editors are busy people; if one asks you for your manuscript right away, you might miss a window of opportunity if you are unprepared. Agents and editors also want to know if you will be cooperative and easy to work with and will be able to meet deadlines.

Most publishers' and agents' websites post guidelines for submitting queries; you also can contact their offices and request their submission guidelines. Follow the instructions exactly. Do not send your manuscript or sample chapters unless they are asked for specifically. After you have sent your query, wait an appropriate period before following up.

## The Four Elements of a Query Letter

Your query letter represents your book. It should be written in the same narrative voice and with the same tone as the book itself. In one page, you must convey your book idea, your knowledge of the publishing industry, and your ability to complete the project and participate in selling your book. Do not be overly creative in your attempt to stand out; the letter should be easy to read and understand.

If you are submitting your query to a publisher, put this information at the top of the page:

**Date**

**Title:** Such as "Manuscript Submission Request"

**Status:** Whether this is a simultaneous submission (you are submitting to multiple publishers) or a proprietary (or exclusive) submission

**Represented by:** Your name, or your agent's name and phone number

A query is composed of four basic elements:

**1) Personalized opening**
Address each query to a specific person by name. Verify the person's title and the spelling of his or her name. Each query should have an individually written opening telling why you have chosen to write to that editor or agent.

**2) Book description**
One or two paragraphs describing the nonfiction book you intend to write, or a brief synopsis of your fiction manuscript. The opening line should "hook" the reader's attention and compel him or her to finish the letter. Describe your book with the same smooth, well-polished phrases that you will use in your publicity materials.

**3) Reasons for publishing your book**
Describe your qualifications for writing the book and the reasons why this book will sell. In this section, you can include information about the market for this particular book or about your plans for selling it. You also can talk about what makes your book stand out from others in the marketplace.

**4) Closing and thank you**
End your query with a thank you and a polite farewell. Be sure to include all your contact information on the page.

## Tip: Follow the rules

Authors who do not follow instructions or attempt to attract attention by being "different" and breaking the rules do not make a positive impression on literary agents or publishing houses. Colorful stationery, cute postage stamps, unusual presentations, and packages containing unsolicited manuscripts all indicate you are an unprofessional amateur. Tactics like these are likely to get your query dismissed before anyone even looks at it.

# Email and Snail Mail

Many literary agents and publishing houses now prefer queries to be sent by email. Look for a "Submissions" link or button on the company website for the email address or upload form. Follow the agent's or publisher's instructions exactly to avoid having your email discarded as spam or screened out by the company's email filter because it has unauthorized attachments. The subject line of the email is important and should include "Query" and the name of your book. Copy and paste the text of your query in the body of the email — do not send it as an attachment.

The text of the email should resemble the body of a written query letter. The reader will have to scroll down to read the entire query, so make the most of the space that is visible when the email is first opened. Place your contact information (your email address and phone number) at the top of the email where it is easily seen. Many agents read their email on smartphones or other small devices, so the first line should be particularly catchy to entice them to read further. Avoid abbreviations and slang, like "U R" and "LOL," often used in email correspondence.

Though email is less formal than a written letter, you still should begin with a salutation containing the name of the agent or editor. Shorten the paragraphs — no one likes to read an excessively long email — but retain any information that lets the reader know you have researched your genre and the market. Some agents and publishers ask you to attach a synopsis, outline, résumé, or writing samples to your email query. Unsolicited attachments will not be opened.

Test your email by sending it to yourself before you send it to anyone else. If you have copied and pasted the text from a word processing program such as Microsoft Word, it may contain formatting that causes strange characters to appear in the email. You can get rid of this formatting by saving the document as "plain text" before you copy it or by pasting the text in Microsoft Wordpad or Notepad (in the "Accessories" menu under "All Programs") and copying it from there.

Some publishers and agents still ask that queries be sent by regular mail. When sending the query by U.S. mail, print and sign the query letter, and mail it with a SASE (stamped, self-addressed envelope) in a standard letter-size envelope. If additional material, such as an outline or synopsis, is requested along with the query, send everything flat in a document-size envelope so that pages do not have to be folded. You will not receive a response if you do not include a SASE. Agents do not have a budget for postage to mail out responses to every query they receive, nor the time to address individual envelopes.

## CASE STUDY: HOW I WRITE A SYNOPSIS

CLASSIFIED CASE STUDIES
*directly from the experts*

Kimberly Llewellyn
www.KimberlyLlewellyn.com
www.cleverdivas.com

Books: *The Quest for the Holy Veil* (Penguin/Putnam), *Tulle Little, Tulle Late* (Penguin/Putnam), *Tender Harvest* (Avalon Books Contemporary Romance), *Pretty Please* (Kensington Precious Gem Romance), *Soft Shoulders* (Kensington Precious Gem Romance)
Genre: Romantic comedy, romance, chick-lit, paranormal romance, nonfiction/YA
Agent: Zoe Shacham, Nancy Yost Literary Agency

The synopsis is a very important tool. It follows your book all along the submission process. Your synopsis will help an agent love your book. Your agent will use it to entice an editor to consider your novel. The editor then takes it to her meetings to pitch to her peers to convince them to buy the book. Once bought, the marketing department uses it for promotion. They also use it to pitch to the sales team, which in turn pitches it to the bookseller, and in turn, they hand sell your book to the reader.

I keep the synopsis as short as possible: five to eight pages. In fiction, the synopsis has to have a beginning, middle, and an end. I like to show the character arc, the growth of the protagonist, and the emotional journey. The synopsis needs to reflect the core of the story, the high points (plot points), and the climax.

Some of my synopses are offbeat or quirky in order to reflect my writing style, especially when writing funny chick-lit. Have your synopsis reflect the tone of your story. If it is a dark, gripping horror novel, let the dark language of the synopsis reflect that. Of course, if it is a romantic comedy, let your comedic voice shine through. If it is a sensual romance, use lush, rich words. It is all about your voice.

To avoid the sagging middle, I summarize that part of the book in a paragraph, writing something like, "Mary encounters more disasters, including a ..." and then I list them. Or, "Further obstacles keep her from her goal, including ..." It is fast and quick, and the agent can move on. Remember, you always have to give away the ending in the synopsis. Saying, "If you want to see how it ends, you will have to contact me" is a sign of an amateur writer.

# Email and Query Etiquette

Publishing is a long process that involves frequent communication between the author and the agent, editor, and other staff at the publishing house. Agents and editors not only are looking for good manuscripts, but they also are looking for good authors who will be cooperative, easy to work with and professional about meeting deadlines and fulfilling requests. From the beginning, the way you communicate shows how professional you are and how well you understand the publishing industry. Here are some tips for communication etiquette:

- Once you have sent off your query, sit back, and wait patiently for a response. Agents and editors have busy schedules and might not be able to review your query right away. Remember that their existing clients take priority over screening new and unknown authors. At certain times of the year, an agent or publisher may be overwhelmed with work, away at a trade show, or on vacation; often a notice on the website announces that the company is closed to new submissions for the time being. In that case, wait until queries are being accepted again before sending yours.

- Most publishers and agents specify an average response time on their websites. Do not attempt to contact them again until this time has passed. Allow an extra two weeks for mail delivery if your query was sent by regular mail. Some publishers and agents do not respond at all if they are not interested in a query. If the specified period has passed and you still have not received a response, assume that the query has been rejected and move on to new prospects. An agent or editor will contact you if he or she is interested in your book.

- After sending a letter or email, you may have doubts and want to reword your query. Resist the temptation to send a correction or a resubmission. This will indicate that you are unsure of yourself, unprofessional, and likely to be difficult to work with in the future. Do not send follow-up email messages like, "Just want to be sure you received the email I sent last week." Bombarding the agent or editor with email messages only will annoy him or her.

- Do not attempt to force a relationship by sending gifts, cookies, or flowers. It is appropriate to send a polite thank you note or a Christmas card, but not a Valentine or a Fourth of July email card.

- Email tends to be more casual than other types of correspondence, but keep your language professional and business-like. Avoid abbreviations, slang, and foul language. Do not vent your frustration after a rejection by sending an agent a scathing email full of invectives and accusations. It will not accomplish anything, and every email becomes a permanent written record. You never know where that email will end up — it could be passed around as a joke among other agents or posted on a blog.

- Most busy people prefer email to a phone call. Phone calls take up valuable time, interrupt workflow, and distract from the matter at hand, which is why you often encounter voice mail or an answering service. Email, on the other hand, can be prioritized and read at a convenient time when the recipient is ready to devote attention to them. Email also provides a useful record of what is being said without the need to take additional notes.

- Less is always more — keep your email messages simple and to the point. Do not turn your business email into a personal diary or a reflection on life. Always ask yourself what you are trying to accomplish with the email, and use as few sentences as possible. Long, wordy emails are likely to be skimmed over or not read at all.

## Query do's and don'ts

**DO:**

- Research each agent or publisher carefully before writing your query.
- Personalize your query for each agent or editor.
- Have your proposal or manuscript ready before you send out query letters.
- Be honest.
- Be concise.
- Keep the same narrative voice as your manuscript.
- Follow the agent's or publisher's guidelines for query submissions exactly.
- Use standard paragraph formatting and a black 12 pt. font.
- Edit and spell check your query several times.
- Have friends and fellow writers review and critique your query.
- Wait for the agent or editor to respond to you.
- Spend your time working on your platform, preparing your next round of queries, and planning your next book.

**DON'T:**

- Take a hostile or aggressive stance.
- Misspell the agent or editor's name.
- Use special fonts, unusual formatting, or colored stationery.
- Send out your query as a mass mailing, a form letter, or email blast.
- Exaggerate your qualifications or your book's sales potential.
- Use clichés.
- Include sample chapters or a manuscript with the query letter unless specifically requested.
- Attempt to "take back" or resend a query email or letter.
- Try to force a relationship by sending gifts or personal messages.
- Phone an agent or editor before they have received a written communication from you.
- Send repeated emails or make phone calls asking about the status of your query.
- Spend your time agonizing over whether a particular agent or editor has read your query, wondering whether to call them or send another email, daydreaming about an acceptance letter, and blogging about the demise of the publishing industry.

# Book Proposals and Manuscript Submissions

An agent or editor has responded to your query and wants to look at your manuscript or book proposal. Congratulations! You are one step closer to finding a publisher for your book. Do not delay in sending whatever has been requested. The previous section mentioned that you should have your polished manuscript or book proposal on hand and ready to go before you send out queries. Screening submissions takes time and effort and is only one of an acquisitions editor's or agent's many activities. The editor or agent may have time to look at submissions right now or may be scouting for new material for the next season's releases. Do not hesitate to grasp this opportunity. Your quick response will make a good impression and build on the interest piqued by your query.

Follow the editor's or agent's instructions and send exactly what is asked for. You may be asked to title your submission in a particular way to conform to the company's filing system. Some publishers or agents might ask for your entire fiction manuscript, others will want only a synopsis and sample chapters. You might be asked to send a nonfiction book proposal of a specific length or to include your résumé and writing samples. Complying with instructions streamlines the reading process for the agent or acquisitions editor. If you send a hard copy of your manuscript or book proposal and want it returned, include a SASE with the correct amount of postage.

## Nonfiction book proposal

Your book proposal is essentially a sales tool. Everything in it should contribute to convincing an editor your book is worth publishing. Some of the elements from your proposal, such as your author bio, will become part of your public relations package later on.

A nonfiction book proposal includes these basic elements:

### Cover page

Your cover page is a plain page with the title of your book, your name, address, and contact information. Text should be centered and balanced on the page to create a pleasing first impression. Put the title and subtitle near the top of the page, followed by your byline. If you have an appropriate image, such as a book cover idea, a portrait of the subject of your book, or your own professional portrait, you can put a low-resolution photo (100 dpi), 1.5 to 2 inches by 2 to 3 inches, under your byline. Your contact information should follow. At the bottom right of the page, put "Copyright" and the year. An agent shopping your book around to publishers will put his or her name and contact information on your cover page instead of your own.

## Table of contents (TOC)

You can use the outline feature in a word processor such as Microsoft Word to generate a table of contents automatically that can be updated with a click of your mouse. *See Chapter 9 for more information on designing your book.* Be sure to update the table of contents just before sending your proposal.

## Book summary

This section should be a polished, well-written overview of your book — its subject matter, purpose, and unique angle. Avoid going into too much detail — that can be covered later in the chapter descriptions. The summary should convey your vision for the book.

## Your platform

This part of the proposal, often titled "About the Author," contains information about your writing background, postsecondary education, professional certifications, memberships in associations, awards, volunteer work — anything that shows why you are the best person to write this book. Do not generalize; list specific accomplishments that can be verified. Include personal details that are relevant to the book, such as your involvement with key people or events, your own experiences, or a hobby related to the subject matter. If appropriate, you can insert your headshot or a one-page bio listing pertinent and interesting facts about you. End with URLs (or links, if you are submitting your proposal electronically) for your website and articles you have written. If you are active in social media such as blogging, Facebook, or Twitter, give those links too. This part of your proposal should convey to the editor that you are media-savvy and knowledgeable about the publishing industry and actively promote you as an author.

## Sample photos or illustrations

If your book contains charts, maps, illustrations, or photos, insert one or more examples here. You can use a rough sketch of your idea if you intend to hire an illustrator for the book, but explain this clearly. For a book that will have photo inserts, select a few of the most interesting photos. Use small, low-resolution images that will not require too much memory or make it difficult to send your proposal by email. The procedure for an art book or a book that is primarily photos is different — follow the editor's or agent's instructions for submitting these. Always send copies and keep the originals.

## Book comparisons

This part of your proposal requires research, but it is essential to give an editor some information he or she can use to evaluate your book and present it to an editorial committee. This is done by comparing your book idea to other books that have done well in the market. Locate three to six recent "comps" (books similar to yours) by searching online booksellers such as Amazon.com and Barnes & Noble for books about the same subject matter or from the same genre. Verify that these books sold well by looking at their sales rankings on online booksellers' sites and checking the *USA Today* and *New York Times* best-seller lists. Next, study the publishers' websites to see how large each company is and how many books it publishes each year. Select books from companies similar to the publishers you want to sell to. Finally, get a copy of each book from a bookstore or library and read it. Note the quality of the printing and binding because you do not want to compare your book to an inferior one. Careful research pays off because an editor will be excited if you can demonstrate there is a genuine demand for your type of book.

Once you have selected three to six "comps," copy a cover image for each one from an online bookseller's website, and type next to it the author, title, publisher, date of publication, ISBN number, page count and whether it is a hardback, trade paperback, or mass-market paperback. Be careful to choose the edition that sold the most copies. Write a brief description of each comp followed by a paragraph explaining how your book is similar but offers something new and different. New developments occur so rapidly in many fields that books often are outdated within two or three years; you can say that your book offers the latest perspective. Your book may present the subject matter for less sophisticated readers or in a more organized manner.

Occasionally, a book idea is so unique that you will have difficulty finding any comps for it. In that case, look for best-sellers in the same genre or for successful books in another genre that use a similar format. Explain how your book will appeal to readers who like that genre or how your format succeeded with readers in another genre.

## Marketing plan

Publishers are interested in what an author can and will do to promote a book. If you do not plan to hire a professional publicist for several months when your book launches, you must specify what you will do to make your book known to the world. List everything you will do to market your book, leaving out no details. Your marketing plan should consider every possible avenue for publicity and sales:

- Do you make regular appearances in the media, on a TV show, or radio talk show? Do you have media contacts that will be willing to interview you about your book?

- Do you have a presence on the Internet, such as a website, a regular column, or a blog? Do you have a high-volume book blog, website, or online store from which you could sell copies of your book?

- Is your book an extension of an existing business, through which you could sell it?

- Do you do give public lectures, seminars, or workshops at which you could promote your book?

- Do you have contacts at major bookstores who might buy your book?

- How much money can you invest in publicity for your book?

- Do you belong to any groups, clubs, professional associations, or religious organizations that could serve as a platform for marketing your book?

- Does your book tie in with an industry or profession that might buy your book in bulk as a gift or giveaway?

- Are you available to do book tours, and how far can you travel?

If possible, provide a reasonable estimate of how many books you could sell in the first year. To support your marketing plan, you might include clippings of recent (within the last five years) newspaper articles about you or a CD or flash drive with recorded radio or TV interviews. You also could include articles that demonstrate public interest in the topic of your book. *See Chapter 11 for more suggestions about publicity and marketing.*

## Chapter descriptions

Detailed chapter outlines show how your book will be structured and what subject matter will be covered. This part of your book proposal takes time to write because you must conduct research and think each section of your book through completely. Be clear and avoid generalities. These chapter descriptions will serve as a guide while you are writing your book. After seeing the chapter outlines, the publishing company might ask you to change some parts of your book to conform to their brand or offer suggestions for improving the book.

## Sample chapters

Include the first 20 or so pages of your book, ending with the end of a chapter or a teaser — a paragraph or situation that entices the reader to want to continue reading. If you feel these pages are not your best writing, go over them until they are. You might want to include a sample from the first chapter and a representative chapter from later in the book. Try to choose material that will interest or entertain the editor.

### Formatting your book proposal

Agents or publishers may specify how they want the book proposal formatted. Otherwise, use the following guidelines:

- 1" margins on all sides
- Times or New Roman 12 pt. text
- A header on each page (except the cover page) with a page number, the book title, and your name

If you are printing a hard copy, use fresh ink or toner so the text is dark and crisp, and print only on one side of the page.

## Fiction proposal

An agent may ask to see a proposal for a fiction book before committing to reading the whole manuscript. A fiction book proposal does not require the same amount of research and planning as a nonfiction proposal. You already have done the work of writing the book, and you do not need to do a market analysis or compare your fiction book to similar novels. Your fiction book speaks for itself, and agents and publishers already know the market for your genre.

A proposal for a fiction book includes:

## Synopsis

A synopsis is a one- to ten-page summary of your fiction book. Write it as though you were writing a proposal for a movie adaptation of your book. The synopsis should be both entertaining and engaging, so the reader wants to read the entire book. It should have the same narrative voice and "feel" as your book. You can include snippets of dialog and description to demonstrate your writing style. A synopsis is not meant to be a teaser that leaves the reader hanging — tell how the story ends and tie up the loose ends of the plot, so the editor can see that it is solid and well thought out.

Some authors find distilling a ten-page synopsis from a full-length novel to be a painful and difficult process. Numerous books give suggestions and step-by-step advice for writing a good synopsis. If you know any writers or belong to a writers' group, ask to read some of their synopses, and have them critique yours. You also can find help and sample synopses online. You will find a list of helpful books and websites in Appendix A: Further Reading. Some authors write a synopsis before they begin writing a novel — it helps them keep track of plot lines and develop their characters. Others jot down notes as they go along. If you have already finished your book, write a summary of each chapter in order. Then, go through and simplify each summary, taking out unnecessary details but retaining important elements. Keep doing this until you have reduced your synopsis to ten pages or less. Ask friends or fellow writers to read and comment on it.

Here are some simple guidelines for writing a synopsis:

- Write in the first person.
- Provide no more than ten pages.
- Cover all the main elements of the plot.
- Start out with a theme or plot question and work around to its resolution.
- Give a brief sketch of all important characters, what their goals are, and how they fit into the story. Details like physical descriptions can be left to the sample chapters.

- Describe the central conflict of the story.

Here are some basic suggestions for formatting a synopsis:

- Put your name at the top left of the first page.
- Under your name, put your address and contact information on separate lines.
- Opposite your name, at the top right of the page, put the novel genre.
- Underneath, give the word count of the novel, aligned with the right margin.
- Below this write "Synopsis."
- Six lines below your contact information, center your title in UPPERCASE letters.
- Leave another two lines between the title and the beginning of your synopsis.
- Double space.
- Indent paragraphs (no extra space between them).
- Write character names in UPPERCASE letters the first time you use the name.

## Sample chapters

Together with the synopsis, include the first three chapters or 50 pages, whichever is longer. Some submission guidelines ask for the first chapter and a chapter from the middle of the book.

## About the author

Include information about your writing background and any personal circumstances that contributed to the writing of the book. You do not need the credentials and qualifications that help to sell a nonfiction book proposal, but you do want to present yourself as professional, knowledgeable about the publishing industry, and ready to work with the publisher to sell your book. Mention previously published books, media exposure, blogs, and any other publicity you might have received.

# Formatting Your Fiction Manuscript

After reading your synopsis, an agent or editor might ask you to send your full manuscript. Some agents ask for the manuscript right away after reading your query. Follow the agent's instructions for formatting and sending your manuscript. You may be asked to mail a hard copy or to send or upload an electronic file.

Proper formatting distinguishes you as a professional writer. Some agents and publishers may have their own formatting preferences. If you are unsure of a specific agent or editor's requirements, follow the common formatting and presentation guidelines outlined below.

- If printing your manuscript, use plain white 8.5- by 11-inch, 20-pound paper.
- Use a standard, easy-to-read font, such as Courier, Times New Roman, Arial, Tahoma, or Calibri; 12 point.
- Text should be double-spaced.
- Indent each new paragraph five spaces.
- Do not justify the right margin.
- Each page should consist of approximately 250 words.
- Include page numbers in the top right corner each page, except the title page and table of contents page.
- Margins are 1-inch all around.
- Do not include any copyright information anywhere on the manuscript.

## The title page

Center the title, subtitle, and your name in the middle of the page. The title is typed in all capital letters and bolded. Below the title and subtitle, double-space and type "A Novel." Below "A Novel," double-space and type "by." Below "by," double-space and type your name.

### BOOK TITLE
A Novel

by

Author's Name

Type your contact information in the top left corner, single-spaced.

Type an estimated word count in the top right corner.

## Table of contents page

Place a header in the top left corner with your last name, and then a slash, followed by the title (typed in all capital letters), followed by another slash, and then the word "Contents." For example: Author's last name/BOOK TITLE/Contents

Center, approximately one-third of the way down the page, the words "Table of Contents."

Four lines below "Table of Contents" list your chapters, each double-spaced in upper- and lower-case letters, flush left. Place the corresponding page numbers, flush right.

Do not number the table of contents page

The margins of the table of contents page are 1.5 inches all around (all other page margins are 1 inch all around).

## First page of each chapter

Begin each chapter on a new page.

Place a header in the top left corner with your last name, followed by a slash and then the title (typed in all capital letters.) For example: Author's last name/ BOOK TITLE

Put the page number in the top right corner and on the same line as the header.

One-third of the way down the page, bolded and in all capital letters, type the chapter number, followed by two hyphens and then the name of the chapter. For example, **CHAPTER 3 - - ON THE ROAD**.

Four to six lines below the chapter title, begin the body of the chapter.

## Subsequent pages of each chapter

Place a header in the top left corner with your last name, followed by a slash and then the title (typed in all capital letters.) For example: Author's last name/ BOOK TITLE

Put the page number in the top right corner and on the same line as the header.

Begin each change of dialogue on a new line, and indent five spaces.

## Packaging your manuscript for submission by mail

To submit your manuscript to an agent via standard mail, place your unbound pages in a manuscript box (manuscript boxes are available from The Writer's Store at **www.writersstore.com** and from office supply or stationery stores.)

Do not staple, paperclip, or bind the manuscript in any way.

If you wish to receive a response from the agent, include a No. 10 self-addressed, stamped envelope (SASE) in the box. If you want the manuscript sent back to you, include a large envelope and enough postage to pay for its return.

### The dreaded "slush pile"

The staff at publishing houses does not have time to read every manuscript that comes through the door. Unsolicited manuscripts and manuscripts that do not follow submission guidelines go into the "slush pile," a sort of bottomless in-box. When junior staff has extra time, or editors are looking for new ideas, they might look through the manuscripts in the slush pile in search of something interesting. For most manuscripts, however, the slush pile is the end of the road. To keep your manuscript out of the slush pile, follow submission guidelines to the letter.

HarperCollins has created an outsourced online "slush pile" called Authonomy (**www. authonomy.com**) where writers can upload their manuscripts to be read by editors, publishers, agents, fellow writers, and interested readers. Readers rank their favorites, and the top five are sent to editors for review each month.

## Children's Books

Children's books differ from adult fiction because they typically are shorter manuscripts with artwork, illustrations, and design elements that are an integral part of the book. If a publisher or agent responds to your query, include a manuscript, typed in a commonly used black font, in the package. Keep the manuscript neat and professional, and do not mix font types or use bold and other unnecessary, distracting formatting.

For a children's graphic novel, the rules are slightly different. Do not divide the manuscript into paginated sections or worry about marking out page breaks. The submission package also will include a print or reproduction of one finished piece of art that stands as a solid representation of your ability as an artist and relates to the submitted material. Some publishers consider text only when it is accompanied by illustrations, and others will consider text alone. Above all, the text for a graphic novel should demonstrate language economy, and the ability to communicate a story through dialogue and onomatopoeias. The illustrations in graphic novels usually tell most of the story. Research your targeted publisher's guidelines thoroughly before crafting a children's graphic novel proposal.

If you are submitting an illustrated children's book, you need to show the publisher how the book will look when it is laid out. This can be done in several ways, including storyboards and dummy books.

## Storyboards

A storyboard is a useful technique for the illustrating children's book author. Storyboards are an excellent way to distribute the book's content — text and illustrations. Composed of a sketch of each page on a single sheet of paper, the layout helps you, as well as the editor and the art director, visualize what is taking place on each page and organize the final layout. The approval of the storyboard leads to the completion of full-size sketches and then, final illustrations.

To create a storyboard:

- Create a series of 17 proportionate double pages.
- Each panel should be divided in half, with page 1 starting on the right hand side of the first panel.
- The blank left hand side of the first panel will carry printed front matter.

- Page 32 is the last and appears on the left hand side of the last panel, which leaves the facing page open for back matter.
- Because of economical considerations, publishers find it more appealing to produce books in the traditional sizes: 7 by 10 inch and 8 by 10 inch. Design the storyboard sketches in a manner that demonstrates to the publisher what type of illustrations the book will contain.
- Color is optional.

## Dummy books

A dummy book can be any size, as long as it is appropriate to your manuscript. It is helpful to sketch the dummy's layout beforehand so that you know precisely how it will go together. After determining page breaks in the manuscript, you will be able to parcel out the text that will appear on each page. Some authors make thumbnail sketches, or small drawings, to plan their books before creating the dummy book. Thumbnail sketches are a good way to visualize page elements and text division. Picture books are usually 32 pages long, so it is good practice to create a 32-page dummy..

To make a dummy book:

- Dummy book pages can be newsprint or drawing paper, with a cardboard cover.
- Books are made of what are known as signatures, that is, sheets of paper folded in half.
- To make a dummy book, make two signatures of eight pages each.
- Fold the pages in half to make two signatures of 16 pages apiece, for a total of 32 pages.
- Trim down the pages if so desired.
- Stitch the signatures in the crease, and then to each other.
- Affix the cardboard cover and the end papers, which also can be decorated.
- Do not forget to include the copyright, dedication, and title page. The front matter, or the material that goes in the beginning of the book and precedes the story, consists of the copyright notice, dedication, and title page.

- Back matter is composed of elements such as production notes, the author's biography, and other matter to be included at the publisher's discretion.
- The dummy book may contain some indications of color, and text is often pasted or printed in place on the pages.
- You may wish to use ruled lines on text pages to "contain" text blocks.
- Create a color cover design.

## Who will be looking at the dummy book?

Usually, an art director and an editor look for the presence of certain elements in the dummy, such as quality of content, logical arrangement of elements and narrative structure, and flow and continuity. While the illustrations do not have to be of finished, print-ready quality, they should stand as representations of the intended final product.

## Submission do's and don'ts

**DO:**

- Send the requested material immediately. Agents are perplexed when authors send material weeks or even months after it has been requested. If an agent is intrigued enough by your query to want to read your manuscript or learn more about your nonfiction project, send it immediately. If you wait, you risk the agent losing interest, forgetting about you and your book, or deciding that you are unprofessional and not worth representing.
- Follow instructions for formatting, titling, and submitting documents.
- Keep images and photos low-resolution and small to avoid taking up too much memory.
- Include any information relevant to selling your book in your author biography and marketing plan, including personal contacts, club memberships, hobbies, and past experiences.
- Create a detailed marketing plan, and indicate your willingness to invest in promoting the book.
- Have friends or fellow writers review your synopsis or book proposal.

- Tell how your story ends in the synopsis; do not leave the editor or agent hanging.
- Use a priority delivery service to send a hard copy of your manuscript. A delivery service ensures the material arrives in a timely manner to the right destination (on the agent's desk and not in the assistant's "slush pile.")
- Include a SASE with the correct amount of postage if you want a hard copy of your manuscript returned to you.
- Include a copy of the agent's request. Often, an intern or assistant will open the package. Inserting a copy of the agent's request for your material, along with a copy of the original query letter or a brief cover letter, indicates the material was solicited and ensures it will be delivered directly to the agent for review.
- **Send only what is requested.** Following instructions demonstrates that you are a professional author who is easy to work with.

DON'T:
- Design a dramatic graphic illustration that takes up your entire cover page.
- Offer a sample chapter from the middle of your book without including at least the introduction or first chapter.
- Exaggerate, make empty promises, or generalize about your qualifications, marketing plans, or the sales potential of your book.
- Send off a hurriedly prepared book proposal or synopsis.
- Place copyright information in your fiction manuscript.
- Send originals of anything: manuscripts, documents, photos, or illustrations. Always keep the original and send copies.
- Insert large, high-resolution photos and images that take up large amounts of memory and make the file too large to send conveniently by email.
- Send the entire manuscript if the editor or agent only has requested the first ten pages.

# If You Have Already Self-Published Your Book

If you have already self-published your book and an editor or agent expresses interest in your query, send a copy of the book along with the book proposal or synopsis. Explain clearly where and how you have been selling the book, how many copies you sold, and any arrangements you have made with bookstores or distributors. Be honest, and do not attempt to hide anything. The editor needs to know how much exposure the book already has received in the market and whether there are any potential conflicts of interest with distributors. The publisher also might be able to build on relationships you have developed with independent bookstores or other outlets for your book.

# Your Manuscript on the Other Side

What happens when your book proposal or manuscript arrives on the desk of an agent or editor? If he or she is excited about the book, or it seems a perfect fit for a particular publisher or project, your proposal or manuscript might be read right away. More often, it will be added to a stack of other proposals and manuscripts waiting to be read. If you failed to follow submission instructions correctly and sent your manuscript in an unusual format or sent the wrong materials, it might be set aside to be looked at someday when the editor or agent has a spare moment, or even discarded.

After reading your manuscript or proposal, the agent or editor might pass it around to other staff members and ask for their opinions. An agent who decides to represent your book will contact you and arrange to send you a contract. He or she then will begin shopping your book around to publishers who might be interested in it. An acquisitions editor who likes your proposal or manuscript typically does not make the final decision to accept your book for publishing. He or she will prepare a presentation for an editorial committee, sometimes gathering sales data from the marketing department and researching the sales potential for your book. Your book may pass through several reviews before it is finally approved. All of this takes time. It may be several weeks before you hear anything. The fact that a publisher or agent was interested enough in your query to ask to see your book is a positive sign, but it does not mean that your book will be selected for publication. As with query letters, it is better to wait patiently and not nag the agent or editor with follow-up email and phone calls. When your book has gone through the reading process, you will receive a response. In the meantime, focus on building your platform, sending out more queries, and writing your next book.

## What are your chances of getting published?

In one year, a literary agent might receive as many as 36,000 queries. He or she might request sample pages or proposals for perhaps 2,500 of those queries and go on to read about 100 full manuscripts. Out of those, the agent might offer to represent nine or ten. Of those nine or ten books, only five will be sold to publishers. If this sounds daunting, do not give up. Most agents agree that the majority of the queries and sample submissions they receive are amateurish, unprofessional, and unresearched. You can improve your chances of getting published greatly by following the suggestions in this book, educating yourself about the publishing industry, and constantly working on your writing.

## Chapter 6

# Working with
# a Literary Agent

A literary agent represents a writer and the writer's work to publishers and helps negotiate the sale of the work. Literary agents represent approximately four out of five manuscripts purchased by major publishers today. Literary agents play an important role for both publishers and authors. Agents know each publisher's specialties and are always on the look-out for promising new material. They screen queries and submissions to make sure only the best quality manuscripts land on the desks of acquisitions editors. Agents act on behalf of authors to negotiate the best possible deals and help in-experienced novices navigate the legal and technical details of getting published. An agent is interested, not just in selling individual books, but in developing an author's career over the long term. A literary agent can market subsidiary rights to your book and is often the best person to sell translation rights, international rights, electronic rights, audiobook rights, and even movie rights.

If you prefer to concentrate on writing and leave the business details to someone else, consider finding a literary agent to represent you. Do not assume, however, that you can just sit back and let your agent do all the work. Your agent will be just as interested as your publisher in your platform and your ability to promote and sell your writing. Agents typically do not take on the role of coaching amateur writers. Like editors, they prefer to work with experienced professionals who know the industry.

# Do You Need an Agent?

Not every book needs an agent. Your agent is paid by commission, typically 15 percent of your earnings from royalties and the sale of subsidiary rights. A book written for a small niche market, such as an academic book, religious book, a book of poetry, or a book on a regional topic, will not generate enough revenue to be worth an agent's time. The majority of agents manage novels and popular fiction. Unless the topic of a nonfiction book appeals to a broad commercial market, such as parents or people trying to lose weight, sales are not likely to be large enough to interest an agent. For this reason, publishers of nonfiction often accept unagented books. If you are writing a picture book and have to share your royalties and advances with an artist or illustrator, there probably will not be enough left over to pay an agent.

You might not need an agent if you have developed personal contacts in the publishing industry and feel comfortable negotiating publishing contracts yourself. Some large publishing houses accept queries, even if they do not accept unagented manuscripts. University presses and small presses generally accept submissions directly from authors, as do many publishers of children's books. You do not need an agent if you intend to publish your work as an e-book or with a POD service and market it yourself. You always can hire an agent to represent you later on, if your project grows beyond your expectations, and you want help managing your career.

However, a literary agent *can* help you break into the publishing industry if you have a well-written, polished fiction or narrative nonfiction book in a genre with broad commercial appeal. A less experienced agent is more likely to be open to new authors but might not have the same clout as an established agent. If you can capture the interest of a well-known agent, you will profit from his or her reputation and network of contacts.

A literary agent can help you in many ways:

- **An agent knows which editors would be interested in your work.**
  Agents continually cultivate relationships with publishing house editors. They know which editors will be most interested in your genre, platform, and writing style based on their tastes and needs. They will submit your

work to the appropriate publishers, the right imprints, the maximum number of imprints, and the correct people within those imprints, which increases your chances of being published.

- **Agents are aware of changes in the industry.**
  The publishing industry is constantly changing. An agent keeps abreast of new media and shifts in the market to better navigate the obstacles and opportunities for first-time authors.

- **Editors prefer agent submissions.**
  Agents have more influence with a publisher than an unknown writer does. If an agent has prescreened the material and is willing to represent an author's work, an editor considers it worthier than if it is submitted directly by a writer.

- **Agents ensure your manuscript is read.**
  Most large publishing houses only accept submissions from agents. An agent will work with you to make sure your material is as strong as it can be before submitting it for consideration.

- **An agent can negotiate a better deal and create a bidding war.**
  Agents will get your manuscript or book proposal seen by the maximum number of publishers. If multiple publishers are interested in the project, a powerful agent can coordinate a bidding war. Without an agent, you might not know what other publishers could be interested in your book.

- **Agents understand publishing contracts and are experienced negotiators.**
  Publishing contracts are written for the benefit of the publishing house, not the author. Agents are familiar with the boilerplate contracts of the publishing houses with which they work. They quickly can assess your offer, decide what is in your best interest, and determine how to proceed in negotiations with the publisher. Your agent makes more money if you make more. He or she is familiar with industry standards and contractual language and knows how to ask for larger advances and royalties and how to change minor clauses of the contract to favor you. A good agent will arrange for your contract to include an escalator clause, which provides a bonus payment should your book accomplish a specific feat, such as making a best-seller list or being picked up by a book-of-the-month club. Without an agent, you have no leverage to negotiate better terms.

- **Agents ensure timely payment from the publisher.**
  Once your manuscript has been completed, submitted, accepted, and finalized, your agent will conduct the necessary follow-up to ensure any outstanding financial balances are handled. The publisher works through the agent, so any money you receive will come directly from your agent after he or she subtracts the negotiated percentage for services rendered.

- **An agent buffers you from the aggravation of business matters**
  The publishing industry is a business. An agent handles the business aspects of the publishing process, so you can maintain a creative relationship with your editor and focus on writing. Agents deal with rejection letters, so you do not have to think about them. Agents track payments and ensure you are paid on schedule. An agent also handles publicity, marketing, and legal aspects of your career and can offer guidance as business issues arise.

- **An agent will ensure you receive better subsidiary rights.**
  Subsidiary rights are secondary rights that can be sold with a book. They include translation rights, audio rights, film rights, book club rights, serial rights, foreign rights, and additional rights. Agents negotiate to retain some of these rights and take responsibility for selling them on your behalf; they take care of responding to inquiries, sending out books, handling paperwork, and arranging deals. They might maintain relationships with foreign agents or publishers. Successful agents use co-agents in Hollywood to try to sell the movie and television rights for your book, which creates additional revenue and royalties. Without an agent, the publisher often will retain these rights.

- **An agent has contacts to help your career.**
  An agent's network can help you land endorsements and forewords from other authors and experts, publicity tie-ins, teaching engagements, speaking opportunities, media coverage, and more writing assignments.

- **An agent is your advocate.**
  Editors may have 30 titles to edit each year and are forced to prioritize them. Titles with agents take priority at publishing houses and receive more attention from editors than books without agent representation. Agents will advocate for quality book cover designs, higher marketing budgets, and better placement. If an editor leaves the company, an agent will work to ensure the new editor assigned to your book is enthusiastic

about it being published. Without an agent, if your editor leaves, you and your project will be orphaned. If your first book underperforms and your publisher drops you, your agent has a vested interest in finding another publisher for you. Without an agent, if your first book is not successful, you will have a difficult time finding an agent or publisher for subsequent books. Your agent may be the only stable element of your writing career.

# How to Find Reputable Agents

As a first-time author, you may have difficulty finding an agent willing to take on your book. Like publishers, agents are deluged with queries every day, and they are busy managing their existing clients. Agents specialize in particular genres and types of books. A query sent to an agent that does not handle your type of material will be rejected automatically. Begin your search for an agent by following the procedure outlined in Chapter 4 for finding a publisher. Make a list of agents you would like to work with that handle your type of book, rank them by priority, and begin sending out personalized query letters.

You can find literary agents through the Internet. Typing "literary agents" in a search engine will bring up a list of agencies and directories. The following online directories list agents along with information about them:

- **AgentQuery (www.agentquery.com)** — Agent Query offers a free searchable database of more than 900 literary agents.
- **Association of Author's Representatives (www.aar-online.org)** — AAR is a professional organization for literary and dramatic agents. It was established in 1991 through the merger of the Society of Authors' Representatives, founded in 1928, and the Independent Literary Agents Association, founded in 1977. Browse its list of member agents.
- *Guide to Literary Agents* **(www.guidetoliteraryagents.com)** — This Writer's Digest Book is a complete resource for writers who need representation.
- *Jeff Herman's Guide to Book Publishers, Editors, and Literary Agents* **(www.jeffherman.com)**
- **Preditors and Editors™ (http://pred-ed.com/pubagent.htm)**
- *Publishers Weekly* **(www.publishersweekly.com)** — A weekly trade magazine targeting publishers, booksellers, literary agents, and libraries

- *Publishers Marketplace* (**www.publishersmarketplace.com**) — A resource for publishing professionals. A $25 subscription, payable monthly, gives you access to its articles and databases.
- *Writer's Digest* (**www.writersdigest.com**)
- **Writers Net** (**www.writers.net/agents.html**) — An Internet directory of writers, editors, publishers, and literary agents

---

## CASE STUDY: HOW I ACQUIRED MY AGENT

CLASSIFIED CASE STUDIES
directly from the experts

Alice J. Wisler
www.alicewisler.com
www.alicewisler.blogspot.com

Books: *Rain Song* (2010), *How Sweet It Is* (2010), Hatteras Girl (2010), A Wedding Invitation (2011), all Bethany House Publishers

Genre: Romance

Agent: Kristin Lindstrom, Lindstrom Literary Management

Ever since I was six, I wanted to write a novel and have it published. I started sending out query letters for a work-in-progress and waiting for agents to affirm me. Then, the rejections came. After one particular rejection letter, which included personal feedback from a well-known agent, I realized that I had another problem besides the fact that I was querying for an unfinished novel: The main character's narrative voice was bland, and she was not likable. I read a few pages from my novel again and realized I did not even like her.

I revised and three months later, I had 20 chapters I was proud of. I sent out a query letter to an agent I found on agentquery.com. By nightfall, the agent asked to see my first three chapters. After she read them, she called to say she wanted the whole manuscript. Two weeks later, I received another phone call. It was the agent — Kristin Lindstrom of Lindstrom Literary Management. "Alice, I love it, and I want to represent you." Within eight weeks, we had a two-book deal with Bethany House. *Rain Song* was published 20 months later, and six months after that, *How Sweet It Is* was released. More recently, two more novels are under contract with the same publisher, thanks to Kristin.

Visit your local bookstore and library and seek out books similar to the one you are interested in publishing. Check the acknowledgment page to see if the author has acknowledged his or her agent by name. If the agent is not acknowledged by name, contact the publisher to get the name and phone number of the agent. Explain that you are a writer and would like to contact the agent associated with that book. If this approach does not work, try asking around in online writer's forums.

## Proceed with caution

Anyone can call himself a literary agent, buy business cards, and accept writer submissions. Beware of scammers that pose as literary agents and prey on inexperienced writers by charging them for questionable "services." You will see their ads and solicitations in magazines and on the Internet. Legitimate literary agents make their money from commissions on the books they sell. Avoid "agents" that:

- **Ask for a reading fee** — If an agent charges you any kind of fee to review your manuscript, steer clear. This practice is not illegal, but agents who do this are considered unprofessional and are making money from the writer, not the publisher.

- **Ask for a retainer** — Reputable agents are able to pay for their own expenses. They only take on books they determine to be marketable and do not ask for up-front fees or retainers from writers.

- **Offer to edit your manuscript, or offer other services, for a fee** — Agents are not editors. They should not be selling you any kind of editing services. Reputable agents only will accept market-ready materials.

- **Ask for a commission higher than the industry standard** — Reputable agents charge the standard industry fee of 15 percent of the proceeds of all rights sold, with higher percentages for certain types of rights (25 percent for foreign rights, and 20 percent for dramatic/film rights). If an agent tells you that you must pay more because you are new and do not have a solid track record in the industry, look for another agent to represent you.

- **Do not belong to AAR** — Although membership in this organization is not a guarantee, the agents who belong to AAR have agreed to a certain standard of ethics and professionalism.

- **Sell mostly to smaller, less reputable publishers** — Do not waste your time pursuing agents who have a large percentage of sales to small, electronic, or subsidy publishers. This does not help your reputation as a serious author. You easily could pursue these avenues yourself without representation.

- **Have no verifiable sales record** — Professional literary agents will discuss their recent sales with a prospective client. They should be able to tell you how many books they have sold, what types of books they sold, and to whom they were sold.

- **Send a generic acceptance form letter** — When a legitimate agent offers to represent a client, he or she makes a personal telephone call or sends a note to the author. A professional agent would never remit a representation offer using a generic form letter containing wording that could apply to any book — only con artists do that.

- **Try to pressure you into making a commitment** — A good agent will answer your inquiries respectfully and allow you to make the final decision concerning their offer of representation. Stay away from an "agent" who refuses to answer your questions, is rude or bullying, or pressures you in any way.

- **Ask you to sign contracts with unprofessional terms** — Avoid agents with contracts that include perpetual agency clauses, claims on clients' future commissions if the agency has no part in selling the property, clauses that allow the agency to bill clients for normal business expenses, provisions that ask for up-front payments, clauses for publishing through print-on-demand, or contracts that offer no advance.

- **Guarantee publication of your book** — Regardless of how well established a literary agent is, he or she can never guarantee your book will sell. Unsavory "agents" use promises of publication to entice trusting writers.

The website Predators & Editors (**anotherealm.com/prededitors**) and Writer-Beware (**www.sfwa.org/for-authors/writer-beware**) each maintain a list of individual agents to avoid.

The best way to get an agent is through a referral from another writer, a friend, or someone in the industry. Ask fellow writers or contacts in the publishing industry for a personal introduction to an agent. Read writers' and agents' blog posts and forums. Join writers' groups, and network as much as you can. When you send a query letter or a cover letter to an agent after an introduction, be sure to mention in the first paragraph that "so-and-so referred me to you."

Conferences, seminars, retreats, book festivals, and workshops provide opportunities to meet agents in person. Agents expect writers to approach them at these events. Some conferences even schedule pitch sessions where authors are given a few minutes each to promote their books to a gathering of agent representatives. The goal is to connect with agents and leave them with a positive impression of your work for when you submit your pitch package in the future. Some agents even may ask you to send them your book proposal or manuscript.

## Getting the most From a writer's conference

Proper planning and organization will enable you to get the maximum benefit from attending a writer's conference. Follow these tips:

1. Review the conference website to determine the agents who will be attending or speaking and create a list of the agents you wish to approach.

2. Create a plan of how you will spend your time at the event. Prioritize what you know you must do and what you would like to do if time permits.

3. Complete your pitch package before attending the convention, so you will be able to send the material immediately upon returning home from the event.

4. When you arrive at the conference, study the map and the program to best navigate the terrain.

5. Plan to attend both educational and social events, and walk the exhibition floor if one is presented. Collect business cards from everyone you meet.

6. Determine the best time to approach your preselected agents. This may be early morning, after a round-table or seminar presentation, or at an opening night cocktail reception.

7. Prepare and practice a pitch speech. Create different versions of your pitch: a 15-second pitch, a one-minute pitch, a two-minute pitch, and a three-minute pitch. Remember, an agent's time is valuable. Keep your speech simple, exciting, and compelling. Leave the agent with a desire to know more about your project or story. Pitch the story or idea first, and then follow with your credentials, accomplishments, and platform, if time allows.

8. Be prepared to answer follow-up questions.

9. Do not ask an agent to read your work or tell him that you will be sending it to his office tomorrow. Wait for an agent to invite you to send your work.

10. As soon as you return home from the conference, send your query letters to the agents who expressed interest. Be sure to mention in the letter that you met them at the conference. Do not send your manuscript, sample chapters, or book proposal unless invited to do so.

# Agent Queries and Pitch Packages

The procedure for submitting queries to agents is similar to the procedure for submitting queries to publishers, outlined in Chapter 4. Follow the same rules for agent submissions:

- Research your list of agents carefully, and narrow it down to those who handle your genre, are open for new submissions, and whom you would like to work with. Learn as much as you can about the agency by studying its website and its list of books published.

- Follow the agent's instructions for submissions exactly.

- Personalize your query for each agent. Check the spelling of each name, find out if it is a Mr. or a Ms., and use a title if applicable. In the opening paragraph, explain why you have chosen to submit your query to this agent.

- Take your time and write a good opening paragraph and pitch paragraph for your book.

- Have your complete, polished manuscript, book proposal or sample pages (your "pitch package") ready to go before you start sending out queries, so you can respond immediately if an agent requests them.

- Maintain a record of all the queries you send out, the date, and the response you receive. You can do this with a simple spreadsheet on your computer. You also can manage your submissions with a software program designed for writers.

## Submission Management Software

| Program | Description | Provider | Cost |
|---|---|---|---|
| Sonar 3 | A manuscript submission-tracking program that tells you which market has each piece, whether a piece has been sold or rejected, and which stories are on hold. | Spacejock Software (**www.spacejock. com/Sonar3.html**) | Free |
| SAMM | Easy storage and retrieval of your manuscript and query information. Maintain a complete history of everything you write and submit. | Sandbaggers (**www. sandbaggers.8m. com/samm.htm**) | Free |
| The Writer's Scribe | A professional submission tracking software for writers that allows you to view all your activities with a standard calendar format. | The Writer's Scribe (**www.thewriters scribe.com**) | $39.00 |

Several online submission trackers allow you to manage your submissions in the "cloud" — a Web-based environment. The information then can be accessed conveniently from anywhere using a laptop or wireless device. Track the markets you approach, the status of the queries you have submitted, estimated response times, publication guidelines, query titles, money earned from each sale, editors' comments, and pay rates.

## Online Submission Trackers

| Application | Description | Provider | Cost |
|---|---|---|---|
| Writer's Database | Helps you keep track of all the relevant markets for your writing and the status of your submissions to each of those markets. Includes contact information, rates, estimated response time, submission guidelines, titles, money earned from each sale, editor's comments, and manuscripts and queries you have sent | Luminary (**www.writersdb. com**) | Free |
| Duotrope® LLC | | Duotrope's Digest (**www.duotrope. com/subtracker. aspx**) | $5 monthly |
| QueryTrack-er™ | An online database that helps you keep track of query letters sent to literary agents and publishers | QueryTracker (**www. querytracker.net**) | Free |

| Application | Description | Provider | Cost |
|---|---|---|---|
| Writer's Market | The Writer's Market is an online database of more than 8,000 listings for book publishers, magazines, contests, literary agents, newspapers, online publications, and syndicates. This system allows you to organize your top markets, manage submissions, manage your freelance rates, and stay abreast of the latest publishing news. | Writer's Market (**www.writers market.com**) | $5.99/ month, $39.99 for 6-month, $39.99 for 1-year subscription |

Divide your queries into batches of eight or ten. While you are waiting for responses to your first queries, write the next batch of query letters. Begin sending them out when you receive the first rejections.

Occasionally, email gets lost or screened out by an agent's spam filter. If a time passes, and you have received no response to your query, follow up with a second email. Most agent websites specify a response time; if not, wait a minimum of three weeks to allow your query to be read before following up. Send a brief message explaining that you sent a query X number of weeks ago and are wondering if your email was received. Attach a copy of the first email, or forward it, and include your query.

When you receive a response from an agent asking you to send sample pages, a manuscript, or book proposal, follow the submission instructions exactly. Some agents ask you to upload documents from your computer to a submission site; others may ask you to attach them to an email or use an online service such as YouSendIt* (**www.yousendit.com**) or Googledocs (**www.google.com**). You might be asked to mail a hard copy of your manuscript. Once these materials have been received, it may take an agent several weeks or months to read and evaluate it. Inform the agent if your manuscript is currently being read by other agents because reading a manuscript involves a considerable investment of the agent's time.

## Your Pitch Package

You pitch package is all the material you will use to sell your book. For fiction writers, a pitch package consists of a query letter, synopsis, and completed manuscript. For nonfiction writers, a pitch package includes a query letter, book proposal, and two sample chapters. In addition, you should gather details about the market for your book and information to support your author platform — your credentials and qualifications, copies of news clippings and interviews, previously published works, and anything else that might build an agent's confidence in you. An agent expects you to know the selling points of your book and be able to convey them effectively. Be prepared to explain how you plan to promote your book. You will not include all of this material with your initial queries, but you should be ready to make a presentation to any agent who shows an interest.

Agents represent writing careers, not authors who write only one book. They look for authors who have a vision and plan for their writing careers. Before approaching an agent, you should have a clear understanding of what you want to accomplish with your writing and the next step along your path as an author.

## Elements of a pitch package

| Checklist for Fiction Writers | Checklist for Nonfiction Writers |
|---|---|
| ✓  Agent file | ✓  Agent file |
| ✓  Query letter | ✓  Query letter |
| ✓  Synopsis | ✓  Book proposal |
| ✓  Completed novel | ✓  Sample chapters or completed manuscript (narrative nonfiction only) |
| ✓  Polished and critiqued manuscript | ✓  Marketable idea |
| ✓  Marketable book | ✓  Author platform and promotional plan |
| ✓  Author platform | ✓  Career map |
| ✓  Career map | |

# Query do's and don'ts

**DO:**

- Try to get a personal introduction or referral to an agent.
- Be professional, courteous, and brief.
- Use email to save on the cost of postage.
- Send a SASE for the response if you are submitting by postal mail.
- Follow exact instructions for submitting queries and pitch packages.
- Include the title of your book in the query.
- If sending an email, include the title of your book in the subject line.
- Research each agent and personalize each query.
- Address your query to a specific agent.
- Include your complete contact information.
- Include information about your background and credentials.
- Keep your query to one page — two at the most.
- Proofread your query several times before you send it.
- Thank the agent.
- Have your pitch package ready before you start sending queries.
- Keep a record of all queries sent and responses to them.
- Wait an appropriate period before following up.

**DON'T:**

- Address your letter "To Whom it May Concern."
- Use decorative backgrounds, cute stationery, or unusual fonts.
- Use a smaller font to try to fit more on the page.
- Use vague generalities or include irrelevant information in your query.
- Use unusual characters, emoticons, or HTML in an email.
- Bold, italicize, or use all caps in your query letters.
- Indent paragraphs.
- Enclose gifts, gimmicks, or other items with your queries.
- Query more than one work at a time to the same agent.
- Telephone the agent — he cannot evaluate your writing over the phone and your call will take up valuable time.

- Send out a mass email to several agents at one time, or cc other agents on an email.
- Send email with attachments, unless specifically instructed to do so.
- Immediately send another query to an agent that has just rejected your first one.
- Expect an immediate response to your query.
- Fail to respond promptly when asked for additional material.
- Have unrealistic expectations of becoming rich and famous from your book.

# Simultaneous Submissions

Submitting query letters to more than one agent at the same time is standard practice in the literary world, and it benefits the writer. An agent may take two to four weeks to review your query letter and respond. The response either will be a rejection letter or a request for further material, in which case the agent will need an additional four to eight weeks to review the manuscript or proposal. If you only query one agent at a time, it could take years to find an agent. Querying multiple agents simultaneously should land you an agent within six months as long as you are approaching the right agents (which you should be, based on your extensive research) and pitching them effectively (which you will be able to do with the knowledge you gain from reading this book.)

Sometimes, rejection can be a gift. If the agent gives you notes, his or her advice can help you make constructive revisions and lead to a better manuscript or improved proposal. Most agents are too busy to write editorial notes. If you are lucky enough to receive feedback from an agent, be sure to send him or her a thank you by email or postcard, and inquire if you may resubmit the work once you have made the suggested changes. Do not be discouraged if the agent will not accept the revised submission; move on, and pitch the next agent on your list.

# Exclusive Reads

When an agent asks to see your manuscript or book proposal, he or she may ask for an "exclusive" for three or four weeks. This means that for the next three or four weeks, while the agent is reading your manuscript, you promise not to submit your manuscript to another agent. This is how an agent avoids wasting time reading and evaluating a book that he or she will not be able to represent. If another agent has shown interest in your book or is already reading it, make that clear from the start. After the exclusive period ends, if the agent wants to represent your book, you are not obligated to accept the offer. If you researched agents before sending out queries, however, they should have gone only to agents you would like to work with.

Most writers handle requests for exclusivity by placing a limit on the time the agent has to review the material, so they are not waiting indefinitely for a response or holding up subsequent requests from other interested agents. Let the agent know that you are giving him exclusivity for a set period, usually two to four weeks for a book proposal or six to eight weeks for a manuscript. If during the exclusive period, you receive a request to review your book proposal or manuscript from another agent you queried, you will have to wait until the exclusive period is over before sending your material to the next agent. The best policy is to be honest and explain the situation.

## When an agent requests revisions

Sometimes, after reviewing the additional requested material, an agent will ask you to make specific changes to your manuscript or proposal and resubmit it. You will need to consider whether you wish to make the changes, if the revisions will benefit the material or project, and how much you want to pursue possible publication with that agent. When an agent takes the time to comment on your material and offer suggestions, it is usually because he or she feels there is good potential for selling the book and is seriously considering representing you. If you feel comfortable with the agent's requests, it is probably in your best interest to make the requested revisions and resubmit the material for a second consideration.

## The author-agent agreement

Each agency has its own form of author-agent agreement. You should understand and feel comfortable with the contract before you sign it. Ask the agent to clarify any terms or clauses you do not understand. You may also request reasonable changes. *An example of an author-agent agreement is included in Appendix B.* A typical author-agent agreement includes the following elements:

- Confirmation that your agent is the exclusive sales representative for your work

- The right of your agent to hire co-agents to help sell subsidiary rights
- The agent's responsibilities
- What work your agent will represent (usually all of an author's literary works in all forms)
- The duration of the agreement. Some contracts have a specific period after which the author has the option to extend the contract or allow it to lapse.
- How notification must be submitted to terminate the contract — for instance, by certified letter with a 30-day notice
- The agent's right to represent competitive books
- The amount of the agent's commission
- Additional expenses you are responsible for (such as messenger service costs, the purchase of review galleys, or attorney's fees)
- A clause stating that, upon request, you are entitled to receive an itemized list of expenses
- The right of the agent to act as a conduit for payments received by the publisher
- The remittance time for issuing payments to you after they are received from the publisher
- You affirm that you have the right to allow the agent to sell the book. (In other words, you confirm that no one else can claim rights to the material.)
- A clause stating that, in the event of your death, you have the right to assign the agreement to your heirs. This ensures that any outstanding royalties or income are paid to your estate.
- Which state's laws will be used to interpret the contract, should a dispute arise. Usually, it is the state where the agent's office is located.
- The method that will be used to resolve disputes — for example, mediation, arbitration, or litigation
- A clause stating that both parties must give a signed approval to any changes to the agreement
- The circumstances under which you can terminate the agreement. For example, this section may note what your responsibilities are if you leave the agency before the contract expires.
- Your agent's rights and responsibilities after the agreement ends. For instance, the agent may retain the right to sell subsidiary rights for any books he or she has sold while under contract.

Some agencies retain and market subsidiary rights, such as film rights and translation rights, separately. They might work with a co-agency that sells publishing rights in another country or with an agency that specializes in selling film rights to movie production companies.

# How to protect yourself

If you are signing with a new agent who does not have an established reputation, you may wish to negotiate some specific terms in the contract to protect yourself if the agent is unable to sell your book or if you become unhappy with the relationship.

- Include an exit clause allowing you to terminate the contract if you are not satisfied with the agent's work. An agent who agrees to this clause probably will include a stipulation that should your book sell in the future to any of the publishers he pitched, the agent is entitled to the commission. The agent also may require an extended termination notice, such as 120 to 180 days.

- Limit the term. If the agent does not agree to an exit clause, then insist upon a term limit that specifies a period (for instance, 18 months) after which, if the agent has not sold the book, the author has the option to seek alternate representation.

- Add a keyman clause. A keyman clause specifies that if your agent leaves the agency for another firm, you have the right to terminate the agreement.

- Request a cap on expenses. If the agreement specifies that you are responsible for legitimate expenses incurred by the agency, ask for a cap to be placed on those expenses (for instance $300 or $500).

## Hiring an attorney

If you choose to hire an attorney to review the agreement, make sure that he or she does not come between you and your agent or publisher. It is important that the lawyer:

- Provide a fast turnaround time. You do not want to keep an agent waiting and risk having the offer rescinded, which is a common occurrence when lawyers become involved in the process.

- Be an expert in book publishing and agent agreements. Do not obtain the services of a general "entertainment" attorney; you need someone knowledgeable about the publishing industry.

- Outline his or her points to you, so you can approach the agent to request the changes. Never have the attorney contact the agent directly.

- Cleary define his or her fee before reviewing the material to avoid surprises later.

## CASE STUDY: EXPERT ADVICE FROM LITERARY AGENT

Barbara Poelle
Irene Goodman Literary Agency
27 West 24th Street, Suite 700B
New York, NY 10010
www.irenegoodman.com
queries@irenegoodman.com

Agency's books and authors include: *The New York Times* best sellers *Seduction Becomes Her* by Shirless Busbee and *Devil In My Bed* by Celeste Bradley and a *USA Today* best seller *The Girl Most Likely To* by Susan Donovan.

*On how to find an agent:* You find an agent the same way you would write a book: research, research, and research. There are so many viable sources in every media these days that a big red flag starts waving if you are sending me a children's book or Christian literature when my profile clearly states I am looking for thrillers, mysteries, historical romances, and humorous nonfiction. I probably cannot trust your work to have much attention to detail.

*On what she looks for in fiction manuscripts:* I look for a unique take on an existing formula buoyed by a solid execution that grabs me by the ears and stuffs me into the pages. Let's face it, there are not any new plots, but there are always new stories.

*On what makes a good query letter:* Three things: The Hook, The Book, and The Cook. You should be able to tell me about your book in a succinct sentence — this is the "hook" — which may also be referred to as a "log line" (for instance, "A great white shark terrorizes a small New England beach town over 4th of July weekend"). Then, you should expand the description into five or six sentences — which is the "book" — and can be used as an "elevator pitch," meaning a verbal pitch when meeting agents, editors, and the basic public face to face. This section of the written query should also have the word count as well as the current compararble titles on the shelf. (And for the love of all that is holy, do not say J.K. Rowling or Stephen King.) And finally, the "cook" — which is you, and it does not matter if you have zero publishing credits — just be able to state in the cook section why this book? Why you? And why now?

*On what she looks for in nonfiction book proposals:* I am looking for platform. How many people already are excited about a book by you? I wish I could tell you that a good story or an interesting topic always will thunder across the finish line victorious, but in today's media driven world, there must be evidence of staying power; having a solid online presence or growing multimedia platform is like stapling a golden ticket to the proposal.

*On paying attention to trends:* I say treat your novel the way you live: with 98 percent passion and 2 percent common sense. Pay attention to trends, but write what you are passionate about.

*Query letter mistakes to avoid:* The mistakes people make in queries are so numerous and hilarious that they themselves could make up an entire book. (Hmm, now there is an idea; anybody know an agent?) Poorly executed queries vary from misinformed to outright insulting, and before we went electronic, they might arrive with "gifts" ranging from homemade food products to bedazzled soda cozies.

*Tips for maintaining a good working relationship:* Like any relationship, respect is the cornerstone. There needs to be a great deal of trust and enthusiasm on both sides of the table but, above all, the understanding that this is a business venture, and everybody wants the results to be wildly successful. I absolutely adore my clients; I find them to be as delightfully different as their genres, but what they all have in common is a great deal of focus and patience in an industry that demands both.

# Selling the Book

Once both parties sign the agency agreement, the author-agent partnership is official, and the process of selling your book to a publisher begins. The time from when you first acquire an agent until you land a book deal and, ultimately, see your book in stores can range from several weeks to several years, depending on the circumstances.

### Step 1: The agent works with you to make edits to the manuscript or proposal.

Agents usually take on new projects they feel are strong enough to send out to publishers immediately. However, sometimes the agent will ask you to make edits and polish the manuscript or proposal further before pitching it to publishing house editors.

Your agent may provide you an editorial letter outlining the requested changes, insert comments directly on your manuscript or proposal, or — if the edits are minimal — discuss it with you in an informal telephone conversation. Depending on your agent's schedule, you may receive this within a few days or within several weeks. You and your agent then will devise a schedule for delivery of the edits. Based on the scope of the changes, your material may go through several rounds of edits and may require a few days or several months to complete.

### Step 2: The agent pitches the project to a list of carefully selected publishers.

Once the material is strong enough to send out, the agent will write a pitch letter (similar to a query letter) and approach several publishers he or she feels are good matches for your book. Most agents will pitch your project to more than one editor at the same time. Your agent may submit it to three editors or 40 editors simultaneously. Each individual agent has his or her own selling technique.

Do not expect your agent to share the list of the publishers he or she has approached or is planning to pitch until after the submission process is complete. An agent's job is to sell your book, and most agents prefer not to consult with authors about whom they should be pitching (unless a specific publisher has expressed an interest). It is best to let your agent do his or her job and not interfere with the pitching process. The timing of the submission stage varies greatly depending on how widely the work is submitted and whether the material that is being read and considered is a 20-page proposal or a 500-page novel.

### Step 3: When an offer is received, the agent negotiates with the publisher on your behalf.

It may be months, or even years, before you receive a publishing offer — or you may land a book deal the same day you hire your agent. There is no way to know how long it will take between the submission stage and the offer stage. Once a publisher does make a verbal offer, your agent will negotiate the major terms of the agreement with the editor. The negotiation process usually takes only a few hours to a few days to complete.

If several publishers are interested in your book, the agent may conduct an auction that lasts several days, during which publishers place their bids, and the agent goes back and forth, getting the best possible offer.

### Step 4: The publisher creates a formal agreement.

Once the terms have been negotiated, the publisher will construct a formal agreement. This may take two to 12 weeks.

### Step 5: The agent may negotiate minor details of the agreement.

Once the agent receives the formal publishing contract, he or she will review the details and may ask the publisher's legal department to make a few minor adjustments to the language contained in the agreement. This may add a few days to a few weeks to the timeline.

### Step 6: The author and publisher sign the contract, after which an advance payment is issued.

Once the final contract is agreed and signed by the author, the publisher will countersign it and issue your agent the initial portion (usually 50 percent) of the negotiated advance payment. Your agent takes his or her commission from the payment and sends you the remaining balance. This stage of the process may take four to six weeks.

### Step 7: The author completes and delivers the manuscript.

The average publishing contract gives the author six to 12 months to deliver the final manuscript. Most nonfiction authors begin writing the manuscript as soon as they receive a verbal offer from the publisher. A fiction author's manuscript already is written when she or he receives an offer; however, the publisher may request a few changes that will need to be completed before delivery of the book. Depending on the project, this stage of the process may take a few days or a year.

## Step 8: Final edits are requested and delivered.

Once you deliver the final manuscript, the editor reviews the book and provides comments for final edits, a process that takes two to ten weeks. Then, you make the final changes and resubmit your manuscript to the editor. Sometimes, several rounds of edits are necessary.

## Step 9: The book is put into production.

Once the editor receives your final changes and the manuscript is "approved," the publisher sends the second half of the advance payment to your agent, who then issues you the payment, minus his or her commission. Now, your book goes into the production process, which consists of copyediting, proofreading, design, and printing. The publication date of your book may be six to 18 months after the manuscript is delivered and accepted (approved with final edits.)

## Timeline for publishing a book

| Stages of the process | Timeframe |
|---|---|
| The agent requests edits to the manuscript or proposal before submission to publishers. | One day to three weeks |
| The author makes the requested changes and returns the material to the agent. | One week to six months |
| The agent pitches the book to editors and receives an offer. | A few hours to two years |
| The agent negotiates the terms of the verbal offer. | One to seven days |
| The publisher issues a formal contract. | Two to 12 weeks |
| The agent negotiates minor details of the agreement. | One to four weeks |
| The author signs the contract, and the initial portion of the advance payment is issued. | Four to six weeks |
| The author delivers the completed manuscript to the publisher. | Two weeks to 12 months |
| The editor reviews the manuscript and requests edits. | Two to ten weeks |
| The author makes changes and resubmits the manuscript. | Two weeks to three months |
| The editor reviews the changes and approves the manuscript or requests additional edits. | Two to six weeks (Plus six to eight weeks if additional edits are requested) |

| Stages of the process | Timeframe |
|---|---|
| The publisher issues the second half of the advance payment. | Four to six weeks |
| The book goes into production and is published. | Six to 18 months |

# Developing a Good Working Relationship with Your Agent

After accepting your book proposal or manuscript and signing a contract, an agent will begin to pitch your book to publishers who might be interested in it. Literary agents spend a good deal of time cultivating relationships with acquisitions editors and other publishing industry professionals, often taking them to lunch or meeting with them to talk about books and projects. The agent knows the best way to present your book and which editors to approach. Even after an agent invests a lot of effort, some books do not sell. Remember that the agent only makes money when you do and is just as interested in selling your book as you are. Be patient, maintain a supportive attitude, and comply with any requests your agent makes. After your book sells, the agent will continue to work with you and the editor, help to resolve business issues, and look out for your interests.

Agents like working with writers who are professional, hard working, and cooperative. Writers can become so focused on writing their literary masterpiece that they forget they are in a business. It helps if you know the guidelines for crafting a good query letter, understand the components of a book proposal, and know how to approach editors and agents. Be open to your agent's advice; he or she will know the publisher, the market, and the genre that matches best with your project. Allow your agent to do his or her job.

Manuscripts rarely go to the publisher on the first submission. Your agent will ask you to rewrite sections of your proposal or manuscript. Do not take a request to rewrite personally; your agent is trying to ensure that you produce the best possible book to receive the best possible return on both of your investments.

Publishing is a deadline-driven industry. If you cannot meet deadlines while working with your agent, will you be able to complete the book on time for a publisher? Chronically missing deadlines or failing to deliver what you promised is unprofessional. Be honest with your agent about difficulties you are encountering. If you are not going to be able to meet a deadline, let the agent know in advance instead of waiting until the last minute.

You are not your agent's only client. Agents have to manage deadlines, contracts, manuscripts, and queries for multiple clients. Avoid contacting your agent unnecessarily. If you are constantly complaining or nagging to your agent, he or she will consider you more trouble than the 15 percent commission is worth.

Communicate directly with your agent. Do not have your secretary or personal assistant contact your agent on your behalf. Keep your agent informed about everything that affects your writing career — send a note or email when you receive an award, schedule a TV appearance or speaking tour, or send off your final edits to the publisher.

Show your appreciation with a thank-you note when the agent lands you a book deal, helps you get a book review, or takes time to offer you suggestions. Be sure to include the agent in your acknowledgments.

# When and how to end a relationship with an agent

If your book attracts public attention, other agents will start contacting you, and larger, more prestigious firms might try to lure you away from your current agent. If your agent is doing a good job for you, think carefully before jumping ship for another agency. Remember, your agent believed in you and recognized your potential long before you achieved success — and helped you become a published author.

However, there may be circumstances under which you may want to consider ending the relationship. Some of these may be:

## When there is poor communication

An agent who does not stay in regular contact with you or does not return your calls or emails may be overwhelmed with too many clients and unable to devote the time needed to further your career. You have a right to receive a response from your agent in a timely manner. If communication has broken down, it may be time to seek alternate representation.

## When an agent lacks integrity

If your agent cannot explain his or her efforts to sell your work, if you find your agent is not telling you the truth, or if you suspect the agent of unethical practices and you no longer trust your agent, it is time to move on.

## When the agent is not productive

If you do not agree with the agent's procedures and policies — for example, if the agent does not share the responses he or she receives from publishers, only pitches to one editor at a time, waits four months for a response, or has an assistant discuss progress reports with you instead of doing it personally — then look for another agent.

## When the agent is not enthusiastic about your book

Your agent should be passionate about your work. You need someone who believes in your writing career and will diligently pitch your manuscript or book idea until it is sold. If your agent is not enthusiastic about your project, find another agent who is.

## When an agent lacks the resources to further your career

After you publish two or three successful books, your agent may not have the contacts, influence, or financial resources to manage your career on a larger scale.

If, after you have discussed the situation with your agent and tried to find a satisfactory remedy, the problems persist, you will need to end the business arrangement formally. Try to exit the relationship with respect and professionalism. You do not want to become known as a difficult author who jumps from agent to agent. If your book already has been sold, your agent still will be entitled to receive his or her earned commissions and represent the subsidiary rights, so you do not want to undermine your relationship. Move on with dignity and grace. Notify your agent of your decision by telephone (or in person, when possible), and then follow up with a certified letter confirming the new terms of your contract.

## Chapter 7

# How to Read a Publishing Contract

The negotiation of your publishing contract is the single most important transaction in the life of your book. You will be signing over your rights to the book in exchange for compensation from the publisher. The publishing contract determines how much you will be paid, how long the publisher will hold the rights to your book, and what will happen if the book is published in another format, recorded as an audiobook, or made into a movie or a TV show.

Every publisher has a standard publishing contract, known as a "boilerplate" contract, but some terms can be negotiated. As an unknown, first-time author, you may not be in a position to make changes to the contract. You must decide if you can accept the terms offered or if you want to walk away from the deal.

Your agent, if you have one, will negotiate the terms of your publishing contract. Most agents deal with specific publishing houses so often that they already have a set contract with the publisher outlining agreed-upon terms. All the agent needs to do is negotiate a few rights and terms particular

to the author. Many of the important terms will not be negotiable, but the agent may be able to get you concessions on lesser points, such as the number of royalty payments, the number of books that must sell before an author receives a higher royalty rate (unit break), and the author's buyback rate (the discounted price at which the author buys books). If you do not have an agent, the publisher will prepare the contract.

Read the contract carefully, and be sure you understand everything it says. As a first-time author, you may be unfamiliar with some of the terminology. Your agent will be able to explain what the contract means in the context of the publishing industry, but an agent is not a lawyer. If you have any doubts about your contract, have it reviewed by an entertainment lawyer who specializes in publishing law. Sometimes, a standard contract uses general language or omits important details that could have legal consequences later. Even standard contracts should be checked for typos and missing words that could change the meaning of a phrase.

Unfamiliar legal language is difficult to understand at first, and it might be tempting to just go ahead and sign the contract without reading it carefully. Like any other language, however, "legalese" can be learned. Persevere, and you will find that once you understand the reasons for various words and phrases, the meaning is clear. Many publishers' contracts have been created over time, and some of the clauses they contain are a direct result of some past mishap, such as an author who disappeared without submitting a final manuscript or a lawsuit for copyright infringement resulting from plagiarism. A publisher wants to protect itself in every way possible from potential loss or damage. A publishing contract is essentially an agreement to allow the publisher to publish and sell your book in exchange for financial compensation.

A typical publishing contract is between eight and 20 pages long and contains all or most of these basic elements:

- Grant of rights
- Term
- Representations and warranties
- Manuscript delivery and acceptance
- Indexing
- Publication
- Editing and proofreading
- Copyright

- Royalties
- The advance
- Statements, payments, and accounting
- Subsidiary rights
- Revisions and updated editions
- Author copies
- Additional books and options
- Copyright infringement
- Noncompete clause
- Termination of contract and reversion of rights
- Bankruptcy
- Miscellaneous

# Grant of Rights

This section names and defines the book and specifies the rights being assigned to the publisher. For example, "The author hereby grants and assigns to the Publisher the exclusive rights to publish in the English language in book form in the United States and Canada, a Work now titled *Title of Book* (hereinafter called the Work)." Exclusive rights means that no one else has the legal right to publish the work in book form in English in the U.S. and Canada for the period specified in the contract.

# Term

The term specifies how long the publisher will own rights to the book. The term may be defined as a fixed number of years, or it may extend as long as the publisher keeps the book in print.

## Watch out for:

A vague "out-of-print clause." Most publishing contracts state that rights to the book revert to the author after the book has been out of print for a specified time. It is important to define the meaning of "out of print" clearly. A book is out of print when the publisher declares it is out of print and updates its ISBN record or when the book is no longer available in any edition from the publisher. A publisher could use POD to keep your book "in print" indefinitely, which means the publisher retains the rights to it while selling few copies and doing little to market it. Make sure your out-of-print clause specifies that your book is "out of print" when it sells fewer than a specified number of copies during a 12-month period.

## Representations and warranties

In this section, the author guarantees that the book is an original work, does not violate any copyrights or civil liberties, has not been published before in book form, that no one else can claim ownership of rights in the book, and that the author has obtained rights or permissions pertaining to all material in the book. The author agrees to participate in any legal defense against lawsuits challenging these rights and to repay the publisher for any losses incurred if his or her representations prove to be false.

Most of the time, the situations covered in this section will never arise, and even editors may not understand the implications of this part of a contract fully. If you ever do end up embroiled in a lawsuit, however, the language in the contract will be important. For example, does the author become responsible for legal fees when a lawsuit is initiated by an injured party or only after a judgment has been passed on the case?

This section of a contract makes you responsible for verifying that no part of your book is plagiarized and that you have obtained permission to use quotes, excerpts, photos, illustrations, and any other original material. It pays to be careful and diligent. *See Chapter 12 for more information on copyright laws and plagiarism in the publishing industry.*

## Manuscript delivery and acceptance

This section specifies how the manuscript must be formatted and the date by which it must be delivered to the publisher. It also stipulates that the publisher is only obligated to accept, pay for, and publish a manuscript that is satisfactory in form and content. Typically, the manuscript is required as a Microsoft Word file, and you might be asked to submit one or two hard copies and originals of artwork and photos.

The language in this clause is sometimes very general to allow for flexibility. If you already know exactly what you are going to write, how many pages and chapters and when they are going to be ready, you can make the description of your manuscript more exact.

If you have an agent, he or she will work with you to ensure the delivery date is practical and realistically can be met. Your agent also will try to insert wording in the agreement that obligates the publisher to assist you in editing a specific number of drafts before the publisher can reject the manuscript.

## Watch out for:

A heavy penalty for late delivery of the manuscript. If a contract has a late penalty, it also should include a bonus for early delivery of the manuscript.

# Indexing

If your book will have an index at the back, the publisher may ask you to provide it. Creating an index can be time-consuming work. *See chapters 8 and 9 for more information about indexing.* Some publishing contracts deduct the expenses of creating the index from the author's royalties. They might charge a flat fee or several dollars per page. It is reasonable for the publisher to require the author to provide an index, but not to charge the author a fee for producing one.

## Watch out for:

A fee for indexing deducted from the author's royalty

# Publication

This section of the contract states whether the publisher is obligated to publish the book within a specified time and may give the retail price. It sometimes contains a clause explaining what recourse the author has if the publication deadline is not met.

## Watch out for:

Vague language that does not give a specific timeframe for publication. Be wary of any contract requiring the author to repay the publisher if publication is cancelled.

## Editing and proofreading

This section sets out the procedure for editing and proofreading the manuscript. It typically will state that the final edit will be subject to the author's approval and give a time limit for the author's review. There might be a clause requiring the author to bear the cost of making extensive changes to the final proof, apart from correction of errors made by the book designer or typesetter. Try to specify a percentage of the cost of correcting the final proof, typically 10 to 15 percent, that the publisher will pay before the corrections are charged against the author's royalties.

## Copyright

The author holds the copyright to a written work, and a publishing contract assigns that copyright to the publisher for a specified period. *See Chapter 13 for more information about publishing copyrights.* At the end of that period, or if at any point the publisher breaches the contract, the copyright reverts to the author.

In the U.S., a publisher owns all rights to a work written as a "work for hire." An employer also owns all rights to a work written by an employee during the course of employment, such as a manual for operating a machine or a report that is written as part of the employee's job.

### Watch out for:

The copyright in the name of the publisher. The publisher may agree to register the copyright as part of the contract, but the copyright always should be in the name of the author. Any legal settlement for copyright infringement goes to the owner of the copyright.

## Royalties

Your agent will ensure you earn royalties for sales of your book that are appropriate with industry standards. Most authors receive a royalty of 10 percent of the book's retail price for the first 5,000 copies sold, a royalty of 12.5 percent of the book's retail price on the next 5,000 copies sold, and a royalty of 15 percent of the book's retail price on all copies sold after that. The contract sets a royalty rate for each format: hardcover, trade paper, mass-market paper, audiobooks, electronic editions, special editions such as book club, bulk sales, and Braille editions. The current royalty rate for e-books is generally 25 percent because the retail price and the production costs are lower. Royalties are not paid on books that are given away for promotion or review or books that are returned by bookstores and destroyed.

## Watch out for:

- Royalty rates that are too low. There are two ways to calculate royalty rates: on net (the profit the publisher nets from the sale of each book) and on gross (the retail price of the book). Royalties paid on net average about half of royalties paid on gross receipts.

- Royalty rates should escalate based on the sales of the book. The number of books sold at which the royalty rate increases is called the "unit break" or "break point." Some publishers do not count books sold in bulk or through book clubs in the total sales number when determining these numbers.

- Your publishing contract may stipulate a lower royalty rate on books that are sold at a deep discount. For example, the royalty rate might be cut in half on books that wholesale for 55 percent or more below the list price. Because the bookstore chains and large retailers that will be selling most of your books typically pay less than 55 percent of the list price, your royalty rate effectively is being cut in half. This can create a situation in which the publisher benefits by selling your books at a deep discount because the reduction the royalties it must pay you offsets the reduction in the sales price.

- High reserves. The publisher holds back some of your royalties as a reserve to cover the cost of books returned unsold by bookstores. The contract should limit this reserve to a reasonable amount, typically 20 percent. Reserves should not be held back for longer than two years at the most.

# The Advance

An advance is the payment you receive before your book's publication. An advance originally was intended to provide financial support while the author was writing the book. The advance often is based upon an estimate of your book's first-year sales. The amount is an advance against future earnings. The amount of the advance depends on many factors, including how much the publisher expects to make from the book, whether the author is well known and successful, and how much is allotted in the publisher's budget for new acquisitions. An average advance for a first-time author is between $8,000 and $12,000.

In the past, the advance typically was broken into two payments: 50 percent issued at the time the contract was signed and the remaining payment issued upon delivery and acceptance of the complete manuscript. Today, many publishers break the advance up into three payments, with the final payment due when the book is published. Some publishers break the advance up into as many as five payments. Your agent will negotiate to get you a higher advance and a fewer number of payments.

Of course, the publisher wants to pay as small an advance as possible because it wants to ensure the entire amount it pays you up front will be earned back through your royalties. Because you do not have to return any of your advance — unless the book is cancelled due to the author breaching the contract — the publisher loses the portion of the advanced amount that you do not earn back through sales of your book.

## Watch out for:

- An advance that is too low. The advance should reflect the author's credentials and writing ability, the amount of work involved in writing the book, and the book's sales potential.

- Advances broken up into too many payments. You might never receive your entire advance if payments are tied to publication dates and the publisher cancels publication after you have submitted the full manuscript.

- Cross-collateralization clauses. Some contracts contain clauses allowing the publisher to charge outstanding amounts from previous advances against royalties from future books. Arrangements like these should be avoided if possible.

# Statements, Payments, and Accounting

This section stipulates how often the publisher will provide a statement of your royalties, usually quarterly or biannually, and how often royalty payments will be made. It often includes a clause requiring the publisher to notify the author immediately of any sale of rights or contract that results in a payment to the author of more than a certain amount (usually $100) and to remit that payment to the author without waiting for the regular accounting period to end. There might be an overpayment clause allowing the publisher to deduct the excess amount from future royalties if it happens to pay the author more than the royalties due for an accounting period.

A contract involving royalty payments generally allows the author, or the author's representative, to conduct an audit of the publisher's accounting records pertaining to the author's works. This is done at the author's expense unless errors are found that amount to more than a certain percentage (such as 5 percent) of the total payments made to the author.

# Subsidiary Rights

Subsidiary rights are all the rights (besides publishing rights) associated with your book that are available to sell. If you are dealing directly with a publisher, the publisher usually buys all the rights to your book and shares the proceeds from selling them. If you have an agent, the agency may reserve some of the rights, such as film rights, and market them separately. In some cases, the author keeps (reserves) certain rights. Subsidiary rights include:

### Reprint rights

Reprint rights grant the right to print the book in paperback edition. In most current publishing agreements, the publisher retains the reprint rights.

### Book club rights

Numerous book clubs specialize in different genres and acquire book club rights enabling them to offer your book to their members. Money made from the sales of book club rights is split equally between the author and the publisher.

## Serial rights

A serial is an excerpt of your book that is reprinted in a magazine or in another book, such as an anthology or compilation. First serial rights allow excerpts to be printed before the book's publication. Second serial rights grant the right to publish the excerpts after the book has been released. It is more common for nonfiction material to be serialized than fiction.

## Foreign language rights

Your agent may use a co-agent in another country to capitalize on selling foreign language rights, which grant the right for your book to be printed in non-English-speaking countries. Some publishing houses already are set up to publish in foreign countries. In this situation, your publisher will retain these rights.

## Electronic rights

Electronic rights grant the right to publish the book electronically. An e-book published on the Internet or a book purchased to read on an electronic device is a form of electronic publishing.

## Audio rights

Audiobooks often complement the printed version of the book. Audio rights refer to books that are published in audio form, such as on a cassette tape or compact disc or delivered as a podcast available for downloading from the Internet.

## Performance rights

Performance rights allow your book to be made into a film, a television show, a video game, a play, or musical. An agent usually charges a 20-percent commission for the sales of performance rights.

## Merchandising rights

Merchandising rights allow the creation of products related to your book, such as bookmarks, calendars, greeting cards, games, party decorations, or toys. The *Harry Potter* series of books by J.K. Rowling and the *Curious George* series by Hans Augusto Rey and Margret Rey are examples of franchises that spawned numerous merchandising opportunities.

## Reserved rights

The contract should include a clause stating that the author reserves (keeps) all rights not specifically mentioned in the contract. This protects the author in case some new form of publication emerges, such as cell phone apps or excerpts published in an anthology that was not anticipated when the contract was written. This clause is important because, with technology and the nature of the publishing industry evolving so rapidly, it is likely that novel ways of disseminating books will emerge.

As a first-time author negotiating with a publishing house, you are probably not in a position to insist on keeping some of these rights. The publisher probably is better equipped than you are to market them, and you will get a share of the proceeds. A well-established agent might be able to negotiate an arrangement for retaining certain rights and help you market them.

## Watch out for:

Delayed payments for sales of subsidiary rights. When the publisher sells subsidiary rights to your book, your share of the proceeds should be paid to you immediately, not at the end of the next accounting period.

# Revisions and Updated Editions

A nonfiction book needs to be updated periodically to keep it current, so the contract may require the author to perform revisions and updates. Make sure the contract limits how many updates can be requested within any given period. There should be a formula for determining how much revision can be done before the book is essentially a new book, subject to a new contract and more money for you.

You should insist on having the right to write revised editions of your book. If you are unavailable or unable to meet a reasonable deadline for a revised edition, and the publishing company contracts with another writer, you and your heirs still are entitled to receive a portion of the royalties. You also can include a clause that ensures later editions will not be published under your name if you are not involved in writing them.

| **Watch out for:** |
| :--- |
| A clause allowing the publisher to deduct an unspecified amount from your royalties to cover the cost of producing revised editions of your book |

# Author Copies

The publisher supplies a specified number of free copies of the book and allows the author to purchase additional copies at a discounted price. The discount typically is increased if you buy larger numbers of books. This discount is particularly important if you plan to sell copies of your book at seminars and lectures. An agent may be able to negotiate more free copies, a larger author discount, or a smaller number of books that must be bought to qualify for the more favorable discount rate.

# Additional Books and Options

Most publishing contracts include a clause giving the publisher the "first right of refusal" on your next book. That means you cannot submit your next book to any other publisher until this publisher has passed on it, made an offer, or let the option period lapse. If your first book does well, the publisher wants to capitalize on its success by bringing out a sequel or another book by a popular author (you). However, an option can prevent you from seeking more favorable terms with another publisher or delay submitting your book to other publishers if this one decides to pass on it.

If possible, protect yourself by eliminating the option clause altogether. If not, try to make this clause as specific and limited as possible. For example, limit the option to one "next book" in the same series or specific genre. The publisher might require you to submit a full manuscript of your next book for consideration; try to change this to a book proposal for nonfiction, or a synopsis and three chapters for fiction. The publisher might state that the option period begins with the publication of the last book in this contract and lasts for 90 days. Try to get the option period to begin when you submit the last manuscript or to shorten it to 30 days.

## Watch out for:

An overly strict option clause, or one that is too vague. The option clause in a contract can become a source of complications and frustration. What exactly is an author's "next book?" In the case of a nonfiction book, would a revised, updated version or a spin-off created by the publisher be considered the author's "next book?" What if the author co-writes a book with someone else — is that the "next book?" Perhaps you already have written your next book. Does that mean the publisher must begin reviewing your submission right away, before your first book even hits the market? Some of these clauses state that the publisher has the option to publish the next book under the "same terms and conditions" as the current contract. If your first book is a best-seller, should you be able to negotiate a higher royalty rate and better terms for your second book? Your royalty rate on the first book goes up when sales pass a target number; do sales of your second book build on that higher rate, or do you have to go back to the lower rate? If the publisher decides it wants to consider your next book for publication, it may enter into weeks of negotiations during which you are unable to seek offers from other publishers. Think carefully about your particular situation when negotiating this clause with a publisher.

# Copyright Infringement

This clause usually states that the publisher might, at its own expense, take legal action in your name against someone who infringes on the copyright for your book. For example, if someone posts sections of your book on a website, the publishing company might have its lawyers send out a "cease and desist" letter threatening legal action if those chapters are not removed. The publisher also might seek damages in court if your book has been pirated or plagiarized. However, the publisher is not required to do this. If the publisher chooses not to pursue legal action, the author can do so at his or her own expense. Any money awarded as damages goes first to pay for the legal costs, and whatever is left over belongs to the author. If the publisher has lost profits because of the copyright infringement, however, the award must be divided equally between publisher and author.

# Noncompete Clause

The publisher may include a noncompete clause that forbids the author from releasing a book on a similar subject without the publisher's permission. Although the publisher understandably wants to protect the uniqueness of its book, you might want to write multiple books on a subject in which you specialize. For example, if you are a psychologist who is an expert on eating disorders, you are likely to write more than one book on the subject. An experienced author knows better than to release two similar books because sales of one could hurt sales of the other. Try to have this clause removed; if it stays, it should be restricted to almost identical books.

> **Watch out for:**
>
> An overly strict noncompete clause. It might be necessary to define the work covered by the contract in a way that allows you to write and publish related books without violating the noncompete clause.

# Termination of Contract and Reversion of Rights

This part of the contract lays down the circumstances under which the agreement can be terminated — for example, if the publisher gives the author notice that it has decided not to go ahead with publication, defaults on royalty payments, or fails to publish within the time allotted by the contract. If one of these circumstances occurs, the contract is cancelled, and all rights revert to the author. When a contract is cancelled because the publisher failed to keep up its obligations, the author keeps the money the publisher has paid him or her.

# Bankruptcy

This section details what will happen to the book and the publishing rights if the publisher declares bankruptcy or liquidates its business. A typical contract returns all rights to the author.

# Miscellaneous

Some standard clauses are found in contracts of every kind. The name or wording may differ slightly, but the purpose is the same. These clauses cover various eventualities that might arise during the course of any formal agreement:

**Arbitration** — A clause setting out a procedure for settling disputes arising out of the contract by arbitration. It usually states where and how the arbitration will take place. Arbitration is a method of negotiating a resolution to a problem without resorting to legal action.

**Law** — A clause stating which laws govern the contract, usually the laws of the state in which the publishing company has its headquarters

**Assignment** — A clause stating that the rights and responsibilities covered in the contract cannot be assigned to another company or person without written consent of both parties. For example, if the publishing company is bought by another company or wants to sell the publishing rights to your book to another company, it must get your signed approval first. Authors usually are allowed to assign the money they receive from a book to another person or entity, such as a charity or an ex-spouse as part of a divorce settlement, without obtaining signed consent from the publisher.

**Waiver** — A clause stating that a waiver of a breach of any of the terms in the contract does not mean that the other terms of the contract are waived or that similar breaches are waived in the future. For example, if a publisher or author is allowed to extend a deadline once, it does not mean that all future deadlines can be extended without breaching the contract or that other terms of the contract do not apply. Waivers must be in writing and signed by both author and publisher.

**Communications or notices** — A clause describing exactly how written notices concerning the contract will be exchanged between the author and publisher. A notice usually is considered delivered (served) if it is hand-delivered or sent digitally (email or other electronic file transmission) or by mail to the address specified at the beginning of the contract. A notice of termination usually must be sent by registered mail.

**Inheritance** — A clause stating what will happen if one of the people signing the contract dies before the term of the contract ends. Typically, the legal responsibilities and the financial benefits of the contract would transfer to "the heirs, executors, administrators and assigns of the author" and to "the successors and assigns of the publisher."

# Collaborations and Co-authors

A publishing contract for a book written by two or more authors is more complicated because it must define the extent of the collaboration and how much each author is contributing to the book. Two co-writers might receive equal shares of the royalties, but in a case where one author is a celebrity or an expert and the

other is a professional writer, the one with fame and name-recognition might be entitled to a larger share because his or her reputation will be a major factor in selling the book. There should be a separate written agreement between the co-authors describing exactly how they are collaborating and their respective responsibilities and obligations.

The publishing agreement typically makes co-authors "jointly and individually" responsible for each obligation in the contract. This could have far-reaching consequences. If, for example, one co-author plagiarizes material, all the co-authors will be held responsible in a lawsuit. One co-author's inability to meet deadlines could invalidate the whole contract.

If one or more of the authors has worked with the publisher, they may have out-standing amounts owed to the publisher from previous advances or marketing costs. Cross-collateralization is an arrangement that allows the publisher to recoup outstanding amounts from royalties for future books. To avoid complications, insist on having a separate account established for this book.

## Publishing contract do's and don'ts

**DO:**

- Read a publishing contract carefully before you sign it.
- Ask the publisher, your agent, or an entertainment lawyer to explain anything you do not understand.
- Think about the consequences of the terms of the contract — whether the deadlines are realistic and the terms are reasonable.
- Run a plagiarism check on your manuscript and get written permission for all borrowed material.
- Negotiate a specific "next book" clause, or try to get rid of it altogether.
- Keep a copy of your contract and any associated documents where you can easily refer to it.

**DON'T:**

- Trust that the acquisitions editor of the publishing company that created the contract is the best person to explain it to you.
- Skim over the text in the contract because you do not understand the language.
- Sign any contract without reading it.
- Let your publisher or agent pressure you to return a signed contract quickly. The publisher or agent can wait another day or two; chances are that once they receive the contract, it will sit in an in-tray for several days before the publisher signs it.
- Get a lawyer who knows nothing about the publishing industry to review your contract. A lawyer who does not understand the usual terms and conventions could jeopardize your book deal by raising unnecessary objections.
- Overlook the implications of signing a contract as a co-author with someone else.

## Chapter 8

# Self-Publishing

The goal of self-publishing is not just to see your name on the cover of a book but to produce and sell a quality product. You are responsible for the writing, editing, production, printing, marketing, distribution, and sales. Self-publishing involves two processes: producing the best possible book and doing everything in your power to sell it. Many self-publishing authors hire professionals including freelance writers, editors, illustrators, photographers, layout artists, and book designers to ensure their books meet the same high standards as conventionally published books. Some also hire publicists and marketing specialists to help them sell their books.

Until the last decade of the 20th century, self-publishing was essentially vanity publishing. A writer invested thousands of dollars and ended up with boxes of printed books to sell in any way he or she could. Then, the advent of POD technology made self-publishing affordable for almost anyone, and online booksellers gave authors direct access to millions of potential buyers. From 2009 to 2010, the number of new titles released in the U.S. increased 132 percent, as the convergence of POD technology, self-publishing services, e-books, and online booksellers fueled an explosion in self-publishing. The Internet has introduced several new business models for self-published writers, including digital books that can be produced and marketed entirely online and books that are spin-offs of blogs or educational websites.

Self-publishers are both writers and entrepreneurs. A number of factors should be considered when deciding whether to self-publish, including your expectations for your book, the size of your audience, your talents and abilities, and how much you can afford to invest in publishing and marketing your book. Self-publishing is a perfect vehicle for certain types of books, and for some, it is a possible entry to the world of conventional publishing. It is not a recipe for overnight success, however, and unless you work hard and exercise your initiative and creativity, you could be disappointed by the results.

# Why Self-Publishing?

You might choose self-publishing for many reasons. It is difficult for first-time authors to break into the world of conventional publishing and attract the interest of publishers and agents, who receive hundreds of thousands of queries every year. Several years could pass before your book is finally printed, and there are many pitfalls along the way. Even when a publisher buys the rights to your book, it might never reach publication. Publishers' marketing staffs and budgets are stretched increasingly thin, which means that your book might not get the publicity needed to make it sell. The burden of promoting a book often falls on the author.

Major publishers tend to concentrate their marketing resources on promoting their well-known authors whose books are guaranteed to sell; books by lesser-known authors are relegated to the shelves in the back of the bookstores where few customers come across them. The methods used by major publishers to market books often follow a general formula and do not target special-interest audiences. Once the initial burst of publicity has ended, sales gradually fade away. A self-published book, promoted using tactics that reach potential readers in a target market, can continue to sell steadily year after year.

A self-published book that sells successfully sometimes is picked up and re-issued by a major publishing company. Once you have built up your platform and attracted a following, you can include this information in your "pitch" to demonstrate that your book has sales potential. You can send a printed copy of your book to an agent or publisher instead of a manuscript or book proposal.

Publishers are interested in books that appeal to large numbers of readers. If you are writing about a highly specialized topic, the book might not sell enough copies for a publisher to make a profit. Publishers have lots of overhead; they have to pay rent, production costs, and payroll. You, on the other hand, can self-publish with a minimal investment and sell the book directly to the people who will be most interested in it. You might want to publish your own textbook for a seminar or a family memoir that will be sold to 30 of your relatives. With POD, you can print just the number of copies you need for a few dollars each.

Self-publishing gives you complete control over your work. You choose your title, book design, and cover, and control all aspects of the publishing process. You retain all rights and full ownership of the book and keep all proceeds from the sales of your book.

Depending on how you produce your book, a self-published book could be available for purchase in just a few weeks. You set your own deadlines, and the only delays are the time it takes to get the book printed or online.

The aggressive promotion of e-book readers has created a new self-publishing business model. The process of publishing an e-book is relatively simple and inexpensive. You can sell your book online and bypass printing it altogether. The amount you make on each sale might not be as high, but because the price is lower and e-books are popular and easy to buy, you probably will be able to sell more books. There are no production, printing, or shipping costs. If you develop a good system for attracting readers' attention, you can generate a steady income from self-published e-books. *See Chapter 12 for more information on publishing an e-book.*

## Why Not Self-Publish?

After spending weeks, months, or years perfecting your manuscript, you will not be receiving a nice advance from a publisher. Instead, you will be laying out your own money to finance production, publication, and marketing. You will be responsible for all expenses associated with producing your book: typesetting, indexing, book cover design, editing, and proofreading. You will pay the cost for printing each book (some self-publish printers charge as much as $10 per book, plus setup fees). You will need money for a website, travel expenses, packaging supplies, postage and shipping, promotional copies of your book, advertising, and printing order forms, one-sheeters, and posters. These expenses will be proportional to the size and scope of the audience you hope to reach. You can save money by promoting your book locally and limiting the number of promotional copies you send to reviewers, but this also limits the number of people who hear about your book. You will have to sell enough copies of your book to recoup these expenses before you start making an income from it. Your books will sell one by one, and money will come trickling in. If you are selling through a distributor or an online bookstore, there will be a lag of several weeks between when the books sell and when you receive payment for them.

When you self publish, you are responsible for all marketing and distribution. Your book will not sell if no one knows about it. Publicizing your book is hard work and takes a considerable amount of time. You must be willing to promote yourself, make appearances on TV and radio, network, blog, and give talks for writers' groups and bookstores. You must find a distributor willing to take on your book, or approach individual bookstores and convince them to sell your book.

Most bookstores will not carry self-published books. Large retailers and bookstore chains buy their books at deep discounts from established distributors. To sell your book through independent bookstores, gift shops, museums, and other outlets, you either will have to go through a distributor or visit each store yourself and meet face-to-face with the buyer. Each outlet only will take a small number of books to sell, and you will be responsible for warehousing your books, shipping out orders, and processing returns.

You are responsible for obtaining an ISBN, bar code, Library of Congress Control Number, and copyright registration. Many self-publishing services offer these as part of their packages, but you still have to pay for them.

Research indicates that 85 percent of self-published POD books sell fewer than 200 copies, and the average number of books sold by a self-published author is 30. A best-seller on Lulu.com is a book that sells more than 500 copies, and that does not happen often.

Mainstream media, such as *Publishers Weekly* magazine, do not review self-published books. Reviews are an important means of making both booksellers and potential buyers aware of new books. Self-published authors have less credibility in the publishing industry than traditionally published writers, though a writer who can demonstrate strong sales for a self-published book is treated with respect.

## *Eragon:* Hard work leads to self-publishing success

When he was 14, Christopher Paolini set out to write the kind of fantasy fiction story he would like to read. At first, he had difficulty creating a cohesive structure for his tale, so he read books about writing and plotted a story line for a whole trilogy, now a series of four books called *The Inheritance Cycle.* After two years, when he finished *Eragon*, he gave it to his family to read. His parents, whose business was producing small publishing projects, believed it was good enough to sell and invested all their resources to self-publish it. The family spent another year copyediting, proofreading, designing a cover, typesetting the manuscript, and creating marketing materials. They self-published through Lightning Source®, a POD subsidiary of Ingram Content Group, a book wholesaler and major distributor for independent bookstores. After the first books arrived in November 2001, the Paolini family spent a year traveling and promoting the book at 135 libraries, bookstores, and schools, with Christopher dressed as a medieval storyteller.

In a January 2004, interview with Kit Spring of *The Observer*, Paolini said, "Selling the book meant putting food on the table… I would stand behind a table in my costume talking all day without a break — and would sell maybe 40 books in eight hours if I did really well…. It was a very stressful experience. I was fried. I could not have gone on for very much longer."

In the summer of 2002, while on a fishing vacation, the stepson of novelist Carl Hiaasen saw the book in one of the stores where Paolini was promoting it. He read it and showed it to Hiaasen, who immediately contacted his publishers. Alfred A. Knopf bought the rights for around $400,000 and rereleased it in August 2003. Though some reviewers were critical, *Eragon* was the third best-selling children's hardback book of 2003 and the second best-selling paperback of 2005, and remained on the *New York Times* Children's Books Best-seller list for 121 weeks. A film adaptation of *Eragon* released on December 15, 2006, ranked as the 16th top-grossing film in 2006 and grossed $249 million worldwide. The fourth book, *Inheritance*, was released in November 2011. To date the four *The Inheritance Cycle* books have sold more than 33 million copies worldwide. *Brisingr* sold more than half a million hardcover copies the day it was released — the greatest one-day sale ever recorded for a Random House children's book title. It was also the largest first-print run (2.5 million copies) in the publisher's history.

# Producing Your Book

A book is more than its content — its aesthetic and physical qualities are part of the experience a reader pays for when he or she buys a book. Go through your own bookshelves, or take a walk around a local bookstore, paying attention to the look and feel of various books. What does the size and weight of the book say to you? How does the cover make you feel when you glance at it? Is this the kind of book you will read once or twice and toss in the recycling bin, or is it a reference guide you will come back to many times? Does the spine of the book scream "1950s mass market," "reliable and respectable," or "something new and different"? Does the front cover promise a racy adventure or no-nonsense instructions? Observe the effects of color and quality and the ways in which various publishing imprints distinguish their books. Open the books and look at how the chapters are laid out, the page numbers, headers and footers on the pages, and special effects achieved with decorations, ornamental fonts, and illustrations.

Now think about your own book. Who are your prospective readers, and what kind of book will attract them? How will your book be used? Will it be carried around in a pocket or handbag and pulled out to read in a spare moment, will it be spread open on a desk, or placed on a coffee table for visitors to admire? A businessman might expect to pay $40 or $50 for a reference book with a hard cover and jacket, while a builder expects to pay $14 to $24 for a paperback air-conditioning manual with simple line drawings. Locate a book similar in size and format to the one you want to produce, and keep it handy as a guide to designing your own book.

Study the titles and cover designs of books in your genre. Your concept of a perfect cover might be different, but mainstream publishers have studied their markets and know what appeals to the readers of certain types of books. The image a prospective reader sees on a bookstore table, or as is often the case now, on a Web page of an online catalog could become the reason your book is chosen over several others. Even the cover image for an e-book needs to look attractive when seen as a tiny thumbnail.

When you have a clear vision for your book, you are ready to produce it. With the Internet, a computer, and today's software programs, you have the tools to do many publishing tasks yourself. However, every writer does not possess the skills or the time to format a book for publication or design a professional-looking cover. You might need to hire a copy editor to polish the text, a book designer to lay out your book, an artist to create original artwork for the front cover, or a Web specialist to help you with social media. Some self-publishing companies offer all of these services as a package, for a price. You must decide how you can produce your vision within the constraints of your budget, which services will contribute the most to selling your book, and which tasks you can do effectively yourself.

As you work on producing your book, develop a timeline, and write on your calendar the dates when certain tasks must be accomplished. You will save your energy and use time most efficiently if you are well organized. For example, if you plan to solicit prepublication reviews, this must be done before your book is made available for sale. You must allow enough time for books to be printed and shipped to you before a public speaking event. Your copyright must be registered within three months of publication to give you the maximum legal protection.

## CASE STUDY: ADVICE FROM A PRINT-ON-DEMAND COMPANY

Charles Rosenberg, president
Rose Printing Company
2503 Jackson Bluff Road
Tallahassee, Florida 32304
Phone: 850-325-6826
Fax: 850-576-4153
charlesr@roseprinting.com
www.roseprinting.com

**How print-on-demand has changed the publishing industry:** Print-on-demand has made it feasible to run short production runs (ten to 150, 250) books at a reasonable price. This enables self-publishers to publish their materials and make a small profit. It also keeps titles in print that otherwise would go out of print due to the longer runs economically required of offset (1,000 copies or more). Publishers can reduce inventory investment and still maintain their backlists.

**The services we offer self-published authors:** Rose Printing offers self-publishers POD services for short runs of ten to 25 books. Turnaround is ten working days, which makes it possible for self-publishers to keep their books in print with minimum inventory investment. We also have added editorial and design services to complement POD services.

**The importance of working with a distributor:** Marketing and sales are critical to publishing. Without broad distribution and promotion, many titles go unnoticed and sales are nominal, which makes unit production costs higher. On the other hand, strong author promotion along with broad distribution will increase book sales and make the publishing venture profitable for self-publishers and publishing houses.

**Common mistakes of self-publishing authors:** Most self-publishers tend to overestimate unit sales of their books and order too many initially. Failure to have good self-promotion and marketing plans adds to the problem. Planning ahead, ar-

ranging signings, newspaper and radio interviews, etc., will help promote the title. Sales will follow, and the book will reach its optimal success.

**What people do not know about printing books:** Most people do not realize how inexpensive it can be to print a short-run or long-run book. The key is a solid sales and marketing plan.

**The future of the publishing industry:** Publishing is more streamlined

and less costly today. The marketing channels also are less complicated. More titles are produced each year as a result.

**Advice to a first-time author:** Read materials on self-publishing and
plan your marketing. Join IBPA and your local publishers association.
Call on Rose Printing for editorial marketing and production help. We
have 80 years of experience in this field.

# Finding a Printer

You will need information such as the trim size (dimensions of your book), number of books, and type and quality of the cover in order to get quotes from printing services and compare prices. Think about how you are going to sell your
book — as hard copies at seminars and lectures, wholesale to bookstores through
a distributor, POD through online booksellers, or solely as an e-book. This will
determine what types of printing and design services you need, as well as how
many copies you should order.

## Types of printing services

There are three basic types of book printing services, POD, digital printing, and
offset printing. Some book printers offer more than one type of printing, and
some are affiliated with distribution networks or offer additional services.

### POD (print on demand)

Books are printed digitally only when needed to fill an order. There are two basic
models of POD publishing companies. Subsidized POD publishing companies
such as AuthorHouse* (**www.authorhouse.com**) and iUniverse* (**www.iuniverse.
com**) package printing with other services such as page design, cover design, an
ISBN, and distribution. The basic package costs several hundred dollars, and you
receive royalties on the sales of your book. You are assigned one of the publisher's
ISBNs, so your book lists the POD company as your publisher. The typesetting
and interior design are typically mediocre but acceptable, and you are given a
choice of several cover design templates. For hundreds of dollars more, you can
have your book professionally edited and indexed, and you can buy various marketing services and publicity packages that include press releases and posters. Your
book is made available through various sales channels including Amazon.com
and book distributors and can be sold as an e-book. These services are an option

if you do not have the know-how to produce your own book or the time to shop for and work with a book designer and cover artist. In a few short weeks, your printed book will be in your hands and available for purchase online. You can buy as many copies as you need and order more at any time. The add-on services, such as paid book reviews and marketing packages, are expensive and of questionable value. They make money from authors for the publishing company and cannot be compared to the publicity campaigns of conventional publishers. You probably will get better results if you write your own press releases and information sheets. *See Appendix B for a sample press release and information sheet.* Spend your marketing budget sending out promotional copies to a targeted list of people whom you know will be genuinely interested in your book.

POD printers such as Amazon's CreateSpace* (**www.createspace.com**) and Lulu* (**www.lulu.com**) offer do-it-yourself POD models. You upload a PDF of your formatted manuscript and your own cover design. CreateSpace also offers cover design templates that allow you to design your own cover online with clip art or your own uploaded images. You can make as many changes as you want to your book for the price of one book (the new proof copy) and shipping. You set the price for your book, and the company takes a cut of each book sale (CreateSpace takes 40 percent of the list price).

The largest POD company, Lightning Source (**www.lightningsource.com**) is a subsidiary of Ingram Book Company, the largest book wholesaler in the U.S. Lightning Source deals with publishers rather than individual authors, so you will have to set yourself up as a publisher to work with them. *See Chapter 14 for more information about registering yourself as a publisher.* Publishing with Lightning Source automatically gets you listed in wholesale book catalogs used by thousands of bookstores. However, because unsold POD books cannot be returned to the publisher, bookstores will not request your book unless a customer orders a copy.

## Lightning Source's catalog is more than 1.6 Million

In early 2010, it was reported that Lightning Source's U.S. and U.K. branches were printing 1.5 million books a month in print runs averaging 1.8 copies per title. Lightning Source makes titles from the catalogs of 11,000 publishers, from self-publishing individuals to large companies such as Simon & Schuster, available to libraries and bookstores overnight. It supplies major U.S. booksellers such as Amazon.com and Barnes & Noble, as well as booksellers overseas.

Making your book available on online booksellers and in catalogs through a POD publisher does not automatically sell it. It is up to you to create a demand for your book and interest readers in buying it. POD simply gives you a product to sell.

POD is an excellent option for many self-publishing authors. You can create an attractive, professional-looking book with POD if you pay attention to details and hire an illustrator or book designer to help you. POD allows you to start promoting and selling hard copies of your book with a relatively low financial investment; your main outlay is the time you spend designing, formatting, and promoting your book. Once your manuscript is ready, you can have a printed copy of your book in just a few days. POD allows you to experiment with publishing and get a feel for your market. It also allows you to print books economically for small niche markets. POD has been behind an explosion in self-published titles over the last four years and the rapid development of the indie book (independent book) industry. Major printers have incorporated POD into their business models by bringing old titles back into print and keeping more recent titles in print after their initial popularity has subsided.

Most POD publishers maintain extensive online communities for their writers, with forums, instructions, blogs, and support groups. They also have their own sales ranking systems and typically, promote authors who have sold more than a certain amount with special recognition.

## A caution about POD

Many subsidized POD companies present a rosy picture of self-publishing and try to flatter authors into buying additional services. Approach POD as a business venture — take what you need and leave the rest. Compare costs and services carefully, and remember to account for shipping costs. There may be trade-offs; you might decide to accept mediocre book design services because they are convenient or pay higher prices per book but make a lower initial investment. Representatives from your POD publisher may call to talk to you about purchasing additional services such as marketing packages. Ask yourself if you really need these services or whether you would be better off hiring your own publicist or managing your own publicity campaign. You also may be urged to buy larger quantities of your printed books to take advantage of discounted prices. Only buy what you need for promotional purposes or direct sale. One of the best features of POD is that you avoid sinking your money into inventory that sits in your garage or warehouse for months waiting to be sold.

Read your POD agreement carefully. In some cases, you are giving the publisher the rights to your book for a specified time. You might not be allowed to take your cover design with you when you change printers or "graduate" to a larger press run or a publishing contract. There may be additional fees for making changes to your book or for accessing certain sales channels. Be sure the POD company's policies will not interfere with your plans for selling your book.

Before you submit your manuscript to a POD publisher or service, do an Internet search for comments about them on blogs and writers' websites. You will learn in advance about complaints and hidden fees and find helpful tips for making the most of their services.

## Digital printing

Digital printers use toner printing (rather than ink) to print short runs of standard-quality books in which there is no light to dark variation from page to page. The books are indistinguishable from offset printing. Digital printing is usually the best choice for a print run of 100 to 3,000. It costs less per book than POD, without the high setup costs of offset printing. Many offset printers have added digital printing technology to their facilities to take care of small orders. You will end up with boxes of books to store or ship to distributors.

## Offset

In offset printing, plates are used for ink printing, and the price per unit decreases as the number of books in the print run increases. There is an initial setup cost for preparing the plates; after that, you pay only for printing. Prices vary but can be around $1.25 per book for a run of 3,000. Offset printing becomes economical when a print run exceeds 2,500.

# Deciding How Many Books to Order

Unless you have a large number of pre-orders, or need large quantities to supply a distributor, do not pay for a first run of more than 500 books. Instead of tying up your money in printed books that must be stored in your home or in a warehouse until you can sell them, order only what you need to get started, and use the rest of your money for book promotion. Additional books can be printed within a few days if you need them. When you finally receive the first printed copies of your book, you inevitably will find typos and other errors that you want to correct for the next press run. Never order more books than you reasonably can expect to sell in a year. They may become outdated or damaged by humidity in a storage facility before you can sell them.

Many first-time authors have inflated expectations about how many books they can sell. Before you order your printed books, have your marketing plan in place. Order only the hard copies you will be selling directly to your readers or retail outlets and those you need to send out as promotional copies. If you are working with a distributor or wholesaler, you may be required to supply a certain number of books.

## Getting Quotes

Look for printers that specialize in printing books. Do not go down to your local printer and ask how much it would cost to print your book — they are likely to outsource the job and charge you a markup, or make mistakes that will cost you more in the long run. A book printer can be located anywhere — just keep shipping costs in mind. Search for book printers on the Internet or through directories of publishing services. Approximately 100 printers in the U.S. are equipped to print books efficiently and economically.

The Book Manufacturing section of the *Literary Market Place (LMP)* (**www. literarymarketplace.com**), lists services for art, word processing, printing, and binding. Many libraries carry the print version in their reference sections. The Independent Book Publishers Association (**www.ibpa-online.org/vendors/suppliers.aspx**) allows you to submit RFQs (Request for Quotes) online, and the Association of Publishers for Special Sales website (**www.spannet.org**) has advertisements and forums about printing. You can find lists of book printers on the websites of Aeonix Publishing Group (**www.aeonix.com/bookprnt.htm**) or on Bookmarket.com (**www.bookmarket.com/101print.htm**).

Printing prices vary according to the printer's equipment and printing capabilities and how full its schedule is. If business is slow, a printer may quote a lower price. Send out RFQs to a number of book printers, and compare the quotes. There may be a number of variables including the time needed to print the book, cover and binding options, and shipping arrangements.

# Trim Size and Number of Pages

To get a quote from a printer, you will need to specify the trim size of your book. The trim size refers to the dimensions of a page after the book has been trimmed to its final size during the binding process. Take the book that you have chosen as a guide for your book design, and measure the dimensions of its pages. That is its trim size.

Digital and POD printers typically offer a choice of several standard trim sizes; offset printers have more flexibility. You should select a trim size that fits the type and genre of your book. Mass-market books are 4 ¼" x 7" because they have to fit in the special display racks in retail stores. Most self-published books are either 5 ½" x 8 ½" or 6" x 9", sizes that are easy to hold and read. If your book is a workbook or an instruction manual with illustrations that needs to be laid out flat on a table, 8" x 10" and 8 ½" x 11" are good sizes. A children's book or an art book could be any size, but if you are using a digital printing service, your options might be limited. If you plan to sell your book through brick-and-mortar bookstores, stick to standard sizes that will fit on shelves and displays.

As an example, Createspace offers the following trim sizes.

| |
|---|
| 5" x 8" |
| 5.06" x 7.81" |
| 5.25" x 8" |
| 5.5" x 8.5" |
| 6" x 9" |
| 6.14" x 9.21" |
| 6.69" x 9.61" |
| 7" x 10" |
| 7.44" x 9.69" |
| 7.5" x 9.25" |
| 8" x 10" |
| 8.25" x 6" |
| 8.25" x 8.25" |
| 8.5" x 8.5" |
| 8.5" x 11" |

To get the number of pages in your book for an RFQ, you will need to format your manuscript as a book layout. *See Chapter 9 for more information on book layouts.*

# Book Covers

It is customary for the book printer to print both the interior pages and the book cover, but there may be situations in which you use a different printer for your covers. For example, you might have a cover design that requires special treatment, such as embossed lettering. Ask the book printer to quote the cover price separately. If you decide to have another company print your book covers, make sure they are shipped well in advance of when the printer needs them for binding. Do not have them trimmed, and order extra covers in case of damage or mishaps during binding. You always can use your leftover covers in your promotion kits.

# Determining the Price of Your Book

Publishing is a business. For your book to be viable, you must sell it for a price that covers the cost of printing, shipping, and marketing it and still gives you a profit. When setting the price of your book, consider what you will have to pay for promotion and marketing. Anyone who helps sell your book receives a percentage of the profit, including bookstores, wholesalers, dealers, and distributors. You will need complimentary promotional copies to send out to reviewers, which may constitute 10 to 20 percent of your total stock. Figure in the cost of advertising and returns on books that are damaged or returned. The price of your book should reflect these expenses, and the time it took you to write the book, in addition to printing costs.

The price of your book should be low enough to entice readers to buy it, yet high enough to meet their expectations. Underpricing your book could diminish its stature in readers' eyes. Think about the socioeconomic status of your readers, and look at the prices of books similar to yours. For example, a book for young adults should cost less than a health book targeting middle-aged women or a business book, because young people are likely to have less spending money and might balk at buying high-priced items.

Two methods can be used to determine a book price: bottom-up and top-down. The bottom-up method accounts for the costs involved in getting the manuscript turned into book form and into the hands of readers. If each book costs $3 to create and your markup (the amount added to the cost price in order to determine profit) is eight times, then your book will be $24, or $23.95. (A book priced at $23.95, even though it is only five cents cheaper, appears to cost much less than $24.) Take into account how you will sell your book. If you are distributing through mail order and bookstores, eight times the cost of production is standard. A textbook should be priced at around five times more than production cost. The top-down method of pricing involves comparing the list prices of other books like yours. Average the prices of five or ten comparable books, and set your price in the middle.

When you are setting up your book price with a POD publisher or printer, your "royalty" is the amount you receive from each sale — the amount left over after the publisher and the online bookseller has taken its cut. The publisher amount is usually a set figure per book, plus a small amount per page, while the online bookseller takes a percentage of each sale. The list price of your book has to be high enough to give you a reasonable return on each sale. There may be several levels of royalties because your book will not always sell at list price — you will get less for books sold wholesale or at a discount.

## ISBNs and Bar Codes

An International Standard Book Number (ISBN) is an inventory and identification code that is issued to each individual book for shipping purposes. Different editions of the same book receive different ISBNs. You will need an ISBN if you want to sell your book in bookstores and place it in libraries. ISBNs are not necessary for books that you do not plan to sell on the open market, such as family memoirs.

You can purchase ISBN numbers through Bowker U.S. ISBN Agency (**www. isbn.org**), individually or in blocks of 10, 100 and 1,000. The ISBN website recommends that publishers purchase enough ISBNs to last them for five years. The more numbers you purchase, the less they cost, and you will be able to maintain the same publisher prefix for a longer period. If you require only a single ISBN, they are offered by Bowker Identifier Services (**www.myidentifiers.com**) for $125, or for $150 with a bar code. Some POD services assign one of their ISBN numbers to your book as part of their publishing packages. This identifies the book as having been published under their imprint and may affect your ability to sell to bookstores (many bookstores will not buy books from POD publishers). If you are planning to publish additional books or operate as your own publishing company, you should purchase your own ISBN numbers so that your books will be properly identified in the supply chain.

In 2007, ISBN numbers moved from 10 to 13 digits to accommodate the growing number of titles. According to the ISBN website, the "X" that appears at the end of the number stands in for the number 10; the last number is referred to as a "check digit." The ISBN-13 has five parts: the prefix, group or country identifier, publisher identifier, title or edition identifier, and the check digit. The publisher must update information associated with the ISBN whenever a book goes out of print.

The bar code represents a translation of the ISBN. Authors or publishers can request bar codes from the ISBN website or after an ISBN has been purchased from **www.bowkerbarcode.com/barcode**. Most retailers use the bar code for scanning during checkout and sometimes for inventory, and most retailers and wholesalers will not carry your book without a bar code. When selecting your bar code, choose the Bookland EAN/13 with add on. This should appear on the lower half of the back cover, which is known as "cover four," on both paperback and hardback editions. The bar code for a book differs from a UPC bar code, which is used for merchandise. UPCs, when they appear on books, are used for mass-market paperbacks like those you may see in grocery stores and drugstores. UPCs cost more (about $300) and are not the type of bar code you require. ISBN/bar codes may cost from $10 to $30.

## CASE STUDY: OFFICE MANAGER AT A BOOK PUBLISHING COMPANY

Crystal Edwards

Crystal Edwards is the office manager for Atlantic Publishing Group, Inc. She has been with the company for five and a half years.

As the office manager, my duties vary widely. I take care of typical office responsibilities such as payroll, customer service, processing orders, and accounting, which take up much of my time. I have expanded my duties to include assisting the editorial department and contributing to the overall editorial process.

My role starts at the beginning of the process. As soon as we decide on the title and content of a book project, I assign it an ISBN number based on a block of numbers our company owns. Then, I research and distribute the basics of the book, such as the title, the general content, the ISBN number, and any other information, to marketing and resale sites such as Amazon Advantage, Bowker (which is also the site from which we buy ISBN numbers), and others. This is a very important step because it gets our books out into the public eye, so we can begin collecting preorders before the book is even finished.

When a new or existing author is hired to complete a book project, I am in charge of writing up and securing the contract, processing any necessary documents, ordering their research materials, and issuing payments. Collecting the research is also a time-consuming, vital task for our company, because these books and articles supply our authors with their first look at some of the scholarly writing behind our topics. Another responsibility I have is to meet with editors on a weekly basis. During these meetings, I update a status sheet that shows what stage their books are in and what is in their editing queue, so we are all on the same page and know how each editor is progressing on their projects. I assist them in prioritizing their editing and help by offering advice on content and general coherency.

Then, once a book project is complete, I collect and add in any photos to the manuscript. This can be accomplished in several ways. Sometimes, I am in charge of setting up collaborations with relevant companies so that we can obtain the rights to print some of their pictures in our books. When I contact companies, I, typically, am looking to get photos of products or processes that will help enhance the book, so readers have a better understanding of the material. Or, I assist our editorial assistants in taking the photographs ourselves. Last, I search online for appropriate photos for which we could obtain a copyright. During this time, I submit the manuscript for Cataloging-In-Publication (CIP) data, which is a critical step to having our books recognized in libraries and bookstores across the country.

Once our books have been designed, we hire freelance proofers to go through them one last time to make sure no errors are published. I work directly with the proofers and our art director to coordinate their projects and payments.

I enjoy working with the different departments within the company because it helps me have a better understanding of the entire book publishing process.

# Publisher Filings

Depending on how you intend to market your book, you should have it listed in several other places.

## Library of Congress Control Numbers (LCCN and PCN)

The Library of Congress Control Number (LCCN) is referred to as a Preassigned Control Number (PCN) when assigned before a book's publication. The PCN is printed on the book's copyright page. It is used to reference a work in all its editions, unlike the ISBN, which is assigned individually to every edition of a book. The PCN is useful for anyone who subscribes to the Library of Congress catalog card service and to librarians searching national databases for the purposes of ordering catalog cards. Catalog cards are obtained from the Library of Congress and from commercial suppliers.

Obtaining a PCN can be useful if you want to make your work available for libraries to purchase. However, a PCN only can be assigned to books that the Library of Congress expects to be purchased by libraries — those for which a demand is anticipated. PCNs generally are not assigned to booklets of fewer than 50 pages, lab manuals, advertisements and brochures, calendars, most textbooks, religious study guides, workbooks, coloring books, some books of poetry, vanity press publications, and similar materials. To apply for the number, you will first have to visit the Copyright Office website (**www.copyright.gov**), complete the Application to Participate, secure a password and account number, and then apply for the PCN. Visit the PCN website (**http://pcn.loc.gov**) or the Library of Congress website (**http://loc.gov**). If the author or title changes or the publishing is cancelled, be sure to notify the PCN office. To ensure that your title is properly catalogued, send a complimentary advance copy to the Cataloging in Publication (CIP) Office at the Library of Congress.

## Cataloging in Publication Record (CIP data)

Another Library of Congress service is Cataloging in Publication (CIP), which helps facilitate processing for booksellers and librarians. The service provides more numbers for cataloging purposes that, like the PCN, appear on the book's copyright page. CIP data is useful for helping librarians know how to categorize and shelve your book. Publishers that have printed three books are accepted into the program. There is no charge for the program, but from time to time, the CIP office temporarily has stopped accepting new publishers due to limited funds. This happened for a period of several months in 1990 and in 1996. Participation of self-publishers is limited. According to the Cataloging in Publication website (**http://cip.loc.gov/eligibility.html**), "Self-publishers (i.e. authors and editors who pay for or subsidize publication of their own works; who often do not publish the works of more than three different authors; and whose works are rarely widely acquired by the nation's libraries) are ineligible." Electronic Cataloging in Publication (ECIP) applications are accepted 20 at a time from a single publisher.

Quality Books, a supplier of small press books to libraries, provides Publisher's Cataloging in Publication Data (PCIP) data for books that do not qualify for the Library of Congress CIP program. Libraries need this data in order to enter books in their catalog systems. To apply, visit the Quality Books website at **www.Quality-Books.com**. Upon processing of your application, you will receive a data block to place on the copyright page of your book.

## Standard Address Number (SAN)

The Standard Address Number (SAN) is used to identify separate mailing addresses for companies with multiple departments, including wholesalers, bookstores, libraries, and publishers. A SAN is useful for distinguishing between shipping and billing addresses. SANs are issued through Bowker (who also issues bar codes for ISBNs). Bowker now charges for the service. You probably do not need an SAN if you are self-publishing and have a single address that you use for handling billing, shipping, and editorial correspondence. Bowker Link" (**www.bowkerlink.com**) is a publisher access system that allows publishers to log in and add or update listings in the database. Visit this site for more information on obtaining a SAN.

## Advance Book Information (ABI)

Bowker also provides Advance Book Information (ABI). This service provides a directory and database listing for your book for booksellers, librarians, and distributors to access. The free service ensures that your title is listed in the *Books in Print* directory, which issues in October of each year. Visit the Bowker Link website (**www.bowkerlink.com**) to submit your title at least 180 days before it is due to be published. Listings are added and updated through the website.

# Distribution

When considering where to make your book available for purchase, first consider how you can target your readers, just as you would with advertising. Are there specialty stores that would carry your book? If you have written a nonfiction picture book about the life of Thomas Edison, you may try contacting, for example, the Thomas Edison National Historical Park in New Jersey to find out whether it would be interested in purchasing copies to sell in the gift store. Such a nontraditional outlet can lead to larger volumes of purchases than would display in a bookstore, although retail outlets are certainly a viable option as well. Other retail markets to consider are chain bookstores, local and independent bookstores, newsstands, grocery stores, hotels, drugstores, gift shops, and airports.

Major online booksellers include Abebooks.com, Alibris.com, Amazon.com, Bookfinder.com, Powells.com, and BN.com. You can list your book for sale as an independent bookseller and send out each book yourself, or you can participate in a sales program where you ship boxes of books to their warehouses, and they fulfill the orders. Many POD services fulfill orders placed through these online booksellers.

Selling directly to individual consumers means you keep the entire profit. However, selling to wholesalers and distributors can mean selling in bulk. The larger quantities you sell, the more books you can have printed at a lower cost.

## Distribution outlets

Bookstores purchase most of their stock from distributors, wholesalers, and large publishers rather than from multiple individual publishers. Wholesalers (which can be national, regional, specialized, or library-targeted) fulfill orders sent to them and do not send reps out to solicit orders. Distributors employ sales representatives to visit bookstores and buyers for chain stores and collect orders. Distributors also publish their stock in catalogs, which typically issue seasonally. Because of their added involvement and increased results, distributors take a larger cut of the profit than do wholesalers. Keep in mind that distributors handle the storage, catalog publication, billing, shipping, and marketing, but not the promotion.

Not only do distributors aid in getting your book into national markets and large retailers, but they also lend credibility to you and your book. The more credibility you have, the greater your chances of having your book reviewed by a reputable source. For this reason, be sure to list your distributor in your press release and promotional materials.

When seeking a distributor, look through several of their more recent catalogs for titles similar to yours. Judging from their selection, if it looks as if your book would be in good company, contact them by phone or email. If you are emailing them, include a synopsis and a book flier as an attachment, as well as any press or reviews you might have received. Most distributors only accept a limited number of new clients each year. When considering your book, a distributor will look for certain qualities, such as:

- The production quality of your book
- Your book's marketability
- Whether your title fits in with any of its target markets
- Whether the title has selling potential
- The reputation of the author
- Whether the author has a promotional plan or marketing budget

If the distributor says no to your title, ask for a referral to a wholesaler or another distributor. An additional option to consider is the trade distribution program from the Independent Book Publishers Association (IBPA). The program sends books through a screening process biannually, and those that make the cut are purchased. Visit the IBPA website for more information (**www.ibpa-online.org**).

After you have made a sale to distributors and wholesalers (or not), shift your focus to other markets:

- Children's bookstore chains (some are permitted small purchases from individual publishers, favoring local and regional authors) such as FAO Schwarz
- National wholesaler Baker & Taylor makes 68 percent of its sales to the library market; it would be beneficial to become one of its stock publishers.

- Places where you might be able to set up counter displays, such as local stores, specialty retailers, and locations frequented by your readers
- A table at a book fair
- Local events and fundraisers
- Independent bookstores
- Gift shops, museums, and tourist attractions

## CASE STUDY: THE LOGISTICS OF DISTRIBUTION AT A PUBLISHING HOUSE

Linda Heilig

*Linda Heilig is the distribution manager for Atlantic Publishing Group, Inc., and has been with the company for five years. She interacts with distributors and customers on a daily basis.*

Once a title has been published, distribution is important to make sure customers and distributors receive orders in a timely manner. Atlantic Publishing's policy is that orders are processed and shipped within 24 hours of receiving them. Timely processing enhances the relationship between the publisher and distributors or customers. We believe efficiency is a key factor to being successful at this.

We have developed a system where a numeric position is assigned to each title. This number corresponds to a pallet position and a position on the production line. When invoices are created in QuickBooks, we sort them in a descending order based on the position number. This allows the employees to go down the production line starting where the paperwork is picked up and working their way to the front where the orders are checked and packaged. This numeric system prevents employees from backtracking and wasting time searching for a specific title. The packaging area in the production line also allows orders to be checked to ensure they are accurate.

Another major factor in distribution is understanding each distributor's or customer's requirements for receiving and processing purchase orders. In many cases, a distributor requires that the publisher use Electronic Data Interchange (EDI). Several companies offer this service and will assist in tailoring the setup that is required to meet the specifications of the publisher and the distributor. Once the EDI setup is complete, purchase orders are received electronically and must be acknowledged and advance ship notices created. Another feature of EDI is the ability to send invoices back to the distributor electronically. This saves on postage and cuts down on processing time.

Equally as important is the shipping method. Atlantic Publishing uses FedEx (Ground and Freight), UPS, and the U.S. Postal Service. Most distributors have specific shipping requirements, which the publisher must adhere to. It can be as simple as adding the purchase order number on the shipping label to requiring an additional label be attached to the carton.

Conclusion:

- Atlantic Publishing Group, Inc., publishes and distributes our books. We have discovered the importance of an effective distribution system. To make sales, you have to be able to get your books out in the most efficient cost effective way.

- Be sure to have sufficient inventory and staffing. It is especially important if you are planning a marketing campaign that you estimate the inventory and staff that is needed to fulfill the orders.

- Selling on Amazon.com Marketplace is a great way to generate sales and sell used or damaged inventory. Great shipping encourages buyers to leave positive feedback, which in turn increases our rating and helps increase confidence or encourages new and potential buyers.

## Shipping and order fulfillment

Orders may come in through mail and electronically. You may find it helpful to set up a merchant account with PayPal (**www.paypal.com**), so you can receive credit card payments online. If you will be receiving checks made out to the name of your publishing company (if you have set one up), rather than your given name, you will need to open a merchant account at a bank. *More about setting yourself up as a publisher can be found in Chapter 14.* You can set up the account with the name of the publishing company and DBA (doing business as) your name. Having your name attached to the account will eliminate any confusion when you deposit checks made out to your name rather than the company name. If you want to be able to process credit card orders offline, the PIndependent Book Publishers Association offers its members a low-rate, no-monthly-transaction-requirement merchant status program. Visit the Independent Book Publishers Association website at **www.ibpa-online.org**.

Include an order form on the website and ordering information for those who are unable to use it for some reason. Give a fax number, business address (invest in a post office box), a PayPal email address, an order email address, and a phone number where orders can be directed. Invest in accounting software or an order entry program such as QuickBooks (**www.intuit.com**). Record all the information pertaining to every order, including the date of order, date of payment, payment method, item and quantity ordered, purchaser's name and address, date shipped, and date received (if applicable).

Charge sales tax on orders from within your own state but not on orders from different states or on books purchased for resale. You will print duplicate copies of invoices and sales receipts. Invoices in multiple copies serve as packing slips and shipping labels. Keep hard copy backups in a binder or folder. Similarly, keep hard copies of incoming orders, whether they originate by mail or email. Save them for three to six months in case you need to refer to them for customer disputes and inquiries.

## Self-publishing do's and don'ts

**DO:**

- Choose a printer that specializes in book printing.
- Send RFQs to several printers and compare prices.
- Remember to account for freight and shipping costs when selecting a printer.
- Study POD contracts carefully before committing yourself.
- Plan your book design and know what you want before you hire a professional to help you.
- Get an ISBN number if you intend to sell your book through retail booksellers.

**DON'T:**

- Get your book printed at a local print shop.
- Choose the lowest quote without comparing all the variables, including shipping costs and additional services.
- Order more books than you can reasonably expect to sell in one year.
- Use the same ISBN number on more than one book.

## Chapter 9

# Designing Your Book

❋

Subsidized POD services typically ask you to submit your manuscript as a Word document and do the book and cover design as part of your printing package. Printers and do-it-yourself POD services such as Lulu and CreateSpace ask for a PDF file of your manuscript, laid out as it will look when it is finished. If you know how to use a desktop publishing program or graphic design software, you can do a tolerable job of designing your book interior and cover, but if you want your book to look professional, hire a book designer. You need a professional product to compete with all those other books in the marketplace. The design of your book will affect your sales.

Book design is an art form requiring specialized skills. Book designers are familiar with design conventions and will deliver an attractive, finished product that is ready to print. A book designer knows how to make the pages of your book well balanced, appealing, and easy to read. When you design your book yourself, you will end up experimenting with several proofs before the result is satisfactory. After you perfect the design of your first book, you can use it as a template to format future books.

You can find book designers the same way you find printers, distributors, and other self-publishing services. Ask other writers for recommendations, read writers' blogs and forums, and look through business directories like the *Literary Market Place (LMP)*. Contact a local book publisher and ask for the names of book designers. Type "book designer" in an Internet search engine, and numerous ads will pop up. Find out how many books a prospective book designer has worked on, and ask to see samples. Get quotes, compare services, clarify how you will communicate with each other, set a timeline for getting the job done, and establish an approval process.

## CASE STUDY:
## BOOK DESIGN

Meg Buchner * Megadesign
14688 HWY 35 N
Ferryville, WI 54628
608-734-3259
www.mega-designs.com
megadesn@mchsi.com

*Meg Buchner has worked as a graphic designer for more than 20 years. She works as a freelance graphic designer and functions as the art director for Atlantic Publishing. She has worked with Atlantic for more than a decade and has been proud to design hundreds of book covers and interiors personally. She designed the* Restaurant Manager's Handbook, *which won the prestigious Benjamin Franklin national award. She has received numerous other awards for book cover design.*

**Why is book cover design important?**

There is an old saying: "Don't judge a book by its cover." However, most people DO judge a book by its cover. Specifically, if the title is hard to read or does not look professional, chances are the book will not be purchased.

When designing a book cover, how and where the book will be sold is a very important consideration. For example, today many books are sold as e-books or purchased from an online retailer. This means that the cover has to draw attention and be readable as a thumbnail on a website, which is less than one inch in width. Most websites have a white background and do not allow borders around the book. If your book cover is white or a light color, it can get lost on the site. People will not click on it for more information.

Many elements go into book cover design including fonts, images, photos, and color choices. You want a cover that has balance, symmetry, and draws attention to the book (not the design). A good cover is pleasing to the eye, and the title is easy to see and read. As a rule, no more than three fonts should be used on the cover. The author's name should be secondary to the title if the author is not well known. (This rule does not apply when the author is accredited or a famous person. In that case, the large name alone will sell the book.)

When designing a cover for an author, I typically discuss the cover in depth with the author before starting. Many times the author has a rough idea already, and a professional designer can create and enhance that. I also present authors with at least three initial cover designs to choose from. Typically, one is the cover he or she has described to me as being "exactly what I want," and the other two are my own variations. Frequently, the cover that gets picked is not the author's vision. Why? A professional designer knows what he or she is doing and often comes up with a design that works or looks better. If you go to expense of hiring a professional, let him or her design.

**Why is book design important?**

Book design is crucial for one simple reason: readability. Your information may be critical, or your novel may be fascinating. However, if it is not presented well, or it is hard to read (especially at the beginning), people will not make the effort to read the book. The quality of the design influences people's perception of the quality of the book.

This applies much more to traditionally printed books than to e-books. However, e-books need to be formatted correctly as well, or they will not work or will look poorly made.

In today's world, readers often look at online samples or other customer's reviews before purchasing. If you have even one review that says your book is shoddy or unprofessional, it can affect your sales.

**What do you do when you lay out a book for printing?**

Book design is a relatively complicated process, but here is a general overview. I layout books in Adobe® InDesign® CS6. This professional design software has a book function with which you can create a book document. The book document is basically a "master" that allows you to collect each document within the book (each chapter of the book is laid out as a separate document) and control elements such as master pages, text styles, and page numbering. You also can use the book document to export to PDFs and e-books.

**Why is it a good idea to have a professional design your self-published book?**

Most authors write their books in Microsoft Word. This is word processing software, not design software. I do not know any professional graphic artists that use Word for design. Most printers do not accept Word documents, and many functions a book requires are not available in Word. Unless you have access to and a good working knowledge of professional publishing software, I recommend using a designer. A good designer should give you examples of books he or she has worked on previously in book, electronic, and printed versions.

Many printers have designers on staff or a prepress department, and they are willing to help you get your book to press. However, this service typically costs $85-$100 per hour. If you supply a file to a printer that is not press-ready, you will be charged to have it fixed. Designers routinely handle many complex technical issues. A good designer will guarantee you a press-ready file and work directly with your printer to fix any problems that may arise. In addition, a designer often will give you a flat rate, all-inclusive cost for book design.

## TIP: Save time and money by doing some of the work yourself.

You can save some money by doing a preliminary layout yourself before you give the manuscript to your book designer. Set margins, place photos where you want them, insert text boxes, separate the chapters, and add comments to let the book designer where you want page breaks or sidebars. The book designer will have a better idea of what you expect and will be able to work faster.

# Design Your Book from the Beginning

Layout is the last step in preparing your manuscript for publishing, but as you write, you should be guided by your vision for your book. The previous chapter suggested finding a book similar to the book you want to create and using it as a guide. Look at the various elements of the book — the title page, the table of contents, the chapter headings, inserts, sidebars, illustrations, glossary, index, and appendices. Decide which of these features you want to incorporate in your book and what they should look like. Planning for these features as you write your manuscript will save time and help you organize your thoughts.

Create a consistent structure for your book as you go along. Use the same font style and size for all of the chapter titles, and another style for each level of sub-headings. Use the same format for numbered charts or drawings, text boxes, photo headings, quotes, and asides. For example, if the first illustration is titled "Figure 1-1: _____," all of your illustrations should be numbered consecutively and in the same way. Quotes and subtitles all should be of similar lengths and styles to help tie the book together.

Most manuscripts are typed in Microsoft Word. You can use the "Styles" feature in Word to set up a set of formatting characteristics, such as font name, size, color, paragraph alignment, and spacing, which either are applied automatically to the document as you type or can be selected with a single click from a style palette. Setting up a style before you begin typing saves hours of work as you write. When you finish your manuscript, it already will be organized and consistent, which makes layout much easier. Create a heading style for each of your subtitles. By using different font sizes for chapter titles and subtitles, you can generate an au-tomatic table of contents in Word and update it in seconds. You also can view an outline of your manuscript or a document map alongside your text at any time.

# Formatting your Book

Take a ruler and measure the trim size of your sample book. Open your document in Microsoft Word, and select a page size the same as the trim size, and a two-page view. Measure the margins of your sample book pages and select "mirrored margins" of similar dimensions in Word. Now, you can get an accurate estimate of the number of pages in your book. Mass-market paperbacks often have small margins in order to fit more text on the page and keep the costs of printing and paper lower. Trade paperbacks often have more blank space on the pages and, consequently, use more pages. Look at a selection of books and experiment with your margins to find an arrangement that complements your genre and subject matter.

When you look at a two-page view of your manuscript, the front of each page is on the left and the back of each page is on the right. Because a new chapter typi-cally begins on the right-hand page, adjust your book so that each new chapter heading is on the front of a page (the left-hand side in two-page view). Remember to insert a blank page at the front of your book, plus title pages, table of contents, and a space for a foreword if you are going to have one. Photos, diagrams, and illustrations also will take up space; if possible, insert them now to see how they will fit on the pages. Page numbers and headers (if you are going to use them) also will take up space. At the end of the book, leave pages for an index, author biography, and anything else you plan to include. Look at your page count — though it may change slightly, this is roughly the actual size of your book.

Many POD printers give instructions for formatting your manuscript based on trim size and number of pages. Once you know the size of your book, you can follow your printer's directions to set up accurate margins and make other adjustments. Some offer downloadable book templates, and you can download generic book templates from the Microsoft.com website, from sites like Bookmark Self Publishing (**www.bookmarkselfpublishing.com/main/book-layout-templates. html**) or purchase templates and design instructions from sites such as Self-pub. net (**www.self-pub.net/templates.html**).

Desktop publishing software is used to create the text, graphics, and overall page design and layout of books and Web pages. Some programs allow you to create drop shadows, place text on a curved path, edit photos, and other design features that normally are handled by programs such as Adobe Photoshop® and Adobe Illustrator®. Widely used desktop publishing programs are Adobe InDesign and QuarkXPress®. Printing professionals often use Adobe InDesign and Quark XPress to lay out and design their pages. Once all of the layout and design elements, such as text, photographs, graphics, charts, tables, and other data, have been added, the file is saved in .pdf or .eps format and sent to the printer. Files intended for online presentation are exported as .xml documents. If you already own a desktop publishing program, you can learn to design your own book with it by taking a short class or an online tutorial. If you have not yet purchased desktop publishing software, it probably will cost less to have your book professionally designed when you consider the cost of the software plus the time it will take you to learn the program and do the work. The cost of book design varies widely but is largely based on the number of pages in your book. Your POD publisher probably offers book design services — these jobs typically are outsourced, and the POD company places a markup on them. You might get a better price and better quality by working directly with a book designer. Even if you do have desktop publishing software and know how to use it, book design is a special skill, and your finished product might not look as professional as a conventionally published book.

# Formatting a Book in Microsoft Word

If you feel up to the challenge, you can design a book in Microsoft Word. It is a painstaking process, but it can be done. This is not recommended if you intend to print more than 200 books. If you do not know how to find or use a particular feature, you can find directions on the Microsoft website (**www.microsoft.com**) and in various forums and how-to websites by typing your question in a search engine.

1. Turn on "Vertical Alignment" and "Justify" features to justify your text on the page.

2. Turn on automatic hyphenation. Set the hyphenation zone to about ½ inch and limit the number of consecutive hyphens to three.

3. Select fonts and font sizes for your title, chapter headings and subheadings, and text and create a customized heading style for each in the Styles palette. If you are trying to copy a font from your sample book and do not know its name, search the online digital font directory Identifont (**www.identifont.com**). Microsoft has several style templates in its Style Gallery. When you select one of these styles, you automatically can see how all the headings in your document will look. If you like one of these, select it, and then make changes to the various headings so that they look the way you want them to. You can download additional templates from the Microsoft website (**http://office.microsoft.com/en-us/templates/default.aspx**). If you want your book to look exactly like the sample book, use a pica ruler to measure the exact size of each font and distance between characters. You can print a pica ruler on transparent film from **http://tinytutorials.wordpress.com/2010/09/16/printable-pica-ruler**.

4. Set the margins for your pages based on the instructions of your POD printer and the measurements of your sample book. Select "Mirrored Margins" and two-page view so that you can see the front and back of each page side by side. The front is on the left, and the back of each page is on the right.

5. Insert a section break for each time you start a new chapter or a new type of page, such as a title page. Select "Odd Page" to ensure that each chapter begins on a right-hand page.

6. Insert headers and footers for each section. To keep page numbers consecutive, go to "Format Page Numbers" and click the box that says, "Continue from previous section." If you want to use a chapter or book title as the heading on each page, use "different first page" for each section. To place a different header on the right and left pages, use "Header and Footer Tools," and choose "Different Odd & Even Pages." You can use the space bar to move page numbers and headers around manually, so they look right on the pages.

7. Insert photos, charts and illustrations, and size them to fit the page. You can wrap text around photos, but it is usually easier to break the text and insert the photo in the middle of the page.

8. Use "Find and Replace" to replace all double spacing between sentences with single spaces and to repair any other inconsistencies in your text. Run a spell checker to locate problems you might have overlooked.

9. Look at the book in "Print Preview" to see how the pages will look.

10. Go through the entire book, look for aberrations, and manually repair any problems.

11. Save your document as a Template, so you can use the same settings for future books.

## Photos and illustrations

The recommended resolution for photos and images in a book manuscript is 300 dpi (dots per inch). Photos that look sparkling and clear on your computer screen may look grainy and fuzzy in your book if the resolution is too low. When you save a file from a photo-editing or graphics program in a JPEG format, the program sometimes lowers the resolution of the photo. Also, when you use Word to shrink or enlarge an image, the quality of the image can be affected. For the best results, size your photo to fit your book while it is still in the photo editing program, and make sure it is exported at 300 dpi.

## Converting a document to a PDF file

Most POD printers ask you to upload your formatted and typeset manuscript as a PDF file. You can save files as PDFs in Adobe Acrobat® and other design programs. To create a PDF file from a Word document select print from your menu and print as a PDF. The file will be saved as a PDF document. You can also use free onlne services such as Print in PDF™ (**www.printinpdf.com**) to convert any file on your computer to a PDF.

# Book Interior

Your book interior consists of several elements in addition to the manuscript itself. If you examine a range of books, you will see that every book has most of these elements, but that they can look very different.

# Front matter

The first pages of your book introduce the reader to what is coming later and set the stage for the rest of your book.

## Title page

The title page includes your book title and the author's name, along with any contributing authors. It often includes the publisher's name and city of publication.

## Copyright page

The copyright page is typically the reverse side of the title page, and contains the copyright notice, publisher contact information, ISBN number, and library cataloging data (CPIN).

## Table of Contents

Not every book needs a table of contents, but it is important for a nonfiction book, because it gives the reader of an overview of the book's contents.

## Acknowledgments

This page acknowledges the people who have helped you with your book and can contain reflections on how you wrote the book.

## Foreword

A foreword is an endorsement of your book written by someone who has a reputation in your genre or is known to specialize in your subject matter. A warm recommendation from a well-known authority can do a great deal to boost the status of your book in the eyes of readers. Use your network of contacts to find someone to write a foreword for your book. Do not be afraid to ask a prominent person to write a foreword for you — if your book has merit, he or she probably will be happy to do it. The author of your foreword will gain public exposure through your book.

# Back matter

The back matter of a fiction book can be as simple as a blank page, or a page saying "The End." A nonfiction book may have a variety of information at the back, some of which adds real value to the book.

## Index

The index helps readers locate information in the book by page number. Word processing programs allow you to create an index by going through your manuscript and marking each word that you want to appear in the index. In Microsoft Word, you can do this with "Mark Entry" or Alt+Shift+X. You have the option of selecting words individually or automatically marking all occurrences of a word. When you run the index, you can select how you want the entries to look. If you want the reader to be able to look up topics rather than individual words, create a concordance — a two-column page with the individual related words in the first column and the topic in the second column. Tab to move from one entry to the next. For example, in a book about international cuisines, you might link words like "curry" and "chutney" to the single topic "Indian." When you create an index using a concordance, all the words will be marked and their page numbers will appear under the topic.

Indexing a book takes time, and it might cost you several hundred dollars to have it done. Many POD publishers include indexing as an additional service.

## Glossary

If your book contains technical terms or acronyms, it is helpful to compile a list of definitions for quick reference. A potential buyer browsing the glossary might be motivated to buy the book because the glossary is so helpful.

## Appendices

Charts, lists, and sample documents such as contracts and forms that are too cumbersome to include in the text, or that might be needed for reference, can be added at the back of the book.

## Bibliography

The bibliography lists all the books, articles, and websites from which you obtained material for your book. Various styles are used for citing literary sources including APA, MLA, Chicago, and Harvard, depending on the type of work. You can look at other books in your genre to see how their bibliographic references are constructed and copy their style. The important thing is to be consistent. You can save time by using an online citation builder such as EasyBib (**www.easybib.com**) or the one in Worldcat (**www.worldcat.org**).

## Author biography

Write a brief author biography that helps establish why you are the right person to write this book. You can put your headshot here, if you want your author photo in the book.

## Order form

A reader might borrow your book from a friend or pick it up in a doctor's office or a bed-and-breakfast and want to get a copy to keep. Many books have a tear-out order form on the last page. If you have a publishing company, you can list all of your books and educational materials on the order form.

# Cover

The cover of your book is an all-important sales tool. The cover will become a symbol of your book, appearing in reviews, online catalogs, posters, and bookstore shelves. Potential readers will see your book laying on someone else's desk or coffee table, or in someone's hand in a park, at an airport, or on a subway train. Every element of the cover design has an important function. For that reason, you should not skimp. Get the best cover design you can afford. It will cost around $2,000 to have a cover professionally designed and produced. If you cannot afford a professional, look for a graphic arts student or freelancer with design software, and supervise the design process closely. POD publishers typically offer you a choice of book cover styles and allow you to submit your own image if you want.

The two essential types of book covers are: textual and graphic. Fiction books often have a front cover illustration that suggests something about the story. A colorful graphic is not appropriate for some types of books; many nonfiction books have a simple front cover with the title and author name, and perhaps a symbol. If a well-known person has written a foreword for you, you can put their name on the front cover to: "With Foreword by _____."

Although you want your book to stand out, remember that mainstream publishers have a lot of experience. Ask yourself why they use certain types of book cover designs. The colors, lines, and fonts used on your book cover are just as important as the words. The title always should be easy to read, and if you are already a recognized authority in your field or the author of a well-known series, your name should be equally prominent. Some books also carry a "hook" on the front cover: a few words drawing the reader into the book or a subtitle that says more about the content.

A book cover has three sections: the front cover, the spine, and the back cover. The spine typically has the book title, the author's name, and an eye-catching graphic symbol. Remember that most books end up on a shelf with only the spine facing out. The publisher's name and/or logo may be on the spine, but it might be better to leave it off if you are using a POD printer or have just created your own publishing company.

## What's in a title?

You might have had a title in mind before you ever started writing your book. One of the advantages of self-publishing is that you get to choose your title; large publishers often reserve the right to change a title to fit their marketing plan. Nevertheless, do not let your emotional attachment to a particular title cloud your judgment. A well-chosen title can help sell your book, especially in these days of search engines and online booksellers. Your title should be catchy and interesting and, at the same time, contain keywords that relate to the content of your book. The title suggests what the reader can expect from the book. A short title like "Guide to Fly Fishing" for a nonfiction book can be followed by a longer, more explicit title, such as "How to tie flies, select the best equipment, and read mountain streams." The title of a fiction book can be more creative, but it should suggest something about the genre. If you are writing a series of books, the title should have a common thread that a reader can instantly recognize.

Titles cannot be copyrighted, but you do not want to confuse your readers by giving your book the same title as another book. Some series titles are trademarked. Once you have some ideas for your title, search it on Amazon.com, in search engines, and on Worldcat to see what other books or publications have similar names.

A title that starts with the letter "A" or "B" will appear near the top of alphabetical lists. Numbers also appear at the top of alphabetical lists, but they are harder to remember.

Finally, ask friends and fellow writers what they think of your title. They might not react as well as you expected or might have better suggestions for a title that sells.

## Back cover and book copy

Readers who pick up your book will flip it over and glance at the back cover to see what the book is about. You have just a few seconds, and about 40 square inches, to catch their interest. The most important part of the back cover is the book copy — a concise, well-written paragraph explaining what the book is about and telling how the reader will benefit from reading the book.

Start with a strong headline that immediately captures the reader's attention. Follow that with a "hook," a sentence that entices the reader into reading more. For example, "Earn a million dollars in one year," or, "For twenty-seven years, she had never ventured more than two blocks from her front door ..." Follow that with a list of what the reader will learn by reading a nonfiction book, or a succinct setup of the plot for a fiction book. End with a call to action; motivate the reader to buy your book.

The book copy also can contain one or two sentences promoting you as the author.

Many writers have difficulty writing strong book cover copy. If you are one of them, ask another writer to help you, or hire a copywriter to write it for you.

Blurbs, if you have them, should follow the book copy. A blurb is a short endorsement of the book or author taken from a book review or made by a well-known person or one who has a professional title. Give the speaker's name and title after each comment. You can obtain endorsements by asking people to review your book or sample chapters, and then ask for written permission to put their testimonials on your cover. If someone introduces you publicly at a lecture or a professional gathering, ask if you can quote his or her on the back of your book. Most prominent people like to have their names published. Never pay anyone for an endorsement, or it will have no value.

The back of the book also should have the ISBN number, bar code, and price of the book.

## Book design do's and don'ts

**DO:**

- Have a vision for your book.
- Find a sample book similar to yours to use as a guide.
- Create a style palette for your manuscript, and use it as you write.
- Keep headings and subheadings, quotes, illustration titles, text boxes, and lists consistent as you write your manuscript.
- Use the outline features in Word or different styles of headings and subheadings to maintain an outline of your book as you write.
- Have as many details as possible ready before consulting a book designer.
- Get quotes from at least three book designers before selecting one.
- Write a good book copy for your back cover.

**DON'T:**

- Design your book yourself unless you are confident you can produce a professional-looking book, or you do not plan to market it commercially.
- Be casual about your cover design or your book copy.
- Use a title that is vague or misleading.
- Take up space on the back of your book cover with an author photo (unless it will help sell the book).
- Use a cover design that is not appropriate for your genre.

## Chapter 10

# Building Your Platform

❋

The concept of an author "platform" has become all-important in the publishing industry. Whether you are marketing your own self-published book or pitching your book to an agent or a conventional publisher, your author platform is a major selling point. Your platform is a combination of your public reputation and your résumé or portfolio — all the unique factors that contribute to making readers want to buy your book. A pastor of a megachurch, a TV talk-show host, a politician, a celebrity, or a well-known fitness guru with a large following already has a platform — a large group of interested followers. An author who has published a best-seller also has an established platform. As a first-time author, you must build your platform from the ground up by investing time and effort to publicize yourself as well as your book. Publishing books is a lifelong career. As soon as you publish your first book, you already should be working on your next project(s). A book is only one facet of your career — it can lead you to publish a series of books, create a franchise, become a public speaker, or position yourself as an authority in your field. Building a platform ensures you always will have a ready-made audience for your next endeavor.

Your platform has to be nurtured and cared for over time. It takes almost as much work as writing books and is just as important. Begin by considering what you already have accomplished. Professional and academic credentials are part of your platform if they give you particular authority to write about your subject matter. So is personal experience — for example, working as a nanny for 20 years, managing a construction company, or taking care of an autistic child. Are you active in a group or association whose members know and respect you? How can you expand on these activities? What can you do to add to your reputation?

Your "platform" is anything you do to make a name for yourself. Book tours, public appearances, speeches and seminars at which you promote your book, and radio and TV interviews all bring you into direct contact with potential readers. Someone

who has met you in person or listened to you speak will not forget your name when they see it on the cover of your book.

The activities you do to build your platform depend on your genre and the type of books you publish. The goal is to make yourself widely known to the people interested in reading

your book. For fiction writers, those activities involve making as many readers as possible aware of their books and developing a following of loyal fans who cannot wait for the next book to come out. In addition to publicity and marketing campaigns, a fiction writer can build a platform by giving talks and lectures, holding book signings in bookstores and retail outlets, and cultivating an online presence. An author of children's books could give talks at public libraries — you could announce them with press releases to local papers and make video recordings to post on a website. A science fiction author could do book signings at science fiction conventions. An author of a book written for a small niche market can focus on establishing a reputation within that market. Every public appearance should be accompanied by media attention and announcements on your website.

A nonfiction author must work on establishing a reputation in his or her field, participating in conferences, contributing articles to journals, and writing for blogs. A nonfiction book can become a springboard for a new career.

## Social Media

The Internet gives you access to millions of potential followers, 24 hours a day. The rapid development of e-readers has made reading and buying books an interactive activity. An interested reader can look up information quickly about the author, his or her other books, and similar books by other authors. Readers like to know more about the background of a book and to read additional material, such as the author's commentary or unpublished sections that were left out of a book. They also enjoy being able to communicate with an author or to participate in a fantasy world based on a book. All of this activity strengthens a reader's loyalty to an author.

Although you have little control over who views your Internet presence or what they do once they are attracted by it, the sheer number of viewers makes it effective. It is worth your while to master the use of social media and take full advantage of it. If you feel you do not have time for social media, hire someone to do it for you. Once your various accounts and profiles are set up, you can manage your social media by scheduling a few hours every week to review and update them. Your Internet presence should be more active when you are leading up to the release of a new book or a public appearance to generate interest and attract web traffic. At other times, you only might need to write some blog posts and check email. If you write nonfiction books, you might invest more time in your website and social media: sending out newsletters, tweeting about your topic, hosting an online journal, or posting a series of how-to articles. Remember your purpose, which is to establish and maintain a reputation that will help sell your books, and tailor your social media activities appropriately.

## Keep your public and personal lives separate

Although your fans like to feel they have a personal connection with you, be careful about what you share about your personal life on social media. Keep a consistent public image, and use privacy settings to protect personal communications from reaching people who should not be reading them. Avoid using obscenities or disparaging language. When someone receives attention from the media, one of the first places journalists look for information is that person's social media accounts. Everything you say could end up on the front page of a newspaper. Unless your book is about your family life (and even if it is!), do not post photos of your children; doing so could attract unwanted attention and even endanger them.

One of the best things about social media is that it costs you nothing except your time and energy. Yet, if used effectively, it can gain you more exposure to potential readers than thousands of dollars in paid advertising. You can access the millions of people who use social networking sites, and in many cases, you are able to direct your efforts directly to the people most likely to be interested in your book. Most social media sites also have apps for phones and tablets.

Entire books have been written about exploiting social media, and courses on the subject now are taught at universities. By setting up several social media profiles and linking them to each other and to your blogs and websites, you can generate activity on the Internet and attract search engine traffic. The following is a brief overview of major social media sites. By the time you read this book, there may be new trends in social media, so you always should pay attention when you hear about the emergence of something new and different.

Spend some time familiarizing yourself with the various social media sites, and select the strategy that will be the best fit for your book(s).

## Facebook

Facebook provides an avenue for communicating with your own personal "platform." Any individual can open a Facebook (**www.facebook.com**) account under a personal name or a pen name. Once you set up a Facebook account, you have two pages: your profile and your home page. Your profile contains the information that you want the world to see, including an area called a "wall" where you can post brief messages. Your home page contains information that Facebook wants to communicate to you, including news feeds of posts on other Facebook pages to which you are connected.

You can invite other people with Facebook accounts to be your friends (friend them). If they accept, you will appear on each other's lists of friends, and your wall posts will appear on each other's Facebook profile pages. Privacy settings control how your information is shared on Facebook; for example, you can create a block list of people who are not allowed to access your site. Because the public will see your Facebook page, it is a good idea to check each person's profile before you accept a "friend" request because if they post profanity or strange comments on their wall, these will appear on your profile.

You can create a Facebook fan page for your book, your publishing company, or even a character from your book. The fan page allows you to post comments and information for your fans and allows them to post comments and communicate with each other. You cannot "friend" people from your fan page; they have to find your page and connect to it themselves. You can attract followers to your fan page by linking to it from articles, blogs, and email newsletters. A fan page allows you to post photos of events and links to books sales pages. To keep fans coming back, you must update your fan page regularly with new information, photos, or comments.

Facebook also sells targeted pay-per-click ads that are displayed to Facebook users. Because you only pay when someone clicks on the ad, it can be an economical way of advertising your book. If you purchase pay-per-click ads, be sure to monitor your account; an intriguing ad might generate more responses, and a higher advertising bill, than you expected.

Facebook also provides an avenue for communicating with your own personal "platform." As of October 2013, Facebook currently had more than 1.19 billion active monthly users worldwide. There is a strong possibility that many people who know you have Facebook accounts and will be curious about your book and your career. Old high school and college friends, business colleagues, people you meet at conferences and meetings, and relatives will find your page on Facebook and might buy your books or recommend them to others. If you have written a family memoir or a highly specialized book, Facebook is a way to communicate with the people who will be most interested in it.

## Google+

Rising in popularity since its 2011 launch, Google+ (**www.google.com**) is a social networking site similar to Facebook. Google+ currently has 300 million active monthy users.

## MySpace

MySpace (**www.myspace.com**) preceded Facebook as a popular social networking site. In October 2013, it had 35 million users. It has evolved into a popular showcase for independent musicians, but its structure makes it difficult for authors to use it effectively.

## Twitter

Twitter (**www.twitter.com**) with 215 active users, allows you to send 140-character text messages (tweets) to everyone who is "following" you. People can sign up to be your followers by clicking a Twitter button that you can place on your website, Facebook page, blog, and on publishing company author pages. Twitter is free. Your Twitter home page contains a form for typing messages and lists of your followers. Your profile page contains information about you and all of your tweeted messages. Twitter can be a good way to remind fans when a new book is coming out or when you are doing a book signing or a public appearance. A tweet can be forwarded (retweeted) to other peoples' followers, so it can be a good way to take your message viral.

Some fiction writers set up Twitter accounts for characters in their books and send out tweets as though the character were communicating with fans. Nonfiction writers can tweet updated information, helpful tips, or recommendations of recent news articles. Because the 140-character limit makes it difficult to type long URLs in a tweet, you might have to use a free online link shortening service such as Bitly (**www.bit.ly**) or Is.gd (**www.is.gd**) — just paste in the URL to get a shortened version that you can use in a tweet.

Avoid sending frequent tweets; that only will annoy people.

## LinkedIn

LinkedIn˚ (**www.linkedin.com**) is one of the fastest-growing sites with the number of users doubling from 120 million to 259 million since 2012. This social-media networking site for professionals allows you to post a business profile, such as your experience, current positions, memberships, alumni status, awards, and accolades. You can connect with other professionals, send direct messages, and "recommend" or be recommended by others you are affiliated with.

## YouTube

YouTube (**www.youtube.com**) allows anyone to upload a video or a film clip to the Internet where the whole world can see it at any time. As of February 2011, YouTube had 1 billion unique users worldwide with an estimated 4 billion page views per day. More than 150 years worth of YouTube videos are watched every day on Facebook. Startling and unusual videos seem to be the most popular, and once a few people notice a video they enjoy, they begin passing the link around until it has been viewed hundreds of thousands of times.

YouTube is the best place to upload your video, lecture or book trailer because it easily can be found there by anyone searching for your name or the title of your book. You can embed a YouTube video on a website or blog. YouTube constantly ranks the most popular videos; if your video achieves this stature, even more people will view it.

Upload several videos and create a YouTube Channel. Fans who subscribe to your channel will receive notification every time you upload something new. You can keep your fans engaged by regularly adding new content. You can increase your visibility by partnering with other authors in your genre. Readers who enjoy one author will want to look at your trailers, too, in hopes of finding new books to read.

# Blogs

While you have been researching your book and learning how to publish it, you probably have come across hundreds of interesting blog posts. A good blog establishes you as an authority in your area of interest and enables people to get to know you — or at least get to know your public persona. A good example of an effective blog is the blog of literary agent Rachelle Gardner (**www.rachellegardner.com**). By offering helpful advice and interacting with her readers, she has gained national recognition for her agency and won the confidence of her potential clients.

You can start your blog by registering on one of the free blog sites, such as Wordpress (**www.wordpress.com**), Blogger (**www.blogger.com**) or LiveJournal (**www.livejournal.com**). Once you have set up your account, you can select a template for your blog and begin posting. The free blogs typically run ads alongside your blog; if you do not want ads appearing on your blog, you can pay a subscription fee. A blog has a place for you to type in your post and then preview it before you publish it. Most blogs allow you to insert hyperlinks to websites in your posts, and many allow photos, videos, and widgets (buttons that run applications or link the viewer to another website).

Getting started is simple. As you add more and more posts, you will need to develop a system to organize your posts by topics or themes. Some blogs double as author websites, and you can set up a system of links to other blogs or send your latest posts out as RSS (Rich Site Summary) newsfeeds to subscribers. Wordpress allows users to program their own code on blogs. A Web designer can create a sophisticated blog template for you if you want to make blogging a central part of your marketing strategy.

No one will read your blog if they do not know it exists. As soon as you have your blog up and running, email your friends and contacts with the URL. Add your blog to your business cards, and mention it to everyone. Tweet a welcome announcement and notifications about interesting posts.

## Blogging do's and don'ts

**DO:**

- Post new content regularly. Blogs are dynamic by nature, constantly refreshed with new commentary, reflections, and ideas. Regular blog posts keep readers coming back and attract search engine traffic. Three times a week (at least) is recommended.
- Start each post with a few short sentences expressing your main points, and then go on to elaborate each point in a paragraph. Serialize longer posts as several smaller posts spread over a period of days. You also can link to your longer article on another page.
- Keep your posts personal and conversational as though you were communicating with friends.
- Check your blog regularly and respond to any comments. People who read your blog want to interact with you.
- Organize your blog posts by theme and topic, and use descriptive tags to help people find what they are looking for.
- Include newsworthy facts, statistics, and other information — this will legitimize what you say and help attract search engine traffic.
- Read and post comments on other people's blogs. You can include a link to your own blog as part of your signature. Keep a list of blogs related to your and post on them regularly.
- Make your blog lively and interesting. Add photos, videos, podcasts, or graphics when appropriate. Use guest bloggers and interviews with knowledgeable people.

- Promote your blog with emails, on your business cards, on your book covers, on your Facebook page, and in your tweets.
- Create posts using short extracts from your books or material from your articles.

**DON'T:**

- Delete a blog post once you have published it. Readers often link to your posts or recommend them to friends in emails; making your post disappear will break all those links and disappoint your followers. If you realize you have spoken in error, issue a correction similar to those used by newspapers, or use strikeout to draw lines through the offending text and show the correction next to it.
- Forget to spell check a post before publishing it.
- Start a blog and then forget about it.
- Fail to respond to comments posted on your blog.

# Writing Articles for Newspapers and Magazines

Another good way to build your platform is to write articles for newspapers and magazines. Send out query letters similar to the query letters you send to agents or publishers to magazine and newspaper editors with your article proposals. Writer's Market (**www.writersmarket. com**) has an extensive directory of publications and their submission guidelines. If your reputation is not established enough yet to land you a regular column in a newspaper, there is still hope — sign up to write for an Internet news site such as About.com (**www.about.com**) or Examiner. com (**www.examiner.com**). You must go through an application procedure, but once you are ac-

cepted, you can develop an entire line of online articles and link them to your blogs, author pages, and book pages.

## Author Profile Pages

Take full advantage of the author pages and profile pages on social media sites, online booksellers, and business networks. Examples include Amazon.com Author Central (**https://authorcentral.amazon.com**), your LinkedIn profile, and your Facebook profile. Upload all relevant information, including your headshot, author bio, and list of books you have published. Remember to update your profiles whenever you publish a new book. Put an article about yourself on Wikipedia (**www.wikipedia.com**) written in the third person.

## Participate in an Author's Group

The wonderful thing about marketing books is that when readers love a genre or a topic, they want to read more. Readers are not exclusive; they do not read books by only one writer. There is always room on their bookshelves for another good author. Author's groups are associations of writers who offer support to each other and collaborate to promote their books. Many are organized around a particular genre. Some author's groups organize group book tours; five or six authors doing a simultaneous book signing make a much bigger impression than one little-known author sitting at a table alone. Members share the work of organizing and publicizing the tour. A new author can piggyback on the reputation of established writers in the group by sharing their limelight.

Members of author groups actively promote each other's books on the Internet. They blog and tweet about each other, write book reviews, and place news about other authors in the group in their email newsletters. Belonging to an author group is like turbocharging your online platform. News about you and your books spreads farther, faster when you collaborate. It is also an emotional boost when fellow authors congratulate you on your accomplishments.

Author groups also increase their blog power by co-blogging. Instead of spending hours of precious time every week developing your own blog, you can schedule one good blog post on a group blog every week or two. A group blog attracts all the authors' fans and gives you more exposure than you can achieve by yourself.

Author groups also offer opportunities for mentoring, encouragement, and referrals to agents, publishers, and other services. Some author groups have an application and audition process or requirements for membership. You can find author groups online by typing keywords like "author group your genre blog" in a search engine. An example of an author blogger group is Storytellers Unplugged (**http://storytellersunplugged.com**).

## Monitoring Your Online Presence

As you work to build an online identity and get the word out about your writing, it helps to monitor the buzz and stay abreast of your online reputation. One thing you can do is set up Google "Alerts." Go to Google.com and select "Alerts" under "Specialized Search." (Get there by clicking "more" and then "even more" on the menu at the top of the Google screen.) Set up alerts for your name and the title of your book and for your main characters if you have them. You will receive an email notification each time those names appear on the Internet.

Some social media tools you may find useful are:

- Social Oomph (**www.socialoomph.com**): This service allows you to set up tweets in advance and schedule them to appear at a certain date and time. Free and paid options are available. The free option includes an email newsletter that lists tweets with keywords and key phrases you specify.

- Search engines for tweets: Sites such as Topsy (**http://topsy.com**) and Twazzup (**www.twazzup.com**) track your retweets and any comments about you; type in your username to search.

- Mentions: Sites like socialmention (**http://socialmention.com/alerts**) and Razor Social (**http://www.razorsocial.com/**) track social media for terms you define, and email you alerts.

- Specialized results: Addict-o-matic™ (**http://addictomatic.com**) provides you with a specialized results page when you type in search terms. Searches news sites, blogs, Google, YouTube, Flickr, Digg, Technorati, Topix, Ask, and others.

- BoardTracker (**www.boardtracker.com**) is a search engine for forums.

- Monitoring tools: SDL SM2 (**http://www.sdl.com**) and Trackur™ (**www. trackur.com**). Social media monitoring tools. Free and paid versions.

- Reputation tracker: BrandsEye (**www.brandseye.com**), Reputation. com™ (**www.reputation.com/myreputationdiscovery**), and Brandwatch (**www.brandwatch.com**) track your online reputation through Twitter, online news sources, and others. Free and paid versions.

# Your Author Website

It costs little to purchase a domain name and set up your own website using a template and the free design software available from companies such as GoDaddy.com (**www.godaddy.com**), Wix.com (**www.wix.com**), Buildfree.org (**www.buildfree. org**), and Weebly.com (**www.weebly.com**). However, a professionally designed website makes a much better impression. Look at other authors' websites. When you come across a website you particularly like, make a note of the URL and look at the bottom of the home page for the designer's name and copyright. Contact that designer and request a quote for designing your site. When you are talking to Web designers, show them examples of sites you like and features you want to include on your website.

Look for a designer or Web design company that has experience with author sites. An experienced Web designer already will know which software programs are most compatible and offer the best value and how to solve glitches that might keep your website from running smoothly. He or she also will know how to optimize your website so it appears near the top of search engines' result pages (SEO: search engine optimization).

## Selling books and merchandise online

Many distributors and POD publishers will allow you to link to your own sales page on their site where customers can purchase copies of your book. They handle all the financial transactions and pay you a royalty or a percentage of each sale.

An online shopping cart gathers and processes information for customers making purchases. Most website design programs include a shopping cart template, so you can add an online store to your site. If you are selling merchandise, you can use shopping cart software that calculates sales tax for online sales and processes orders for as little as $30 per month.

You also will need a payment gateway, a service that takes credit card information and validates it before transferring funds to your bank account. Flagship Merchant Services® (**www.flagshipmerchantservices.com**), GoEmerchant (**www.goemerchant.com**), FastCharge Payment Gateway™ (**www.fastcharge.com**), Merchant Warehouse (**http://merchantwarehouse.com**), Instamerchant™ (**www.instamerchant.com**) or Durango Merchant Services (**http://durangomerchantservices.com**). Consider paying extra for chargeback insurance to protect you from losses due to purchases made with stolen credit card numbers.

You can open a merchant account to receive the funds from online purchases with almost any bank. All of these services charge various service fees, transaction fees, and/or monthly subscriptions. Shop carefully, and purchase only the services you need. Make sure your shopping cart software, payment gateway, and merchant account are compatible before you make any commitments.

If you make only occasional sales, and you are not ready to set up a full-fledged e-commerce system and commit to monthly subscription payments, you can use a third-party payment system such as Paypal (**www.paypal.com**), 2Checkout (**www.2checkout.com**) or ClickBank® (**www.clickbank.com**). These companies act as payment gateway and merchant account rolled into one. Instead of monthly subscriptions or service fees, they take a commission from each transaction. These commissions are higher than the transaction fees charged by merchant accounts, but you only have to pay when you make a sale. Many third-party payment systems also process payments from customers in foreign countries.

Protect your website and your marketing efforts by registering your URL with all the appropriate endings: .biz, .co, .net, .info, .org, .us, and .mobi. Also register alternative spellings and possible typos; you can redirect these other domain names to your website. Many spam merchandisers and ad sites attempt to capitalize on legitimate website addresses by registering misspellings of popular URLs. Any fan who looks at your website is a potential customer; you do not want to lose even one opportunity because someone misspelled or mistyped your name. You can reserve a domain name for six to ten dollars per year, a small price to pay for protection of your name. Domain name registrations must be renewed every year. Ensure that you do not lose your domain name by setting up automatic registration with your vendor.

## Planning your website

Before you begin speaking with website designers, have a clear concept of how you want your website to look and function. A website designer will be guided by your vision — his or her job is to provide the technical and artistic expertise. Spend some time exploring the websites of other authors and publishing companies. Observe how each website is organized, where the navigation menus are located, and the ease with which you can find information. Note the way in which the author and books are presented, the color schemes, and the use of video interviews and audio excerpts. Look for features and functions you want to include in your own website.

The overall design of your website should match your genre and your unique qualities. Your input is important, but your personal tastes and preferences might not be the most effective for your website. For example, you might want your website to open with an impressive animation using Adobe Flash˚, a multimedia platform that allows streaming of audio and video. However, visitors to your site probably want to access information as quickly as possible and may not be able to view the Flash presentation clearly on a handheld device or an older computer. A simple home page may produce better sales results and encourage visitors to view more pages on your website. An experienced website designer knows how to appeal to an audience and how to make the website easy for visitors to use (user-friendly). Listen to the suggestions of the website designer before you decide on a final design.

Your website should be created so you or someone on your staff can add new pages, edit text, update each section, maintain blogs and newsletters, change photos, and manage sales and reports without having to rely on the Web designer. Make this clear in your Web design contract, and define exactly what, if any, ongoing maintenance the Web designer will provide and the procedures for making changes to the website design. Website maintenance can take up a lot of time; streamline the process by making all your websites consistent and easily accessible to the staff member who will be updating them.

## Home page

Your home page is both a snapshot of your entire website and a statement about you and your book. In a few seconds, someone who opens your home page will understand what kind of book you are promoting and what information is available on your website. Your home page should be exciting and informative. The top portion of your home page, which appears in the browser screen when someone opens your website, is the most important because many readers do not stay on your website if they do not see something that interests them right away. According to Nielsen Online, the average time spent looking at a Web page is 56 seconds. You have less than a minute to grab a fan's attention.

At a glance, a visitor to your home page should see your name and the title(s) of your book(s), a captivating image of at least one book cover or an attractive headshot of you (if you are going to display your photo), and a list of the sections of your website. Do not make the images too large because that space is valuable. Most author home pages have a permanent portion that displays their name and navigation menu and an area with a blog or news articles and reviews that is changed at frequent intervals to keep fans coming back. Detailed information, biographical material, and book excerpts can be placed on other pages or in a lower section of the home page and linked to an introductory sentence or navigation bar at the top of the home page.

## Navigation

Navigation refers to the way in which visitors to your website move from one page to another. Website designers know that a certain percentage of visitors leave a site each time they are required to click on a button or link to open an additional page. It is important to organize your website so your visitors quickly find what they are looking for and are able to return easily to pages they have already viewed.

For example, you can place a button (a small image that can be clicked to open a new page) for buying your newest book near the top right-hand corner of your home page. Divide the functions of your website into distinct sections: an area for fans, an area for sales, an area for media and business contacts, and so on.

A navigation menu across the top or down the side of your home page links your visitors to the various sections of your website: a list of your books, your online store or sales pages, press releases for the media, reviews, contact information, and maybe a link for people who want to send you an email.

## News

A section with regularly updated news about your book and your career, such as the release date of your next book, book tour dates, and clips of newspaper articles helps engage your fans, but more important, it attracts attention from search engines such as Google and draws traffic to your website. As part of your marketing strategy, your website can be used to build up anticipation for upcoming releases. This information typically is located prominently on the home page and is updated frequently to keep fans interested.

## Store

A store displays information for items sold on the website, including books, audio-books, and e-books, and provides a shopping cart so customers can place orders and pay for purchases. If you write how-to books, you might increase your income by selling additional charts and posters or sell supplies through an affiliate program with a merchant who will process and ship the orders for you. Your store can link to your author pages on your POD publisher's site, or you can place these links directly on your home page.

## About Us

If you are setting up as a publishing company, include an "About Us" section with information about you, the history of the company, a mission statement, and anything else that you want to communicate officially to the public. This is a good place to put your résumé and qualifications. This section also might include links to your contact information or media press kits.

## Community

Some authors encourage readers to become involved in an online community by posting comments in a blog or message board and signing up for social media. A community section also can contain information about book tours, your latest projects, or general news items about the publishing industry. When visitors to your website are allowed to contribute to an online community and interact with other readers, they develop a stronger loyalty to you and your books. Maintaining a community requires a regular investment of time, but it can help build your Internet presence and establish your reputation as an authority in your genre. This area can connect fans to you on Twitter or Facebook.

## Email newsletters

Email is a powerful way to communicate with loyal readers. Encourage them to add their email addresses to your address list, and send out newsletters informing them about your book tours, media appearances, and upcoming releases. Email recipients often forward interesting newsletters to their friends and family. You also can use your email list to learn about your fans by documenting their responses to special offers and their use of coupons.

## Media and press kits

Create a section specifically for the news media where you can post press releases, announcements, and official photos for use in newspapers, magazines, and newsletters. If you do not want to make this material available to the public, put a request form on this page, so journalists can contact you and get a special login to download photos and documents. When you send out email notifications or press releases, you can refer journalists to this area of your site to get photos and additional information. This will save you from having to respond to dozens of individual requests.

## Favorite links

Your website can include an area where you put links to your favorite websites, blogs, and articles. Putting links to useful resources and articles on your site shows that you want to help your readers with their own research and can increase your reputation as an authority in your field. A list like this can help you build a community around your website, and it allows you to exchange links with other authors and websites, who reciprocate by putting a link to your site on their websites. Traffic to and from your site to other websites is one of the factors search engines use to rank the popularity of your site. Remember, though, that when a visitor clicks on one of those links, he or she is going to someone else's website and leaving yours.

## Extras

Depending on your genre and the type of books you write, you can offer bonus material for your readers, such as book excerpts, text that was cut out of the original manuscript before publication, additional stories about your characters, maps and pictures, or free mini e-books written just for this purpose. If your book is nonfiction, you can include links to useful websites, updates, downloadable graphics such as plans and patterns, templates for contracts and forms, and other material that ties in with your book but was too cumbersome to be included in it. Make the extras fun and be creative — you could create playlists of music to go along with your book that readers can listen to on Pandora* (**www.pandora.com**) or Playlist.com (**www.playlist.com**), recipes that match the theme of your book, drawings of the clothing and fashions worn by characters in a book, historical backgrounds, or scrapbooks or journals "created" by your characters.

## Videos and book trailers

Just as a movie trailer gives audiences a taste of what they will experience when they watch a movie, a book trailer gives readers a taste of your book. A book trailer is a video promoting your book. It can be a video of you (or someone else) reading your book copy or excerpts from your book, a short movie related to your book, or a slideshow. You do not need an elaborate book trailer; a well-made home video can be effective. You can have more than one book trailer for the same book.

## Contact Us

This is a very important page. It establishes how the public can communicate with you. If you do not want to receive phone calls, you can supply visitors with a form for submitting email inquiries. You or someone on your staff should check inquiries every day — you do not want to miss an opportunity for publicity.

## Advertising

Although most author websites do not carry advertising, you could make extra income by selling advertising space on your site for products and services relevant to your book topic. You also can advertise your own books or merchandise in a space along the side of each page.

## Business and distribution

Depending on your distribution channels, you may need an area on your site where distributors or individual retailers can place orders, make payments, and print out invoices and statements. If you are selling through your POD publisher, you can set up discount codes for wholesale orders and put links from your website to the POD publisher's order forms.

## Website analytics

Once your website goes live, monitor it regularly to see how many fans are coming to your site and which areas attract the most attention. The analysis of website traffic is a science in itself. You probably do not need to go into it in depth, but a few simple observations can be useful. Page views refers to the number of times someone opens a page on a website. Click-through paths show how visitors to your site move from your home page to the other areas of the site. A click-through rate is the percentage of visitors who click a link on one page to open and view another page. If one page or area of your site is receiving a large number of page views, it might indicate that your readers are especially interested in that topic. It also could mean that you are receiving attention in a news article or another website that is directing readers to your website. You may be able to capitalize on this interest by making this part of your website more prominent.

Low click-through rates from your home page to other areas of your site could indicate that visitors are losing interest after they see your home page and that you need to try a different "look" or approach. Low click-through rates also could indicate technical problems, such as a page that takes too long to load in a browser. Test this by trying to open the page in other browsers and on other computers with different operating systems and software. When visitors enter your shopping cart and then fail to complete orders, they might be having difficulty with their credit card payments.

Most website design software includes some reporting and traffic analysis features. Google Analytics (**www.google.com/support/analytics**) allows you to track conversion data, analyze the flow of visitors through your site, and identify elements of your site that could be changed to improve visitor retention; it is free for websites with fewer than 5 million page views per month. If you decide you need a detailed, in-depth analysis of traffic through your website, you can purchase a website analysis software program or service from a company such as Webtrends (**www.webtrends.com**), Alexa (**www.alexa.com**), or Adobe Web Analytics in the Adobe Marketing Cloud (**www.adobe.com/solutions/digital-analytics.html**).

Your website is a central focus of your online marketing strategy, but it is only one component. It will not make your book successful all by itself. A website is a tool that can be used, together with social media, aggressive media promotion, and live appearances, to gain recognition in the publishing industry. Schedule regular website maintenance on your calendar so your website remains up-to-date and attracts visitors with fresh information that corresponds to your most recent press releases.

## Chapter 11

# Marketing and Publicity

**W**riting your book and getting it into print is only half of a successful publishing endeavor. Many good books fall off the radar soon after they are released because not enough is done to make readers aware of their existence. In order to succeed, you need to sell books — lots of them. While you are still in the earliest stages of writing your book, you already should be thinking about how you are going to sell it. Who is going to read your book, and how are you going to reach them? If you are self-publishing, you will need to begin your marketing efforts long before the book goes to print by building your public image and planning to send out press releases, books for prepublication reviews, and announcements of your book launch. Even if you land a conventional publishing contract, you cannot rely solely on the publishing company's marketing efforts to sell your book. Earlier chapters have described how large publishing companies invest their marketing dollars in promoting authors who are sure to sell large numbers of books. Books by first-time authors often end up tucked away in the back shelves of bookstores waiting to be noticed. Overworked promotions staffs at publishers often promote new books by sending out announcements and review copies to standard lists of addresses without considering who is most likely to be interested in a particular book. Increasingly, authors are expected to pay for their own book tours and events and to organize their own promotions.

The money you spend to promote your book is a business investment, one that you expect to bring in a profit. The size of your marketing budget should be determined by the size of your potential market and your plans and expectations for the book. If you want to sell large quantities of your book to a broad-market audience, expect to spend thousands of dollars promoting it. A book for a niche market might have a much smaller budget. Some authors are focusing all their efforts on selling e-books online and taking advantage of many free opportunities for publicity, but even these methods require a good website, eye-catching graphics, know-how, and hours of time.

You cannot avoid spending money to promote your book, but you can choose how to spend that money most effectively. For example, paid advertising of any kind is expensive, and most ads are seen by only a tiny percentage of your target audience. Sending out a hundred books to reviewers costs less than an ad campaign and is likely to be much more effective. A single book review in a newspaper, magazine, or online journal, on the other hand, puts you in front of hundreds of book lovers. TV and radio interviews and direct encounters with readers at book signings are more likely to attract interest than an impersonal paid ad. Depending on the nature of your book, there are a number of ways to stretch your marketing budget and get more for your money.

# Create a Media Portfolio and a Promotions File

A media portfolio is a collection of all the materials you will use to promote your book and yourself as an author. It includes your book copy, press releases, headshot, author bio, a graphic of the front cover of your book, book reviews and endorsements, videos, book trailers, and press clippings. Anytime you write something about your book, such as a book description for an online bookseller, file a copy away in your media portfolio, so you can use it again the next time you need a similar description. Your query letters are good sources for this type of copy. Your media portfolio should be stored on a computer, with a backup copy on a flash drive or online storage. Keep a folder of all news clippings about you or your book, along with reviews and anything that has been said about you on blogs. Prepare a file you can quickly email to anyone who asks for information about you.

Your promotions file should include contact lists of media and book reviewers to whom you send out press releases and book review queries, along with records of their responses. These lists will be invaluable to you as you pursue your writing career. Develop a media contact list of people who can help you promote your book, and try to develop relationships with them. Keep records of your interactions with them, and note any personal information they divulge, so you can bring it up when you speak to them again.

# Set a Publication Date

Choose a specific date in the future as your publication date. It does not have to be the date your books first roll off the press or appear for sale online — it is a point in time around which you can structure your publicity campaign. You will need to give the publication date in directory listings, and you will mention it in your press releases, on your website and in any announcements you send out. Send out a round of press releases announcing the publication of your book on that date. Try to arrange for interviews at local TV and radio stations. If appropriate, hold a launch party on that date in a local bookstore and invite members of the press. Because you are a local resident, you probably will receive some recognition, and you can begin adding those newspaper clippings to your website and your media portfolio. Once the publication date has passed, remove references to it from your press releases, and focus on a new angle to promote your book.

# Book Reviews

Book reviews are (almost) free publicity. They can be powerful marketing tools. Excerpts from reviews provided before the book's release can be used as blurbs (the quoted promotional copy that appears on the back jacket and sometimes in the front matter, or beginning pages,  of books), and on your blog, Amazon Author Page, or personal website. You can include (positive) review copy with your listing on Amazon, Powell's Books, or the Barnes & Noble websites and quote portions of a review on the back cover. Remember that a review is copyrighted material just like any other published printed matter, so use excerpts sparingly and always be sure to include proper attribution.

Define your target audience and think about the newspapers, magazines, newsletters, and websites they read. Make a list of publications that might be interested in reviewing your book, and gather mailing addresses and email addresses for their book reviewers. Be creative. For example, if yours is a nonfiction book with a historical subject, send review queries to publications that review nonfiction as well as those concerned with the subject matter, such as historical societies and organizations. A mommy website might review a book about nutrition for children, or a church newsletter a book about dealing with grief. Send out review query letters, and mail a hard copy of your book (or email an electronic copy) to those who respond positively to the query letter rather than blindly sending copies of your book out to publishers and organizations that might not provide a review. Some reviewers will not review e-books, POD editions, or self-published works; it is wise to view submission guidelines before sending in your work. *See Appendix B for a sample review query letter and a sample review slip.* This is included with any editions of your book you send out for review.

There are different types of reviews:

- Prepublication reviews: Written for those in the book industry, such as wholesalers, bookstores, and libraries. These reviewers expect to receive bound galleys. A galley is a prepublication book copy that usually is printed in black and white. For major review outlets such as *Publishers Weekly*, that review fiction, nonfiction, mystery, children's, mass market, and other select titles (but no self-published material) send a press release with a cover letter and a bound galley three to four months (four is preferred) before publication. Follow up one to two months later by sending a final copy of the book.

- Early reviews are packaged with a review slip, press release, copies of other reviews, and other materials, such as brochures, to convince reviewers of your book's credibility. *See Appendix B for a sample review slip and press release.*

- Postpublication reviews are intended for the consumer and appear after the published book is available in bookstores and retail outlets.

## The difference between a book critic and a reviewer

A book critic reads the whole book and provides educated and in-depth commentary.

Some book reviewers may not read the entire book and often, will write their reviews based on the press release, front and back matter (what appears on the front and back of the book), and from skimming through the book.

Book reviewers might do 15 reviews a week and do not have time to read a book completely. For this reason, the book copy and the press release you include with your book are important. The reviewer may use excerpts from them as part of the review.

Follow up with a nice letter or email to anyone who takes the time to review your book, and let him or her know you appreciate it, even if the review is negative. Be professional, and avoid tongue-in-cheek comments. Remember that anyone who reviews your book has put time into reading it and most likely was not paid for doing so unless they work for a major publication.

A book review will cost you the wholesale price of your book plus postage. As with any sales initiative, the more review copies you send out, the more reviews you are likely to get. Send out as many review copies as you can afford. Invest in a rubber stamp that says "REVIEW COPY." Before sending them out, mark your review copies by rubber-stamping the edges of the pages, so that the stamp can be seen without opening the cover of the book. Unfortunately, review copies often are sold online as "slightly used" books, and sometimes they are returned to booksellers for credit. Although the review stamp may not prevent the book from being sold, it will ensure that it is not returned to you for credit.

# Paid Book Reviews

Some sources, such as *Kirkus Reviews*, offer paid reviews for self-published and independent authors. A review with a seven- to nine-week turnaround costs $425, or $575 for an expedited review, which is returned in four to six weeks. According to its website (**www.kirkusreviews.com**), Kirkus Reviews is distributed to more than 5,000 industry influencers, including bookstore buyers, librarians, publishers, agents, film executives and foreign publishers. A self-published author can opt to have the review published on the *Kirkus* website, then use the copy for promotional purposes. Authors may include (positive) review copy with their listings on Amazon, Powell's Books, or the Barnes & Noble websites and may quote portions of a review on the back cover.

## Crossover novelist uses crossover marketing tactics

In an interview with *Entertainment Weekly*, Singer/songwriter Josh Ritter says his debut novel, *Bright's Passage*, was inspired by an idea for a narrative song. When the book was released in June 2011 by The Dial Press, an imprint of Random House, it received numerous reviews, including a Sunday book review in *The New York Times* by author Stephen King. Random House orchestrated an extensive marketing campaign based on Ritter's fame as a musician, while Ritter, a veteran who began his career selling self-published CDs at open mic nights and live performances, turned to the same tactics musicians use to sell their music. He released a free download of the first chapter for his fans through TopSpin® Media (**www.topspinmedia.com**), which collected their email addresses in the process. The link for the download was placed on his website and on NPR's *All Songs Considered*, with a share button so fans could recommend it to each other. He recruited Hollywood friends, family members, and fans to take turns reading the first chapter of the novel for a 20-minute video, which was hosted on the website of *Entertainment Weekly*. Another video of him reading from his book during an interview with PBS was posted on YouTube. On his website, Ritter sells *Bright's Passage* merchandise, including T-shirts, bookmarks and stickers, just as he sells merchandise tie-ins with his CDs and live performances.

Book review by Stephen King (**www.nytimes.com/2011/07/03/books/review/book-review-brights-passage-by-josh-ritter.html?_r=1**)

Video of friends and family reading the first chapter of *Bright's Passage* (**http://shelf-life.ew.com/2011/07/14/josh-ritter-brights-passage**)

PBS Interview (**www.pbs.org/newshour/art/blog/2011/07/monday-on-the-newshour-josh-ritter.html**)

YouTube video (**http://www.youtube.com/watch?v=xVUuNIHoa08**)

# Directory Listings

Like obtaining an ISBN and bar code, and registering your copyright, listing your book in a directory helps to legitimize your work and makes it easier for booksellers to find and order it. Visit the websites of the following directories for instructions on how to submit a listing:

*American Booksellers Association (ABA) Book Buyer's Handbook* (**http://www.bookweb.org/resources/bbh**) For publishers with at least three books in print

Book Dealers Dropship Directory (**http://worldtradedirect.tripod.com/id23.html**) Used by online and mail-order booksellers

*Books in Print* (**www.bowker.com**)
You will automatically be listed in Books in Print when you obtain an ISBN number from Bowker.

*Book Trade in Canada* and *Canadian Publishers Directory* (**www.quillandquire.com**)

*International Directory of Little Magazines and Small Presses* (**www.dustbooks.com/d.htm**) For self-publishers and small press listings

*Small Press Record of Books in Print* (**www.dustbooks.com/sr.htm**)

# Press Releases

A press release is easy and inexpensive to send out and can result in magazine or newspaper coverage for you and your book. Press releases can go out whenever you have some kind of news to announce: the publication of your book, a book signing in a local book store, your appearance at a charity event or conference, or your book's relevance to a current event or social issue. Press releases are the source of approximately 20 to 25 percent of the content in most newspapers and magazines.

Editors always are looking for interesting content to print. Study each publication and try to tailor your press release to match its tone and style. Do not make a news release sound like advertising copy. Write using a journalistic approach so the text literally can be inserted directly into a news article. Keep your sentences short (about 23 words) and use clear, down-to-earth language. Start with an attention-grabbing headline and an interesting "hook" in the first sentence. The news release can focus on you or on your book, but always be sure your book title is mentioned. Most press releases are one page; if you want to add more material, separate your author bio and attach it as a second press release. Newspapers like to print photographs along with articles; your chances of getting noticed are greater if you provide a good-quality image of yourself, your book cover, or something to do with your topic. Include a link where a high-resolution image can be downloaded from your website. *See a sample press release in Appendix B.*

A press release can be sent by email, and many publications have online submission forms. Always copy and paste text from a Word document rather than typing it directly into a submission form, so you can spell-check it and keep a record of what you have sent out. Keep your press releases organized. For example, you can give each one a number or a date. On a spreadsheet, note the publication, email address or submission URL, the date, and the number of the press release you sent.

## Individual marketing plan for a self-published book

Douglas R. Brown, founder and editor of Atlantic Publishing Group, Inc., suggests the following marketing plan based on his own company's marketing strategy:

### PR / Publicity — Develop a Press Kit

1. Write a press release. Follow the press release sample in Appendix B.
2. Set up a press kit folder on your author website.
3. Consider adding audio and visual segments.
4. Include both high- and low-res images of your book cover.
5. Include a table of contents (TOC) of what is included in your press kit.
6. Include a two- or three-paragraph summary of the book to use for advertising purposes.
7. Include press clippings of publications and articles as they come out.

### Amazon Advantage Program

Two weeks before the arrival of the published books at your distribution center, add book to:

1. Amazon Advantage
2. Amazon CAP program

### Direct Mail

Consider highly targeted (small) traditional direct mail campaigns.

### National Papers, Radio, and TV

1. Seek out media book reviewers.
2. Send out press releases to appropriate media.
3. Develop a book contact list using Google alerts to discover when someone mentions your book in the press.

### Testimonials and Endorsements

Put testimonials from book (if obtained) on:

1. Amazon.com
2. BarnesandNoble.com
3. Other reseller sites

**Radio**

Plan an email and or postal campaign to radio stations for author interviews

**Authors**

Set up your author page on Amazon pages:

 So You'd Like To

 ListMania

 About the Author

Also, create author profiles on:

 AuthorsDen.com

 Authonomy.com

**Internet Marketing**

Main website

1.  Optimize your main website to feature your new book
2.  Have Internet deals or otherwise try to obtain visitors' email addresses for direct email marketing
3.  Encourage direct sales with discount offers

**Resellers E-Books**

Upload e-book to all e-book resellers, including Amazon, Sony, B&N, and Google Books.

**Article Submission**

Develop short articles on each book, and post them on Ezinearticles.com and articlesbase.com.

**Amazon.com and other reseller sites**

Hire at least five to ten book reviewers and have them post to Amazon.com, B&N.com, any relevant blogs, and other reseller sites.

**Ensure bibliographic information about the book is correct including:**

1.  Cover image
2.  Price
3.  Description (with no typos)
4.  Release date and product details page

**Blog and social networking**

1. Update Facebook profile.
2. Update LinkedIn profile.
3. Set up a lens on squidoo.com.
4. Set up channel on YouTube for book related videos.
5. Post free information and useful documents on Docstoc.com.
6. Send out a Twitter announcement.
7. Start a blog, and invite other authors and business people to be guest bloggers or interviews.

**Word of mouth and viral marketing**

Add a Tell a Friend button to website

Add video to Amazon page

Video: Develop short video with excerpts from the book — advice, etc.

Post on

1. You Tube
2. Author Link On Amazon Book Page

**Measure and optimize marketing activities**

1. Use Google Analytics to track traffic and conversion rates and measure success.
2. Measure Google Adwords campaign and tweak as necessary.
3. Measure traffic to blog and use keyword finder to blog with searchable terms.
4. Measure traffic to website.

# Radio and Television Interviews

A radio or television interview brings you into intimate contact with potential readers, right in their homes, cars, or workplaces. For a few minutes, you have their full attention. This makes interviews an effective way to promote your book.

Major radio or TV stations usually want to hear a sample interview or audition video before committing themselves to an interview. Make a start, and get some practice by seeking interviews on college radio and TV stations or at small local stations. Once you have recorded that first interview, you can send the recording along with your other interview requests.

Before contacting a radio station, try to find out what shows it runs and whether any relate to the topic of your book. Start by looking at its websites for scheduling and programs. Try to come up with a "hook" that is newsworthy, timely, or informative or that relates both to current events and to your book or topic. If your book takes place in a certain locale, stations in that area probably will be interested in helping to promote a published work of local interest. Your role on the show will be to  entertain listeners, so promote your interesting or unique idea rather than overtly promoting your book promotion. Your book title will be mentioned in the introduction, and you may have a chance to refer to it once or twice, but the topic is what will hold your listeners' attention. Radio interviews sometimes are done over the phone, and they can be live or taped.

Contact local television stations and pitch your idea to them, and if you are traveling to their area, let them know you are on tour and your availability. Once you have notified the local media of your talk, tour, reading, signing, or event, you never know when they will send out a reporter or camera crew, so be prepared. Before contacting any media outlet, learn about its audience, and tailor your idea to fit its needs. Targeting a dozen stations selectively is better than blindly sending press releases to hundreds of stations. Try to address your cover letter to a specific person.

Try to stay relaxed during the interview. Get plenty of rest the night before, and have clothes picked out ahead of time (no busy patterns). Visit the Internet for tips on radio and television interviews so that you have some idea of what to expect. Women should wear makeup a little darker than normal for television and arrive ready for taping. Your personal grooming and overall appearance are important. On air, be yourself, and stay focused on your topic. Be prepared for chitchat and banter, and prepare what you want to say ahead of time. Be flexible, and prepare to work your comments in at a different angle than you may have anticipated. You can ask ahead of time if a television station can prepare a graphic for you, which is sometimes called a Chyron (ky-run) — you can email an attachment of the book cover and information about the book, such as a press release, so they have something to draw from. Bring a copy of your book with you to the show, and mention where and when any events or readings will be. After the taping, send a thank-you note.

# Advertising

Some forms of paid advertising can be worthwhile if they are particularly suited to your book.

- Direct marketing — Paid radio and television ads, direct mail inserts, and order forms placed in catalogs and books can bring good results if they are targeted to people who will be interested especially in your book.

- Email marketing — You can purchase a mailing to a targeted email list or create your own mailing list of people who sign up on your website to receive email, e-newsletters, and other updates. Avoid sending spam; unsolicited email should be avoided because it can damage your credibility. You also can get email exposure by purchasing an ad in someone else's online newsletter — for example, if you belong to a professional or trade association that sells advertising in its newsletter.

- Online ads — Paid ads on Amazon.com, other booksellers' websites (such as Powell's Books at **www.powells.com**) and through Google Adwords (see **http://adwords.google.com**).

- Sales aids — These are indirect forms of advertising usually included along with your book when it is purchased. Aids can be posters, bookmarks, and in-store displays (called "dumps").

# Business Cards and Email Signatures

Print business cards with your name, the title of your book, and your website address, where people can learn more about you and order your book. Carry them with you wherever you go, include them in press kits and with cover letters, and leave them on counter displays in stores where your target audience shops.

Most email programs allow you to create an online signature that appears in every email you send out. Create an email signature with your name, the title of your book, a link to your website, and perhaps a short quote.

# Book Publicists

Book publicists are public relations experts who specialize in promoting books. Even authors whose books are published by conventional publishing companies hire book publicists to help them market their books. *Publishers Weekly* estimates that there are about 200 book publicists in the U.S. A book publicist has established contacts that can get an author interviews on national radio and TV stations, and appearances on talk shows. The book publicist also coaches an author for success, identifying qualities of the book and the author's personal life that will make good talking points and attract public attention. An author typically works with a book publicist for a minimum of six months. These services can be expensive and are beyond the reach of most self-published authors.

You can get professional help with your marketing campaign by hiring a freelance publicist to help you create a marketing plan and media contact list, write press releases and fliers, and arrange public appearances. Freelancers are paid by the hour or by the job, and you can purchase their services, as you need them.

# Book Signings

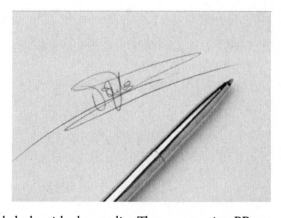

Book signings are a much bigger draw when an event is planned around the signing. Contact both independent and chain bookstores, and ask if they host events. Larger bookstores most likely will have a PR manager or community relations coordinator who handles author events and deals with the media. The community, PR, or marketing coordinator is often out in the field. If you have to leave a voice mail, clearly state your book title and the ISBN number, and mention that you will send a press release. Then, fax or mail one, and wait for a response. If you have not heard anything back in two weeks, follow up with another call. Ask about holding a reading, book party, or publicity event. Consider the possibility of incorporating your book signing in events held regularly by bookstores, such as story times and readings by store facilitators or book club meetings. Once you have determined what you would like to do at the event, decide how you will advertise it. Will you put together a press release and send it to the local media? Are you willing to spend money on advertising? Let the PR coordinator know how you plan to spread the word, and he or she will be more willing to participate in advertising as well.

At the event, meet and greet customers, and let them know of the events to take place. Bring along a flier to pass out at least 30 to 45 minutes ahead of time to draw interest. If you arrive an hour early, you will have time to meet with the PR manager or coordinator or the store manager and talk with them about what you plan to do. Provide a copy of your flier and let them know that you would like to mingle and pass them out. After the event is over, send a nice thank-you note to the community relations coordinator and store manager.

Visit bookstores in your area and offer to autograph copies of your books. Sales associates can place an "autographed" sticker on the books (which sometimes sell for a higher price, especially for well-known authors), and can place them in high-visibility areas near the cash register, on displays, and in the store windows. Do this before or after a signing or event, or drop by a bookstore the next time you are passing by, and ask if they carry copies of your book. If so, offer to sign them. If not, bring a copy of your book along and encourage the manager to order it. It cannot hurt to provide a press release and publisher contact information as an insert along with the book, as well as a sheet containing excerpts from book reviews, if you have any. Give the manager a complimentary copy to keep the title fresh in his or her mind until the next time orders are placed. You can encourage librarians to order copies in a similar fashion.

# Book Tours

Book signings in bookstores bring you into direct contact with your readers, increase the goodwill of the bookstore, and give you the opportunity to hand sell (sell directly to customers) some of your books. However, unless you are already a famous author, you cannot expect to sell large quantities of books at a book signing, and the profit from those sales will not pay the expenses of traveling around the country and staying at hotels. Publishers usually arrange book tours only for certain authors whose books sell in the hundreds of thousands of copies. As a first-time author, you must consider whether a book tour justifies the travel expenses and how far your budget will allow you to travel. Restrict your book signing tours to bookstores in your local area or to areas where you can stay with family or friends to keep your expenses to a minimum. Many authors who go on tours keep them brief or relatively close to home. Also, be on the lookout for book fairs where you can set up a table and for author and illustrator festivals.

If you are willing to travel, let your publisher know this, and ask about upcoming events such as holidays, anniversaries of important events, and famous author or historic figures' birthdays. Do what you can to promote your book, and the publisher will help you by letting you know of events upon your request. Do not expect the publisher to assist with defraying expenses if you are a new author. Be sure to send out press releases to local media everywhere you go.

## Promotion do's and don'ts

**DO:**

- Think about how you are going to promote your book as soon as you think about writing it.
- Identify your potential readers and learn as much as you can about them. Find the best ways to get their attention, and focus your marketing efforts in those areas.
- Set aside a budget to promote your book.
- Get free publicity through news articles and book reviews.
- Create and send out press releases tailored to the publications receiving them.
- Try to get your book reviewed by any publication your readers might see.
- Send a review query first, and only send a copy of your book to reviewers who indicate their interest.
- Mark review copies with a rubber stamp, so they cannot be returned to booksellers for credit.
- Send a press release out with each review copy.
- Be selective about spending money for paid ads.
- Build up a media file containing all the materials you use to promote your book.
- Develop a key media contact list.
- Prepare yourself to give radio and TV interviews.

**DON'T:**

- Expect your book to sell itself.
- Send out the same standard, boring press release to every publication.
- Send out hundreds of books for review without checking whether each reviewer is interested.
- Spend money you do not have on a book tour.
- Purchase marketing services from a POD publisher without finding out exactly what you are getting for your money.
- Lose your temper and act unprofessionally towards a media representative.
- Wait until your book is published to start promoting it.

## Chapter 12

# E-Books

Electronic files of books have been available to read on the Internet as word documents or PDFs for decades, but the debut of convenient e-reading devices that could be carried around and read on commuter trains and at the beach signaled the start of the e-book era. Amazon launched the first Kindle edition on November 19, 2007, but it was not the first e-reader to hit the market; it was preceded much earlier by the Rocket eBook, released by Nuvo-Media in 1998. After the original stock of the first Kindle sold out in five and a half hours (some sources say it was six), scores of back orders were taken, and the stock was not replenished until April 2008. Two years later, Kindle launched the third edition — the DX. Today e-books can be read on tablets such as Apple's iPad, iPhones, and Android™-powered devices and e-readers such as Amazon's Kindle Paperwhite and Touch, Sony® Reader, , Barnes & Noble's Nook GlowLight, Kobo Glo.

Both booksellers and technology manufacturers are eagerly pushing e-reader technology. Here is a device retailing for anywhere from $80 to $300 that everyone has to have — the market for e-readers is everyone who can read. An e-reader is also an impressive and affordable gift for any friend or relative who loves books. In January 2011, many e-book authors noted a sudden jump in their sales. Though the reasons for this are not fully understood, analysts believe it was partly due to large numbers of e-readers and e-book gift cards being given as Christmas presents in 2010.

E-books confer many benefits on self-published authors. There is no investment in printing hard copies, shipping, storing, packaging, or fulfilling orders. Though the price of an e-book is lower than the price of a paperback book or a hardback, the author gets as much as 70 percent, which often amounts to more than the royalties from the sale of a hard copy. An e-book can be sold directly through a link in an email, from a blog, a website, a newsletter, or an online bookseller. E-book conversion services charge around $100 to format a book for electronic publishing, and someone familiar with HTML can do it him or herself. Some POD printers offer an e-book option as part of their packages.

E-books are ideal impulse buys. They sell more easily than hard copies because of their low prices (often $2.99) and because they are available to read in seconds. It is doubtful that e-book buyers ever read all the books they download, but their intentions are good. People sit at their leisure with e-readers, browsing through lists of fascinating titles and thinking, "Ooh, I want to read that!" and, "Oh, I should read that ..." They do not have to overcome the distractions of walking to the front of a bookstore, waiting in line, pulling out a wallet, and parting with a $20 bill.

A growing number of self-published authors are selling several hundred e-books per month. A successful e-book author can command higher advances from traditional publishers than a typical first-time author.

## CASE STUDY: COZY-MYSTERY WRITER SUCCESSFUL IN KINDLE PUBLISHING
Gayle Trent
www.gayletrent.com

*Gayle Trent is a cozy mystery author living in Southwest Virginia. She writes two cozy mystery series, the Daphne Martin Cake Decorating mystery series and the Marcy Singer Embroidery mystery series.*

I have always loved writing. My first book was published in 1999 after much trial and error. I love reading mysteries of all sorts, but the cozy mystery is my favorite genre to write because it is just so much fun. The characters are quirky, and they get involved in some crazy situations.

I have written e-books in the past, but my book that has been most successful in e-publishing is *Murder Takes the Cake*. *Murder Takes the Cake*'s publisher, Bell Bridge Books, participated in a Kindle promotion wherein publishers gave free Kindle downloads of their books for a limited time. *Murder Takes the Cake* was very successful; in fact, it became a Kindle best-seller. I was skeptical of the book's success because it was free. Who would not want a free book? However, I saw the trade paperback version of *Murder Take the Cake* rise to an Amazon Sales Rank of 5,814 in books and No. 31 in Mystery Series on January 2, 2010. *Dead Pan*, the sequel to *Murder Takes the Cake*, also is doing well in the Kindle Store — although it is not free.

As for self-publishing, investigate all your options, and remember that marketing is key. If you are not willing to market and publicize your book, and if you are not sure who your audience is, then do not self-publish.

# How to Sell Your Book as an E-Book

There are several ways to produce your book as an e-book and make it available for sale. The easiest way is as an add-on service from your POD printer: for an additional fee or for a cut of the royalty on each book, your POD service will convert your manuscript to an e-book format and make it available for sale. The easiest way is not necessarily the best. Your POD provider may only make it available on its own sales network and not on other e-book stores. The cut it takes from each sale is probably higher than the percentage charged by an independent e-book service. If the POD provider owns the rights to your book, it also will claim the rights to your e-book for a certain period, which means that you cannot take it elsewhere. A POD service provider is likely to use a conversion process that meets minimal standards and produces a sloppy e-book. It may charge an additional fee for making changes to your e-book.

Numerous e-book conversion/retail sites such as Smashwords™ (**www.smashwords.com**) and Amazon's Kindle Direct Publishing (**http://kdp.amazon.com**) allow you to upload and convert your manuscript free, in exchange for a percentage of each sale. Other sites charge an up-front fee. You can find them on the Internet by typing "e-book conversion" into a search engine. You follow their guidelines to format your manuscript, and upload it along with a cover image. Some sites give you the option of offering your book for sale on Barnes & Noble, the Apple iBookstore, and other outlets for a decreased royalty.

If you do not want to spend the time formatting your manuscript, or if your book contains complex graphics or illustrations, you can pay for a more expensive e-book conversion service that will take your Word document, convert it to various e-book formats, and upload it to e-booksellers. A conversion service also can turn your book in to an iPhone app or an e-book app — a small computer program that plays videos or allows database searches as part of the content.

You also have the option of converting your manuscript to various e-book formats yourself and selling it on your own website. This is not advisable because you probably will not be able to list your books on e-book retailer sites. Readers will never find your books unless they find your website first. J. K. Rowling is an exception — she recently began selling e-books of the Harry Potter novels on her own website, Pottermore.

## Pottermore heralds a new era in electronic publishing

On June 23, 2011, J.K. Rowling made headlines by announcing an online venture called "Pottermore." For years, Rowling had withheld the publication of her seven Harry Potter novels as e-books and downloadable audiobooks. Her new site bypasses Amazon and Apple by selling the electronic versions of her books directly to consumers in multiple languages. Bloomsbury, Rowling's U.K. publishers, and Scholastic, her U.S. publisher will receive some revenue from licensing, but the e-books books are being published under the Pottermore Publishing imprint. Pottermore CEO Rod Henwood says, "We want to make sure anyone who buys it can read it on any device," which means Pottermore must reach an agreement with Amazon, whose Kindle controls about 60 percent of the e-reader market.

The venture employs every available strategy to engage Rowling's fans. Rowling launched Pottermore (**www.pottermore.com**) with an announcement on YouTube. Visitors to the Pottermore site will be able to read 18,000 words of additional Harry Potter content that was not included in Rowling's novels. The site opened officially in 2012. Pottermore is available to users in English, French, German, Italian and Spanish (Castilian). Visitors also can interact on the site and upload their own artwork.

Experts believe that Pottermore is poised to attract a new generation of young readers, along with existing fans who want to read electronic versions of their favorite novels and share them with their children. They predict millions in sales.

| COMPANY | Kindle Direct Publishing (www.kdp.amazon.com) | Smashwords (www. Smash-words.com) | Lulu (www.lulu.com) | Book Tango (www.book-tango.com) |
|---|---|---|---|---|
| COST | FREE | FREE | FREE | FREE |
| DISTRIBUTION PARTNERS | Amazon | Amazon, Apple, B&N, Diesel, Kobo, Baker & Taylor, more | Amazon, Apple, B&N | Amazon, Apple, B&N, Kobo, Scribid, Google, Sony, Books on Board |
| ROYALTY | 70% or 35% | 85% (35%-60% with partners) | 90% (35%-60% with partners) | 100% ((35%-60% with partners) |

**Free e-book conversion company comparison**

# E-Book Cover Images

An e-book cover image needs to be a graphic that is interesting and clearly visible as a thumbnail image. Along with your title, it is your one opportunity to catch a reader's attention and convince him or her to pay for your book. Many readers will skip over listings that do not have cover images.

You can find templates for designing your own e-book covers on sites such as EBook Template Source (**www.ebooktemplatesource.com/free-ebook-covers.html**), Cover Factory (**www.coverfactory.com**), and My eCover Maker (**www.myecovermaker.com**) (subscription-based templates).

# ISBN Numbers

You are not required to have an ISBN number for an e-book, but you might want to get one for several reasons. You cannot list your e-book on Apple's ibookstore or certain other e-book retail outlets without one. You also will need ISBN numbers to list your e-books in catalogs and directories such as those used by libraries to order e-books. You cannot reuse the ISBN number from your print book; you will need a unique number for your e-book.

Some book conversion services will sell you an ISBN number; if they give it to you free, they probably take a larger percentage of your sales. Free ISBN numbers are registered to the e-book retailer, so your e-book will appear under their imprint. You can purchase your own ISBN for $125, or buy a block of ISBNs to use for future books. *Refer back to Chapter 8 for more information about buying ISBN numbers.*

### Joe Konrath, e-book legend

Joe Konrath (**www.jakonrath.com**), author of the Jack Daniels mystery series and one of the top-selling authors in Amazon's Kindle store, described in a famous blog post in January 2011 (**http://jakonrath.blogspot.com/2011/01/time-invest-ment.html**) how hard he worked to promote his first three print novels, *Whisky Sour,* *Bloody Mary* and *Rusty Nail.* In 2005, he spent $4,000 and 80 hours of labor to send signed *Bloody Mary* drink coasters and a sales brochure to 6,500 libraries. In 2009, for another book, *Afraid,* he appeared on 100 blogs in 30 days and toured 200 book-stores. To promote *Rusty Nail,* he drove almost 11,500 miles, visited 504 bookstores, and signed 4,066 books. In four years, he earned $42,000 in royalties from *Rusty Nail.* In January 2011, he made the same amount in one month selling his self-published e-books through Kindle, Smashwords, CreateSpace, and Barnes and Noble while do-ing no promotion at all. In his blog post, he announced that he would no longer be doing promotional tours and would be devoting all of his time to writing more books.

# Formatting Your E-Book

Most e-book conversion/retailer services give you the option of uploading your e-book as a PDF file or a Word document. Unless you intend to sell your e-book only as a PDF, it is better to upload a Word document because it will convert more consistently to HTML, the format used for e-books.

Before uploading your Word document, you should clean up the formatting as much as possible, so the e-book will look exactly like the document you create. You do not have to do this if you are using a more expensive conversion service, as they will be doing all the formatting for you. When you formatted your book for POD self-publishing, you inserted section breaks, blank pages, and page num-bers. Now you have to remove all those things to publish your manuscript as an e-book. Read your e-book conversion/retailer's formatting guidelines carefully before you begin.

How to clean up formatting for an e-book manuscript:

- Delete blank pages, headers, and footers. Take out any page breaks you inserted to keep paragraphs together and any hard returns that you used to position quotes or inserts.

- Your book should now begin with the title page. On the copyright page, type in the new ISBN number and insert the following information:

[Service provider] Edition, published [date] by [your name or the name of your publishing company]

- Make sure you use the same style throughout the document. You may have created new styles accidentally while trying to format.

- Change your margins to 1" or less and line spacing to 1.5 so the manuscript takes up less space in the reader screen.

- Make your manuscript HTML compatible by setting the font size at 10 point or 11 point and choose Arial, Tahoma, or Verdana as the font. Remove any strange characters or symbols. HTML is much simpler than modern word processing programs. It accommodates indented text blocks, bulleted or numbered lists, simple tables, and bold and italics, but not much more.

- Create a hyperlinked table of contents using the Word Table of Contents feature. *Refer back to Chapter 9 for information on how to do this.* Select "Use Hyperlinks Instead of Page Numbers" and set the drop-down levels to "1."

# Electronically Publishing Through Amazon

Publishing a book for Kindle is free; Amazon keeps a percentage of each book sale. It is accomplished through Amazon.com's Kindle Direct Publishing. The KDP is a publishing tool located at **http://kdp.amazon.com** and is accessible once you have entered your username and password. If you do not yet have an Amazon account, you can sign up for free by clicking the "Sign Up" button on the right side of the page. Users who are familiar with HTML can use Mobipocket eBookbase (**www.mobipocket.com/eBookBase/en/homepage/default.asp**) for publishing on mobile devices.

# Selecting a Price

The lower you price your book, in theory, the better its chances of selling. Some strategies have been proven to work, along with, of course, the proper marketing. After all, just as with a top notch website, if people do not know it is there, nobody will visit it no matter how helpful, creative, or professional it is. The same concept applies to your e-book. Let people know it is out there, and your sales will benefit directly.

If you are selling an article, short story, or other short-form work, in general, price on the lower end, from 99 cents to $2.99. If you are selling a book, you can start low, and then adjust as needed. However, pricing above $9.99 is not recommended for a typical novel-length work. Price a book available in paperback from $2.99 to $7.99. If your book is only available as an e-book, use your discretion when pricing. Some books demand a higher price, especially content that is highly technical or graphics-heavy or for which you have to pay contributors.

# Promotion tips

## Set a low introductory price

Some authors choose to price their e-books at 99 cents to begin with, and raise the price gradually as the title gains in popularity — and sales. Others try more creative ways of pricing, such as donating a portion of the profits to charity. In general, lower prices generate more sales.

## Sell low-priced excerpts

To encourage sales of longer works for the Kindle, consider excerpting standalone information and pricing it lower. This tidbit of information is a teaser that will encourage people to buy the work in its entirety. If yours is a nonfiction work, you can excerpt some particularly helpful or little-known information from the book. If it is a novel, memoir, or other fictional work, excerpt a high-interest portion, whether it is from an escalated action point or another highlight from the book. Whatever people read in the excerpt should make them want to read the rest of the work. Excerpts often sell in the Kindle Store from 99 cents to $2.49 and are generally article-length, from one to five pages. The first chapter of all Kindle books is free, and some authors offer free excerpts to entice buyers.

## Serializing your title

If you have a long-form work, consider serializing it, or breaking it up into smaller sections and selling those separately from one another in the Kindle Store. As a general reference in regard to the length of a work, novelettes are typically considered anywhere from 7,500 to 17,500 words in length; novellas are 17,500 to 40,000 words; and anything more than 40,000 words is considered a novel. Of course, your work does not have to be fiction to be serialized, but it should be long-form, or at least long enough to be broken up into smaller subsections. Consider the possibilities of serializing a memoir or a nonfiction book. Each chapter should stand on its own and should end in such a manner that it generates interest for whatever comes next. A large number of notable works have made their entrance into the world of publication in this manner, such as many of Charles Dickens' novels.

You may choose to complete the work in its entirety and then begin serializing it or write it as you go. Once your e-book has been serialized from start to finish, you can publish it as a single volume. An obvious benefit of serialization is that it generates interest for your work; if someone reads each chapter and is interested enough to want to read more, he or she will look forward to the next installment with anticipation. This method also holds great marketing appeal — create a buzz around the serialization, and ideally, you will generate enough to bring in new readers. If your work is good enough, you can rely to some extent on word-of-mouth and social marketing promotion.

CASE STUDY:
INDIE WRITER GOES THE WAY
OF THE EPUBLISHER

April L. Hamilton
www.AprilLHamilton.com
http://AprilLHamilton.blogspot.com
indieauthor@gmail.com

*April L. Hamilton is an author, blogger, Technorati Blog Critic, leading advocate and speaker for the indie author movement, and founder and editor in chief of Publetariat, the premier online news hub and community for indie authors and small imprints. She has spoken at the O'Reilly Tools of Change conference and the Writers Digest Business of Getting*

*Published conference and has also judged self-published books for competitions run by Writer's Digest and the Next Generation Indie Book Awards. She has been quoted in* The Wall Street Journal, MSN Money, *and* The Washington Times, *profiled by ABNA Books and The Writing Cast podcast, and her book,* The IndieAuthor Guide *(2010) has received favorable mention on* CNET *and* The Huffington Post.

In January 2010, I read that Martin Amis and Ian McEwan have elected to go indie with e-book publication of their back catalog titles, rather than have them rereleased through a mainstream publisher, largely because they can earn a 70 to 75 percent royalty going the indie route. Standard e-book royalty percentages offered by traditional publishers only run about 25 percent, or sometimes 50 percent for more established authors.

As to the "why," I would say it is a combination of factors. First, there is the fact that trade publishing is in crisis. Between struggling brick-and-mortar booksellers, the industry's unsustainable returns policies, the pressures brought about by the e-book revolution, and the recent flood of inexpensive and free e-books, the Google Books settlement, and their already historically narrow margins, trade publishers are facing simultaneous, unprecedented challenges. As a result, they have become more risk-averse than ever and have reduced author advances and marketing budgets, all of which leads to a much less author-friendly environment — especially for debut authors. The second major factor consists of recent improvements in e-book and print-on-demand technologies that have made it possible for self-publishers to duplicate the quality of mainstream-published books without having to pay large up-front fees to a vanity press or sign away their publication rights. E-book publication is even simpler, and authors who publish their own e-books enjoy royalties 25 to 50 percent higher than those whose e-books are published by mainstream publishers. The third major factor is Amazon, which lists self-published books right alongside mainstream-published books and offers indie authors all the same sales tools and marketing opportunities as mainstream authors. It is no surprise that Amazon is now positioning itself as a publishing channel alternative to mainstream publishers, and I do not doubt the move will be entirely successful for the company. The final factor is the decline of the chain, brick-and-mortar bookstore. Chain, brick-and-mortar booksellers always have been reluctant to stock self-published books, but now that those booksellers' market share is shrinking day by day, it is no longer critical to get one's book stocked by them. All of these factors are merging to make indie authorship a very attractive alternative to mainstream publication.

The decision of whether to self-publish is one that ought to be made on a manuscript-by-manuscript basis. It all comes down to three questions. First, what is the author's goal for the book? It is not always just about sales; sometimes it is about building readership or supporting a related activity, such as a speaking tour. Second, can a traditional publisher help the author reach his or her goal more quickly and effectively than the author could? And finally, is the traditional publisher *going* to do the things that will help the author reach his her goal more quickly and effectively than the author could? For most authors, debut authors in particular, the answers to the latter two questions are increasingly "no."

However, a niche manuscript can be a great match for an independent, niche publisher. For example, Writer's Digest Books published a revised and updated edition of my originally self-published book, *The Indie Author Guide*, in fall 2010. In this case, I decided that because my goal is for the book to be made available to as many indie authors (and potential indie authors) as possible, WD Books would help me reach my goal more quickly and effectively than I could do on my own. Writer's Digest is an established and trusted brand among authors and aspiring authors; WD Books' catalog is limited to books for and about writers; WD is a forward-thinking company that is open to exploring new technologies and promotion avenues; and WD has numerous established outlets through which it promotes its authors and their books (including magazines, websites, conferences, classes, and book clubs).

So, in this specific instance, I elected to go mainstream. However, I doubt I would do the same with one of my novels because I think they would be lost in the crowd if I sold them to a mainstream publisher — especially a publisher that is just one arm of an entertainment mega-conglomerate, such as Viacom. Smaller, independent publishers have small catalogs, and, as a result, they have more riding on every single title they release. They are just as invested as the author in a given book's success.

Because my fiction is not really "niche" or genre fiction, however, it is not likely to appeal to a small publisher with a specific target demographic.

I started out going down the mainstream path and did not have much difficulty getting a strong agent. Like most aspiring authors, at that point I thought the hardest part of the process of getting published was behind me, but I was wrong. My novel *Adelaide Einstein* got a stack of glowing rejections from the big publishers' editors, all of whom offered some variation on, "Of course I love it, but the American book-buying public does not want comic fiction right now. Send me something darker." So, I wrote a dark comic mystery, *Snow Ball*. My agent did not like it and declined to go out with it at all. Life went on, and I forgot all about my novelist aspirations until a few years ago, when I entered *Adelaide* in the Amazon Breakthrough Novel Award contest on a whim.

After accumulating 36 positive Amazon customer reviews for *Adelaide*, I concluded New York editors do not have any idea what the American book-buying public wants and made the decision to go indie. I published both novels independently, first in Amazon Kindle editions and then in trade paperbacks via CreateSpace, Amazon's POD service. The experience was definitely a learning process for me, and because I have extensive experience with technical writing, I decided to document all I had learned in another book, *The Indie Author Guide*. I became an outspoken advocate for indie authorship, which led me to found Publetariat (**www.publetariat.com**), an online news hub and community for indie authors and small imprints. The site was an immediate hit, so I documented my processes for design and launch of the site in another book, *From Concept to Community.*

I do not see much of a future for myself as a novelist in commercial terms, though I have a couple of fiction works in progress and hope to finish them eventually. I have come to the conclusion that promoting indie authorship and helping my fellow writers accomplish their goals through indie authorship is what I am meant to be doing, and I certainly have found it very fulfilling.

## Chapter 13

# Copyright Law and Plagiarism

Accrding to the U.S. Copyright Office (**www.copyright.gov**), copyright is a form of legal protection grounded in the U.S. Constitution and granted by law for original works of authorship fixed in a tangible medium of expression. A copyright gives the owner the exclusive right to make copies, license, and otherwise exploit a literary, musical, or artistic work in printed, audio, or video form.

Copyright covers both published and unpublished works. You do not have to register a copyright to protect your work; it is under copyright protection the moment it is created and fixed in a tangible form that it is perceptible either directly or with the aid of a machine or device. Copyright registration is voluntary, but you will have to register if you wish to bring a lawsuit for infringement of a U.S. work.

## Copyright Notice

A copyright notice should be placed on the reverse side of the title page of your book: the symbol © (the letter C in a circle), or the word "Copyright," followed by the author's name and the year the book was first published. Revised or derivative versions should have the year the revised version was first published.

Example: © 2014 Author Name

The copyright symbol, rather than the word "copyright," is necessary for international recognition and protects your work worldwide. The copyright is attributed to the owner of the work, which can be the author, publishing company, or the purchaser of the work.

In addition to this, you can put "All rights reserved" or a more detailed statement that no part of the book can be reproduced without written permission, along with contact information for obtaining that permission. Look at the copyright pages of several books to see how they are formatted.

The copyright notice should appear on every copy of your book. Always check proofs and promotional copies to make sure it is there, and check books before they go out for distribution.

# Duration of Copyright

In the U.S., a work that was created (fixed in tangible form for the first time) on or after January 1, 1978, is automatically protected from the moment of its creation and ordinarily is given a term enduring for the author's life plus an additional 70 years after the author's death. In the case of "a joint work prepared by two or more authors who did not work for hire," the term lasts for 70 years after the last surviving author's death.

For works made for hire and for anonymous and pseudonymous works (unless the author's identity is revealed in Copyright Office records), the duration of copyright is 95 years from publication or 120 years from creation, whichever is shorter.

# Copyright Registration

No publication or registration or other action in the U.S. Copyright Office is required to secure a copyright. "Copies" are material objects from which a work can be read or visually perceived either directly or with the aid of a machine or device, such as books, manuscripts, sheet music, film, videotape, or microfilm. "Phonorecords" are material objects embodying fixations of sounds (excluding, by statutory definition, motion picture sound tracks), such as cassette tapes, CDs, or vinyl disks. For example, an essay (the "work") can be fixed in a Word document ("copies") or recorded as an audio file ("phonorecords"), or both. If a work is prepared over time, the part of the work fixed on a particular date constitutes the created work as of that date.

Copyright registration is not a condition of copyright protection. Registration is a legal formality intended to make a public record of the basic facts of a particular copyright. However, registration provides several legal advantages:

- Registration establishes a public record of the copyright claim.

- Before an infringement suit may be filed in court, registration is necessary for works of U.S. origin.

- If made before or within five years of publication, registration will establish prima facie evidence in court of the validity of the copyright and of the facts stated in the certificate.

- If registration is made within three months after publication of the work or before an infringement of the work, statutory damages and attorney's fees will be available to the copyright owner in court actions. Otherwise, only an award of actual damages and profits is available to the copyright owner.

- Registration allows the owner of the copyright to record the registration with the U.S. Customs Service for protection against the importation of infringing copies (pirated copies). For additional information, visit the National Intellectual Property Rights Coordination Center at **www. iprcenter.gov**.

Registration may be made at any time within the life of the copyright. Unlike the law before 1978, when a work has been registered in unpublished form, it is not necessary to make another registration when the work becomes published, although the copyright owner may register the published edition, if desired.

# Filing an Original Claim to Copyright with the U.S. Copyright Office

An application for copyright registration contains three essential elements: a completed application form, a nonrefundable filing fee, and a nonreturnable deposit — that is, a copy or copies of the work being registered and "deposited" with the Copyright Office. A copyright registration is effective on the date the Copyright Office receives all required elements in acceptable form, regardless of how long it takes to process the application and mail the certificate of registration. The time needed to process applications varies depending on the amount of material the office is receiving and the method of application.

Register a claim with the Copyright Office within three months after the book's printing. A book is registered by mailing an application form (Form TX) along with two copies of the book and a fee to the Copyright Office. The fee is $35 if you do so online and $50 if you submit form CO by standard mail. You can obtain the form from the Library of Congress website (**www.loc.gov/copyright/ forms**). Once your application in processed, the Copyright Office sends a copy stamped with a seal and signed by the Registrar containing a date and registration number. Keep this for your records. Processing may take three to five months for electronic filing and six to nine months for paper filing, as the number of annual applications processed by the office hovers around 600,000.

## Online registration

Online registration through the electronic Copyright Office (eCO) is the preferred way to register basic claims for literary works, visual arts works, and performing arts works including motion pictures, sound recordings, and single serials. Advantages of online filing include a lower filing fee, fastest processing time, online status tracking, secure payment by credit or debit card, electronic check or Copyright Office deposit account, and the ability to upload certain categories of deposits directly into eCO as electronic files. You still can register using eCO and save money even if you will submit a hard-copy deposit, which is required under the mandatory deposit requirements for published works. To access eCO, go to the Copyright Office website at **www.copyright.gov** and click on "electronic Copyright Office."

## Registration with fill-in Form CO

The next best option for registering basic claims is the new fill-in Form CO. Complete Form CO on your personal computer, print it out, and mail it along with a check or money order and your deposit. To access Form CO, go the Copyright Office website and click on "Forms." Do not save your filled-out Form CO and reuse it because it contains a unique barcode.

## Registration with paper forms

Paper versions of Form TX (literary works), Form VA (visual arts works), Form PA (performing arts works including motion pictures), Form SR (sound recordings), and Form SE (single serials) are still available by postal mail upon request. Online registration through eCO and fill-in Form CO (see above) can be used for the categories of works applicable to Forms TX, VA, PA, SR, and SE.

# Copyright Infringement and Plagiarism

Copyright infringement and plagiarism are not necessarily the same. Plagiarism is representing someone else's words as your own without giving proper credit. It would not be copyright infringement to claim that you wrote one of Shakespeare's sonnets because his works are too old to be under copyright. Plagiarism is not technically illegal except under the rules of schools and universities. However, you would lose credibility as an author, and no one would respect you or take your work seriously. On the other hand, even if you openly give another writer full credit, you are guilty of copyright infringement if you do not obtain his written permission to use an excerpt from his work in your book. Ignorance of copyright law is not an acceptable excuse in court. Always get written permission to use someone else's written words, photographs, or illustrations.

Ideas and facts cannot be copyrighted, only the words with which they are expressed. Try not to repeat more than three words in a row as another person writes them. If you would like to use the words (more than one sentence) or images of another person, obtain his or her permission in writing.

Section 107 of the U.S. Copyright Law (title 17, U. S. Code) allows the "fair use" of copyrighted text for certain purposes, such as literary criticism, comment, news reporting, teaching, scholarship, and research. However, "fair use" is not clearly defined; there is no specific number of words, lines, or notes that safely may be used without permission for these purposes. In a legal challenge, four factors are used to determine fair use:

- The purpose of the use and whether it is for commercial purposes
- The nature of the copyrighted work
- The percentage of the copyrighted work that was used
- The effect of the use on the commercial value of the copyrighted work

It is better to cover all the bases by getting written permission than to risk paying legal costs to defend yourself in court and possible damages if you lose.

Facts, ideas, and systems cannot be copyrighted, only the way in which a person expresses them. A quote of something spoken in a public setting can be requoted because it is essentially a "fact." An entire speech cannot be quoted in this manner, though. It is always safest to get permission to use quotes, unless the doctrine of fair use clearly applies — for example, a professor including quotes from an author in a lecture about that author's work. No publisher wants to be sued for copyright infringement.

Consider copyrights when you are selecting art and illustrations for your book, and be very careful when using images found on the Internet. If you use original illustrations that you or someone else created specifically for your book, and you have the creator's full permission to use the images, you are within rights. Ensure that you credit the source properly within the book — that is, on the cover, title page, and copyright page. You automatically own the rights to anything you create. You also own the rights to anything created for you as a "work for hire." Be sure to get a signed agreement acknowledging that the creator relinquishes all rights.

## Public domain

Intellectual property laws such as copyright, trademark, or patent laws do not protect creative materials in the "public domain." The public owns these works, and anyone can use them without permission. There are several reasons why a work might be in the public domain:

- Copyright has expired. Copyright has expired for all works published in the United States before 1923. Under current copyright law, nothing published after 1923 will enter the public domain until 2019.

- The copyright owner failed to renew the copyright. Until 1964, the owner of a work had to renew the copyright at the end of 28 years or lose it. Consequently, thousands of works fell into the public domain.

- The copyright owner deliberately has placed the work in the public domain, a procedure known as known as "dedication." Creative Commons (**http://creativecommons.org**) is a nonprofit that helps authors, photographers, and artists dedicate their works to the public domain. Do not assume that something that has been dedicated is free to use; the person who authorized its use might not be the true copyright owner. Always try to get written permission.

- Certain types of work are not protected under copyright law. Facts and theories are not protected under U.S. copyright law, although a specific compilation of facts might be. Short phrases, names, titles, and common idioms are not protected. Any work created by a federal government employee or officer is in the public domain as long as that work was created in that person's official capacity.

## Music and song lyrics

Most popular song lyrics are covered by copyright. In order to use even one line of a song in your book legally, you might have to purchase an expensive license. Before you include popular song lyrics in your book, check with a music licensing service such as License Music Now.com (**http://licensemusicnow.com**). Even lines from hymns or folk songs could be under copyright protection.

## Images

A wealth of royalty-free images is available through various sites on the Internet. When you purchase a royalty-free image, you can use it as often as you like in your book, on posters and advertising copy, and on your website. Royalty-free images are sold on sites such as Thinkstock˚ (**www.thinkstockphotos.com**), Jupiter Images˚ (**www.jupiterimages.com**), Getty Images˚ (**www.gettyimages.com/CreativeImages/RoyaltyFree**), iStockphoto˚ (**www.istockphoto.com**), FotoSearch˚ (**www.fotosearch.com**), Big Stock (**www.bigstockphoto.com**), Time Tunnel (**www.timetunnel.com**), and Photos.com (**www.photos.com**). Public domain images can be found on Creative Commons (to locate images on Creative Commons, visit **http://search.creativecommons.org**). The disadvantage of royalty-free images is that they are available to anyone, and you may find the same image on someone else's website or in another book.

The use of a rights-managed image is sold exclusively to one buyer for a specified time. When that time has expired, you have to renew the license to continue using the image. Rights-managed images are available from companies such as Katzman Stock (**http://katzmanstock.com**), Illustration Works˚ (**www.illustrationworks.com**), and Mira (**http://library.mira.com**).

## Copyright do's and don'ts

**DO:**

- Put a copyright notice on every book.
- Register your copyright within three months of publication.
- Get written permission to use other people's words and images in your book.
- Acknowledge other people's work on your copyright page.

**DON'T:**

- Pay a lawyer to register a copyright for you. You easily can do it yourself.
- Use quotes or excerpts from someone else's work without their written permission.
- Assume that a work is in the public domain without checking to see whether it is copyrighted.
- Plagiarize.

## Chapter 14

# Business and Taxes

When you write and publish books, you are essentially self-employed, and you must report your income from book sales to the IRS as taxable income. Failing to report income amounts to tax evasion, and tax evasion can incur severe penalties and fines. Self-employment carries other tax obligations, including payment of Social Security and Medicare tax. On the other hand, as a self-employed individual, you can deduct business expenses from your taxable income and might even be able to deduct part of the cost of maintaining your home if a portion of it is set aside as a dedicated business office. If you do not want to run afoul of the IRS, and you want to claim as many legitimate tax deductions as you can, you need to understand self-employment taxes.

Income taxes are not the only potential pitfall. State governments require you to pay sales tax on retail sales of your book. Local jurisdictions might require you to pay a business tax or purchase a business license. Because your first book is only the beginning of your writing career, it is a good idea to learn as much as you can while you are getting started to avoid making serious mistakes that could cost you later.

## Hobby or Business?

The IRS is aware that taxpayers will attempt to reduce their taxable incomes by reporting self-defined "business losses," so it has developed a procedure for determining whether a particular individual is engaged in a hobby or a business. For example, a business might be expected to report losses for one or two years, but consistent losses year after year are suspect because, logically, the purpose of a business is to make money. If you intend to report your book-publishing activities as a business, you must establish that you are trying to make a profit.

Hobby income is reported on *IRS Form 1040*. The total expenses a hobby seller can deduct from income cannot exceed the amount of revenue generated by his or her book sales. Expenses that are more than the income you made from your hobby are considered personal losses and cannot be deducted from your taxable income. Hobby expenses must be itemized as a miscellaneous expense on *IRS Schedule A (Form 1040): Itemized Deductions*, and you only can deduct the amount of miscellaneous expenses (including medical expenses, charitable gifts, and mortgage interest) that exceeds 2 percent of your annual income. An author who writes and publishes as a business, however, can deduct most of the expenses associated with book publishing, as well as business losses, from his or her taxable income, even if they far exceed the income from book sales for that year.

The IRS uses two methods to determine whether you are engaged in a hobby or a business. The first is an objective, bright-line (clear standard) test that says an activity is a business if it generated a profit during at least three of the last five tax years, including the current year. This test, known as the "3/5 year test," cannot be applied to first-time authors or those who have not generated a profit for three of the past five years. Individuals who do not meet the 3/5 year test must rely on the following facts and circumstances to determine if their book publishing endeavors are considered a hobby or business. The IRS, looking for evidence that you treat your writing as a business and expect to generate a profit from it, considers:

- Whether you conduct your publishing activities and book sales in a business-like manner
- The amount of time and effort you spend on your writing
- The extent to which you depend on the income generated from book sales for your livelihood
- Whether you have the knowledge and experience to carry on a successful publishing business
- Whether you make adjustments to your methods of operation to improve profitability, such as seeking to lower your publishing costs or trying new ways of marketing your books
- The amount of personal pleasure involved in your activities. You must be able to demonstrate you are deriving more than simple enjoyment from your writing. If you continue to publish books with vanity presses and never sell or promote them, the IRS would consider your writing a hobby.
- The nature of the financial losses you claim on your tax return. A startup business typically experiences substantial losses in its first year of operation,

then moves closer to being profitable each year afterwards. If your losses from publishing are repeated year after year, the IRS will question whether you really intend to make a profit. Your business will be expected to make a profit in some years, even if it suffers losses in others.

# Recordkeeping

Good recordkeeping maximizes available tax benefits by ensuring you do not overlook legitimate business expenses that could be deducted from your income. It also provides you with evidence to support any deductions you claim on tax returns. Accurate records show how much you have spent to publish and promote your books and exactly how much you can claim for certain business expenses, such as vehicle mileage and office supplies.

It is important that you learn to keep accurate records. If you have little or no experience with accounting, help is available from many sources. An accountant can show you how to set up your bookkeeping system and help you file your taxes. Ask fellow writers to show you how they manage their accounts and recordkeeping. The Small Business Administration (SBA) offers free online classes on its website, **www.sba.gov/content/recordkeeping**, as well as mentoring and training programs through its local branches (**www.sba.gov/content/find-local-sba-office**).

Several components make up a recordkeeping system. You will need to keep written records of all the money that comes in and goes out of your business. This can be done with ledger books or spreadsheets, or with an accounting software system. In addition, statements from banks, credit cards, and online booksellers contain information about the transactions occurring in each of them. Every transaction is supported by documents, such as receipts, invoices, and packing slips. All of these documents must be filed and organized, so you can refer to them when needed. At first, your recordkeeping system might be simple, but as you publish more books and expand your sales and promotional activities, it will become more complex. Set up a filing cabinet to store all your documents. At the end of each month, sort all your receipts and file them in envelopes according to the type of expense.

## How long should you keep documents and receipts?

It is recommended that you keep all supporting documents for six years. Once you have compiled the records for a year and used them to prepare your tax return, you should retain these records in a centralized place for six years after the due date of the return. Consider keeping an electronic and a hard copy of your records. If you find it too onerous to maintain hard copies because of the number of records, consider backing up your records to an external hard drive or online data cloud storage site, such as Mozy® (**www.mozy.com**) or SugarSync (**www.sugarsync.com**). SugarSync offers 60 GB of storage for $7.49 per month and Mozy charges $5.95 per month for 50 GB.

# Establishing Your Business

Many writers operate as what the IRS calls a sole proprietorship, a type of business entity owned and operated by one individual. There is no legal distinction between the individual running the business and the business itself, and earnings are treated as the owner's personal income. An individual who runs a sole proprietorship reports income from the business and business losses on a *Schedule C* form attached to his or her personal income tax return (*Form 1040*).

Sole proprietorships are cheap and easy to form, which makes them an attractive option for online sellers. You can set up a sole proprietorship, obtain licenses, and operate a business using just your first and last name. If you are planning to operate the business under your own name, you will not need to take any extra steps to form your sole proprietorship. For some self-publishers, though, it is better to set up as a publishing company with a unique trade name.

## Should you start your own publishing company?

It is easy to start your own publishing company. All you have to do is register a business name with your state and open a separate bank account for your business. In most states, the fee for registering a business name (fictitious name) is reasonable. Find out the procedure for your state on the SBA website (Register Your Fictitious or "Doing Business As" (DBA) Name, **www.sba.gov/content/register-your-fictitious-or-doing-business-dba-name**).

There are several reasons why you might want to start your own publishing company:

- You plan to self-publish a series of books and would like to establish a brand or a unique identity for your series apart from your author name.
- You plan to produce and publish books by other authors in your genre and promote and sell them alongside your books.
- Your books will have more legitimacy if you purchase your own ISBNs because they will be registered under your own publishing company name instead of a POD self-publishing company.
- You can put your publishing company name and logo on the spines of your books and create brand awareness for your products.
- Once you have published three books, you will qualify for registration in the *ABA Book Buyer's Handbook* and the *Small Press Record of Books in Print.*

## Choosing a business name

You will need a name for your publishing company that is catchy, easy to remember, and short enough to be legible when it is printed on the spines of your books. Ideally, the name should be only one or two words. Try to pick a name that reflects your genre or the image you want to project.

Conduct a thorough search to confirm no one else is using the name. Start with the Yellow Pages and the Internet. Type the name into several Internet search engines, including Google (**www.google.com**), Microsoft's Bing˚ (**www.bing.com**), and DMOZ Open Directory Project (**www.dmoz.org**). Before you can register your company name with the secretary of state's office in your state, you must prove no other business in that state is using the same name. Most of the state websites where you can submit a business name registration begin with a name search of all businesses registered in that state. Your local county clerk has a record of all the fictitious names (or assumed names) registered in your county.

Register your assumed name (fictitious name) with the office of the secretary of state in your state and locally with your county clerk. The only states that specifically do not require any type of filing when conducting business under a different name are Alabama, Arizona, Kansas, Mississippi, New Mexico, and South Carolina. Washington, D.C., makes it optional, and Tennessee does not require such filing for sole proprietorships or general partnerships.

## Claim an Internet domain name

Check to see if your business name, or something similar to it, is available as an Internet domain name. Your website will be an important marketing tool for your business; you want people to be able to find it easily. You can search for available domain names on the InterNIC website: **http://internic.net/whois.html**. Register your domain name immediately with an inexpensive registrar, such as GoDaddy.com® (**www. godaddy.com**) or Network Solutions® (**www.networksolutions.com**), along with possible misspellings and obvious variations. Each domain name costs only $7 to $10 per year (some of the new suffixes cost more). When you set up your website, you can arrange for all of these other domain names to redirect to your site. Be sure to renew your domain names on time or set up automatic renewals, so you do not lose the investment you have made in your website later on.

# Business Registration

You will have to register your business locally with the city or county that has jurisdiction over the area where your office is located, and depending on your activities (such as storing and packaging books in your home), you might be required to get certain licenses or permits. Failure to register your business correctly could result in fines or penalties. Every county has its own rules for business registration; contact the office of your local county clerk or look up the regulations on its website. If you are running your business out of your home, you might be required to purchase an occupational license that must be renewed every year. Typically, you fill out an application at your local city or county clerk's office and pay a fee. After the zoning department determines that your business complies with local zoning laws, you will be issued a license. If you are using an assumed name for your business, make sure the correct name is listed on the registration.

You can use the SBA.gov's *Search for Business Licenses and Permits* online (**www. sba.gov/content/search-business-licenses-and-permits**) to get a list of the federal, state, and local permits, licenses, and registrations you will need to operate your business.

Many local jurisdictions have zoning restrictions, and even the rules of your Homeowner's Association could affect you if you plan to conduct your business in a residential area. For example, there may be a limit to the number of employees who can work with you in your home, parking restrictions, limitations on delivery trucks, and prohibitions against storing merchandise in your home or garage. Your local Small Business Administration can advise you about the licenses you need for the specific state and zone in which you reside.

# Get a Post Office Box

Whether you are working from an office at home or have a separate physical address for your business, it is a good idea to secure a post office box (P.O. Box) at your nearest post office. Having a dedicated post office box helps keep your business correspondence separate from your personal correspondence and keeps your home address private. Most important, it will prevent you from having to change your address on all your business documents and Web pages should you ever relocate your office. Continuity in any business means stability.

You can rent a P.O. Box online at the U.S. Postal Service website (**www.USPS. com**). Look under "All Products and Services" for "PO Box Service."

# Standard and Itemized Tax Deductions

Tax deductions are amounts you are allowed to subtract from your taxable income to compensate for certain expenses. The IRS provides two ways to calculate deductions: You can either take a standard deduction or itemize your expenses by listing each one individually. You only will benefit from taking the standard deduction if it exceeds the total amount of your allowable itemized deductions. The amount of the standard deduction is adjusted each year for inflation. The amount of your standard deduction will depend on your filing status and your age. Standard deductions are higher for someone who is older than 65, blind, suffered a net loss due to a federally declared disaster, or paid excise taxes on the purchase of new vehicle. If your publishing business has been very active during the year, or you have experienced personal circumstances such as high medical expenses, there is a good possibility that you will be able to deduct more by itemizing deductions. Tax preparation software walks you through each possible deduction, and based on the information you enter, it calculates whether you should take the standard deduction or itemized deductions. You also can report your itemized deductions manually on *Schedule A* and attach it to *Form 1040*. If you qualify for the higher standard deduction for new motor vehicle taxes or a net disaster loss, you must attach *Schedule L*. Tax Forms and instructions are available on the IRS website (**www.irs.gov**). You also can order them by phone or pick them up from post offices and public libraries.

# Business Expenses

A business expense is not deducted directly from your taxable income but from your business income. The IRS allows you deduct the cost of carrying on a trade or business from the income produced by that business as long as the business is operated to make a profit. You can reduce your taxable income by subtracting business expenses from your business income to diminish your net profit from the business. Many costs can be deducted as business expenses if you are aware of them and document them properly.

Business expenses are reported on *Schedule C* and attached to your *Form 1040*. Tax preparation software will help you identify and calculate your business expenses.

You must keep receipts and documentation to verify each of your business expenses. Some taxpayers try to reduce their taxable income by fabricating or inflating business expenses. The IRS watches for red flags — abnormal expense amounts that suggest a taxpayer is being dishonest. If the IRS audits you and finds you have falsified your expense records, you will have to pay penalties in addition to the income tax you owe on the disallowed expenses.

# What you cannot deduct

One of the most frequent tax errors made by self-employed individuals is taking a deduction from business income for personal compensation and time spent working in the business. Although you spend much of your time writing and tending to your business affairs, you cannot deduct payment for that time as a business expense because you are self-employed.

Other expenses you might think you can deduct as business expenses, such as estimated tax payments, life insurance premiums, meals, campaign contributions, grooming expenses, and commuting expenses, are considered personal expenses by the IRS and cannot be deducted from your business income.

Capital expenses are treated differently from the everyday costs of running your business. Capital expenses are purchases of fixed assets used to operate your business, such as computers, desks, or fax machines. A good rule is that an asset is a capital expense if it has a useful life of more than one year. For example, office supplies are not a capital expense because you ordinarily use them up within a short time. Capital expenditures typically are depreciated over the life of the asset — for example, you subtract a portion of the value of a computer each of the five years that it remains in service. Instructions for tax forms include formulas for calculating depreciation, and tax preparation software calculates it automatically.

The expenses used to figure the cost of goods sold by your business should be recorded as inventory and are not part of your business expenses. If you use a POD service to self-publish, your setup fees would be a business expense, but the books you buy for resale are inventory. Books you buy to send out as review copies or give away for promotion are a business expense because they are part of your marketing costs. If your POD publisher is handling all the sales and distribution and paying you a commission or royalty, you will not have any inventory or cost of goods sold.

# Business Use of Your Home

The IRS allows many kinds of business expenses. The expenses you can claim depend on the way you conduct your business. You might be able to re-characterize a personal expense as a business expense by making some simple changes, such as setting aside a dedicated room in your home for your business.

*IRS Publication 535: Business Expenses* (**www.irs.gov/businesses/small/article/0,,id=109807,00.html**) explains in detail how to determine which expenses are deductible as business expenses.

If you are doing your writing and publishing activities in your home, you could be eligible for a home office tax deduction. The deduction for business use of your home allows you to deduct a certain amount from your business income to account for the fact that part of your home is really a business facility, and the expenses for that part of your home are part of your cost of doing business.

To qualify for the home office deduction, you must use your home as your "principal place of business" or as a "place to meet or deal with your clients or customers in the normal course of your trade business." You will need to have a dedicated area in your home that you use as an office or storage space. The amount you can deduct will depend on how much of your home you are using for your business.

The strict and detailed rules for calculating the deduction are explained in *IRS Publication 587: Business Use of Your Home* (**www.irs.gov/pub/irs-pdf/p587. pdf**). As with all tax matters, you will get the maximum allowable deduction only if you keep accurate records and file supporting receipts and documents. Receipts for maintenance and repairs, the purchase of replacement parts, utilities, HOA assessments, carpet cleaning, and pest control are all important because a portion of those costs can be deducted as business expenses. The IRS allows you to deduct more if your gross income exceeds your total business expenses than if you experience a business loss.

When selecting individuals for audit, the IRS is inclined to target taxpayers who take the home office deduction because there are many opportunities for fabrication and abuse. You have nothing to worry about, however, if your deduction is legitimate, and you have hard evidence to back up your claims.

You must use a specific area of your home only for your business. This does not have to be an entire room, but it must be separately identifiable as your work area. It does not have to be separated from the rest of the room by a partition. You must use your home office or workspace on a regular basis. Make sure it does not appear as though you only use this space occasionally or incidentally. There is an exception if you are storing inventory or samples for your business in part of your home — you still qualify if you use the storage area for personal activities. For example, you could store boxes of books in your basement and still use it to watch TV. The storage area must be separately identifiable and suitable for storage, and your home must be your only fixed place of business.

You also can deduct business expenses if your business is in a separate structure from your home, such as a garage or studio, if you can prove that you use the space solely for business purposes. It does not have to be your principal place of business or a place that you meet customers, but it must be connected to your business in some way. An example of this would be storing books in a shed behind your house.

# Figuring the deduction

A self-employed business owner who files a *Schedule C (Form 1040) Profit or Loss from Business* can figure out the home office deduction using *Form 8829, Expenses for Business Use of Your Home.*

You first must determine how much of your home is used for business. Your business percentage is found by comparing the size of the section of your home you use for your business to the size of your home as a whole. You can use any method to do this, but the IRS gives two common examples of methods for determining your business percentage. If the rooms in your home are of similar size, and you use one or more entire rooms for business, you can divide the number of rooms you use for your business by the total number of rooms in your house. You can also measure the length and width of the area you use for your office or for storage, multiply them to find the area, and divide this number by the total area of your home. (The area of your home can be found on tax documents and title deeds.) This will give you the percentage of your home that is used for business. Suppose the area of your home is 1,400 square feet, and you use a bedroom for your office and a space in your garage for storage.

| Total Area of Home | | 1,400 sq. ft. |
|---|---|---|
| Office in Bedroom | 10 ft. X 10 ft. | 100 sq. ft. |
| Storage Space in Garage | 5 ft. X 7 ft. | 35 sq. ft. |
| Total Space Used for Business | | 135 sq. ft. |
| **Business Portion of Home** | | **9.64%** |

Some expenses related to your home can be deducted from your personal taxable income, whether or not you use your home for business. These include qualified mortgage interest, mortgage insurance premiums, real estate taxes, and casualty and theft losses. If you deduct expenses for the business use of your home, you must separate the business and personal portions of these deductions. The business percentage is recorded as a business expense, and the personal portion is still a deduction on your income tax return.

Other expenses such as depreciation, insurance, rent, and repairs can be deducted from business expenses only if you use your home for business. The three types of home business expenses are: direct, indirect, and unrelated. Direct expenses relate only to the business part of your home and are deductible in full. Examples would be installing storage shelves only in the section of your home that houses your business or renovating a bedroom into an office. Indirect expenses are the general costs of maintaining your house and running your entire home. You can deduct a portion of these expenses equal to the percentage of your home used for business. Unrelated expenses relate only to the part of your home not used for business and are not deductible.

Repairs such as patching walls and floors, painting, wallpapering, repairing roofs and gutters, and mending leaks keep your home in good working order over its useful life and are deductible as business expenses. Improvements that add to the permanent value of the house, such as a kitchen makeover or new windows, are not deductible and must be depreciated instead. It is important to distinguish between permanent improvements, which are depreciated, and repairs, which are reported as business expenses. If repairs are part of an extensive remodeling project, the entire project is treated as an improvement.

Expenses for utilities and services, such as electricity, gas, trash removal, and cleaning services, are primarily personal expenses. However, if you use part of your home for business, you can deduct the business portion of these expenses. To calculate the deduction, multiply the amounts on these bills by the percentage of your home used for business.

## Making the most of your home office deductions

You can maximize your home office deductions by being aware of all the possible expenses that could be deducted and keeping receipts and accurate records. It is easy to overlook the cost of new light bulbs or a carpet cleaning service, but every expense adds up. Study *IRS Publication 587: Business Use of Your Home* (**www. irs.gov/pub/irs-pdf/p587.pdf**) and read articles and blogs on the subject to get some ideas.

Increase the portion of your home expenses that you can deduct by expanding the area devoted to business in your home. If you have a spare bedroom, use the whole room as your office instead of just a desk or a corner. Remember that the space must be used exclusively for business and used on a regular basis to be eligible.

You can lower taxable income for the year by being proactive and paying for planned repairs and maintenance before the end of the tax year. It is always a good idea to keep your property well maintained. Regular inspections and repairs contribute to energy efficiency and increase the value of your home when you eventually sell it. Knowing that a portion of these costs can be deducted as business expenses is an incentive to go ahead and spend the money. Of course, expenses paid for this year cannot be deducted on next year's tax return, even if the services are performed over a period of several months.

# Self-employment Tax

When you work for an employer, employment taxes are automatically deducted from your paycheck. You pay half, and your employer pays the other half. The employer collects the taxes and submits the money to the IRS, which transfers it to the Social Security Administration (SSA). When you work for yourself, you are responsible for paying both your portion and the employer's portion. You usually must pay self-employment tax if you had net earnings from self-employment of $400 or more during the tax year. The amount you pay is set by law: 13.3 percent (in 2011) of your net earnings for Social Security and 2.9 percent for Medicare. This means you will pay 16.2 percent of your net earnings every year to the federal government. The taxes are calculated based on 91.9 percent of your net earnings. The other 8.1 percent is subtracted before the calculation to account for the half that usually is paid by the employer from your net earnings.

Self-employment Tax is Calculated Based on Your Adjusted Net Earnings

| Net Earnings | Net income minus business expenses | $25,000.00 |
|---|---|---|
| MINUS | 8.1% of net earnings | $2,025.00 |
| Adjusted Net Earnings | | $22,975.00 |
| Self-employment Tax | 13.3% of adjusted net earnings | $3,055.68 |

You also can deduct half of your Social Security tax on *IRS Form 1040*. The deduction must be taken from your gross income in determining your adjusted gross income; it cannot be an itemized deduction and must not be listed on your *Schedule C: Profit or Loss from Business*.

# How to pay self-employment tax

Self-employment tax is calculated and reported on *IRS Schedule SE (Form 1040): Self-Employment Tax* (**www.irs.gov/pub/irs-pdf/f1040sse.pdf**). You must file *Schedule SE*, *Schedule C* and *Form 1040* by April 15 after any year in which you have net earnings of $400 or more. If you do not owe any income tax, you must complete *Form 1040* and *Schedule SE* to pay self-employment Social Security tax. This is true even if you already get Social Security benefits.

To pay self-employment tax, you must have a Social Security number (SSN) or an individual taxpayer identification number (ITIN).

## Calculating your net earnings

Your net earnings are essentially your business profit from *Schedule C* minus certain deductions. Under Section 2042 of the Small Business Jobs Act, self-employed individuals can deduct the cost of health insurance in calculating net earnings from self-employment. Wages or salaries from employers who are already withholding Social Security and Medicare tax are not included in your net earnings on *Schedule SE*. *Schedule SE* takes you through the process of calculating your self-employment tax on paper. Tax preparation software and some accounting programs will do the calculations for you based on your answers to certain questions.

## Quarterly Estimated Tax Payments

The United States income tax is a pay-as-you-go tax, which means that tax must be paid as you earn or receive your income during the year. You can either do this through withholding tax from wages or other payments you receive or by making estimated tax payments. If you do not pay your tax through withholding by an employer or do not pay enough tax that way, you might also have to pay estimated taxes. Estimated tax payments are made in four installments, known as quarterly estimated tax payments, throughout the year. First-time publishers are sometimes unaware that they must make these quarterly tax payments, and they end up faced with unexpected tax bills and penalties. The IRS charges a penalty for underpaying estimated taxes and for late payments. To avoid penalties, determine early in the year whether you are required to make these quarterly payments, and be sure to send in your payments before the deadlines.

Sole proprietors, partners, S corporation shareholders, and self-employed individuals generally have to make estimated tax payments if they expect to owe tax of $1,000 or more when they file their tax returns at the end of the year and if the amount withheld by an employer will equal less than 90 percent of what they owe. You can pay your self-employment taxes as part of quarterly estimated tax payments.

You do not have to pay quarterly estimated taxes if you owed no taxes for the previous 12-month tax year. If you had a tax liability for the previous year, you might have to pay estimated tax for the current year.

## Ask your employer to withhold more taxes

If you are working for an employer who is withholding taxes from your paycheck, you can ask to increase the amount withheld to cover taxes on the income from your online sales business. You will not need to pay the quarterly estimated tax if your employer is withholding 90 percent or more of what you will owe at the end of the year. To do this, file a new *Form W-4: Employee's Withholding Allowance Certificate*, with your employer. If you receive a pension or annuity, you can use *Form W-4P, Withholding Certificate for Pension or Annuity Payments*, to start or change your withholding from these payments. You can choose to have federal income tax withheld from certain government payments. For details, see *Form W-4V, Voluntary Withholding Request.*

The IRS gives you two methods for estimating your tax liability, the "Safe Harbor" Method and the "SWAG" method. The Safe Harbor method increases your tax liability from the previous year by 10 percent and divides the result by four to get the amount you must pay each quarter. At the end of the year, any amount you have overpaid in earlier quarters will be deducted from your final payment or refunded to you. The SWAG method requires you to evaluate your accounts and try to estimate how much you owe the IRS for the upcoming quarter. Instead of a fixed quarterly payment, you pay income tax based on how much you earn from one quarter to the next. This method can be risky because if you underpay during the year, then you will owe the remainder in one lump payment to the IRS on April 15, and you may owe penalties. In spite of the risk, most authors use this method because there is no real way to determine how much income you will make in any one quarter. You might earn much more in one quarter than you did in another. With the Safe Harbor method, you are likely to overpay in earlier quarters, which means that you are sinking money into taxes that you could have used to promote your books. Of course, you will get it back at the end of the year, but it is money that could have earned additional profit for your business.

*IRS Publication 505: Tax Withholding and Estimated Tax* (**http://www.irs.gov/ pub/irs-pdf/p505.pdf**) contains a worksheet for figuring your estimated quarterly tax payments. Your tax preparation software will walk you through the steps and calculate it for you automatically, and you also can use some accounting programs if they contain information from your previous year's tax return. There is also a worksheet for recalculating your quarterly payment if your circumstances change. Make sure you pay enough each quarter to avoid underpayment penalties. Penalties are calculated separately on each quarterly payment. You could owe a penalty even if you are due a refund at the end of the year.

The due dates for quarterly estimated taxes are typically April 15, June 15, September 15, and January 15, or the next business day if one of these dates falls on a weekend. You can pay the entire amount in advance for the year on April 15 if you wish. The final payment, which is due on January 15 after the end of the tax year, can be ignored if you file your annual tax return and pay the balance in full before January 31. You can find information about making electronic payments on the IRS website at the Electronic Payment Options Home Page (**www.irs.gov/ efile/article/0,,id=97400,00.html**).

# Sales Tax

If you are selling your books directly to retail customers, you will be required to collect sales tax on books sold or shipped to someone in the state where your business is located. To collect and remit sales tax, you must get a reseller's license or a sales tax certificate from the taxing authority in your state, usually called the State Department of Treasury, State Department of Taxation, or State Department of Revenue. You can find links to each state's taxing authority on the website of the Federation of Tax Administrators (**www.taxadmin.org/fta/link**). Many states allow you to sign up online. Your taxing authority will provide you with an online account or send you paper coupons and envelopes, so you can submit a monthly sales tax return and your payment. Be careful to submit your payments on time every month, or you will be charged late penalties. You also can obtain detailed information from the taxing authority about items that are subject to sales tax in your state.

A sales tax certificate serves several purposes. It allows you to obtain wholesale merchandise for resale without paying sales tax on it. Most wholesalers will not sell to you unless you give them a copy of your sales tax certificate, and you must show the certificate to gain entry to wholesale trade shows and merchandise marts. Many banks require one to open a commercial bank account.

Customers living in the other states where online sales are taxable are responsible to report and pay sales tax themselves for items they bought online. When the customer pays sales tax directly to his or her state, it is called a use tax. Use tax can be reported and paid online at most state taxing authority websites or submitted using a paper return. Some states, such as New York, include a line on their state income tax returns for use tax on Internet, mail order, and out-of-state purchases. It is difficult for states to enforce a use tax on every online purchase. Many people are unaware that use tax exists. Even if they are aware, the likelihood that they will remember to keep a record of every small online purchase is slim. Because so many purchases are now made online, states such as California are conducting campaigns to educate their residents about use tax.

## How to collect and record sales tax

In response to the recent flurry of state legislation concerning sales tax on Internet purchases, several online marketplaces have launched applications that allow sales tax to be added to an item during checkout if it is being shipped to an address in the state(s) where the seller has nexus. You must set up your own account with sales tax preferences. Read the instruction for your online marketplace carefully. The money comes directly to you, and you are responsible to remit it to your state taxing authority.

Sales tax is recorded in your accounts as income, but it becomes an expense when you remit it to the state. It passes through your accounting system and does not appear in your final calculations of profit and loss. You should keep a separate ledger or spreadsheet to record sales tax collected for each transaction and the amounts remitted to your state taxing authority. Most bookkeeping software allows you to set up a sales tax account to capture these amounts automatically when you import sales data to your records. Any amount that you overcharge for sales tax, either accidentally or because amounts are rounded up to the next cent, belongs to the state. You cannot get extra money from customers by overcharging for sales tax.

If you collect payments through PayPal, you can program it to automatically collect sales tax from customers in your state. However, PayPal takes its commission based on the total amount of the sale, so you will be paying commission on the sales tax as well as the retail price of the book. To compensate for this, you can add a few cents to the shipping and handling fee for your book when you list it.

For electronically downloaded products, such as e-books, music videos, and MP3 files, the ZIP code of the billing address for the credit card used to pay for the purchase determines whether sales tax is charged. If you are selling a book or music that you published through CreateSpace (**www.createspace.com**), Amazon's on-demand publishing arm, the sales tax will be collected and processed by Amazon.

## Tax Do's and Don'ts

**DO:**

- Learn about tax laws and how they might affect you while you are setting up your business.
- Keep accurate financial records.
- Keep all receipts and supporting documents for business expenses and organize a system for filing them.
- Keep your receipts and records for at least six years.
- Calculate whether you owe quarterly income tax payments and make them on time.
- Collect and remit sales tax for in-state retail sales.
- Set up a dedicated office space in your home for your publishing activities.

**DON'T:**

- Try to artificially inflate your business expenses with false claims.
- Wait until April 15 to discover that you should have paid quarterly income tax and now owe a penalty.
- Forget that you have to pay self-employment tax on the income from your book sales.

# The Future of Publishing

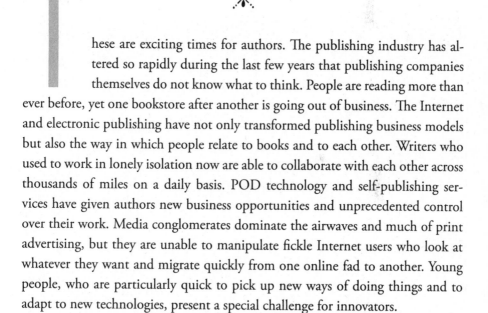

These are exciting times for authors. The publishing industry has altered so rapidly during the last few years that publishing companies themselves do not know what to think. People are reading more than ever before, yet one bookstore after another is going out of business. The Internet and electronic publishing have not only transformed publishing business models but also the way in which people relate to books and to each other. Writers who used to work in lonely isolation now are able to collaborate with each other across thousands of miles on a daily basis. POD technology and self-publishing services have given authors new business opportunities and unprecedented control over their work. Media conglomerates dominate the airwaves and much of print advertising, but they are unable to manipulate fickle Internet users who look at whatever they want and migrate quickly from one online fad to another. Young people, who are particularly quick to pick up new ways of doing things and to adapt to new technologies, present a special challenge for innovators.

This book has presented numerous options for an author who wants to publish a book, from seeking a contract with a megapublisher to marketing self-published e-books entirely online. One thing is clear — if you are determined enough, you will succeed. There is a way around every obstacle if you choose to pursue it. Publishing is hard work, but all of the tools and services are at hand. It is up to you to take an objective look at your work, determine what you must do to succeed, and find the people to help you do it.

It is difficult to predict how the publishing industry will look a decade from now. E-book readers and other digital devices present opportunities to incorporate audio files and animated graphics in books. The publishing industry may follow the model of the music industry, in which musicians release multiple versions of the same songs and videos on the Internet using inexpensive technology, instead of investing hundreds of thousands of dollars to produce a single music video. Writers may begin producing books that change every day, or change in response to input from their readers. Readers may demand more interaction with authors and even begin contributing to the books they read. The rate at which new information becomes available every day makes it almost impossible for many nonfiction books, including textbooks, to stay up-to-date for longer than a few months. Nonfiction authors might begin selling subscriptions rather than books and devote themselves to constant revision.

## Japanese Keitai (cell phone) novels dominate best-seller lists

Japan has had Internet-capable cell phones since early in 1999, and many young people browse the Internet using cell phones rather than prohibitively expensive computers. In 2000, a Web hosting company, Maho no i-rando (Maho i-Land), observed some of its customers writing stories on their blogs and created an application allowing people to upload texts directly from their cell phones. Users began uploading stories written in short installments during train commutes and lunch breaks. When cell phone service providers began to offer unlimited texting for flat rates in 2004, the phenomenon exploded. Today, numerous sites host cell phone novels. Maho no i-rando carries more than 1 million books and has almost 6 million readers and authors.

Cell phone novels can be read, as well as written, on a cell phone screen. Chapters usually consist of about 70 to 100 words each, and each page is limited to 1,000 characters. They typically are written in the first person, as diary entries or dialogue, employing unique cadences and conventions of text messaging familiar to young people who have grown up with cell phones. The story lines resemble comic books and mostly revolve around adolescent romance, sex, and characters with fatal diseases. Part of the appeal of cell phone novels is the apparent intimacy between writer and reader. Readers are able to post their feedback and, often, guide the plot development.

Writers are not paid for their novels, and readers can download them free, although some websites charge a low subscription fee. Traditional publishers soon noticed the trend, however, and began publishing cell phone novels as books. The first published cell phone novel, *Deep Love* by Yoshi, sold 2.6 million copies in Japan, and became the source of a TV series, a manga (comic book), and a movie. In 2007, 98 cell phone novels were published as books, and five made the Japanese top ten national best-sellers list, averaging sales of 400,000 each. The top three best-sellers were cell phone novels by first-time authors. Cell phone books have grown into a $36 million (annually) industry. Several Japanese websites offer prizes to authors and buy publishing rights to popular keitai novels.

Literary critics fear cell phone novels mean the demise of literature, but publishers say they are reaching an untapped audience. Many cell phone novelists have never written fiction before, and many of their readers never read novels before. In Japan, a majority of readers are junior high and high school girls who have grown up reading comic books and watching TV.

The popularity of cell phone novels has spread to China, Taiwan, South Korea, Sweden, Germany, South Africa, and most recently, North America. The cell phone novel may never become as popular and successful in these countries as in Japan, but it has a definite appeal to young readers. German small screen publishers Blackbetty™ Mobilmedia and Cosmoblonde (**www.cosmoblonde.de**) have been active since 2007. The Shuttleworth Foundation, based in Capetown, South Africa, used a cell phone novel in a 2009 project to encourage teens to read, creating Facebook identities for the characters and rewarding readers with cell phone minutes. Textnovel (**www.text-novel.com**), the first English-language cell phone novel website, launched in 2008. Both Textnovel and Figment (**http://figment.com**) run contests as incentives for their writers.

Blockbusters and best-sellers still bring in millions of dollars in sales, but as readers turn increasingly to online booksellers, will new releases still be able to take the front stage? POD makes over seven million titles available — readers can select from a wide range of books on a single topic instead of being confined to two or three newer releases on a bookstore shelf. Large publishers may attempt to buy up online booksellers so they can carry out their marketing campaigns and, once again, exclude older books and lesser-known authors. According to a January 2014 article by Mike Shatzkin, "Publishers now face a world where there is a single dominant bricks-and-mortar retailer (Barnes & Noble), a single dominant internet retailer (Amazon), and, as noted above, a single dominant publisher (Penguin Random House)." The shift to ebooks has improved publisher profitability and they have have discovered "dynamic pricing" — lowering prices on a book temporarily to spike sales and awareness.

Following another trend in the music industry, there is already a glut of self-published titles for sale online. It will not be long before online booksellers will initiate a screening process to eliminate books by unknown authors and those of poor quality. It then will become harder for first-time authors to access online markets.

The ability to extract data from automated sales and the enthusiasm with which readers have accepted e-books has made large publishing companies aware of the potential market for books by independent authors. They already are developing new business models that will attempt to tap into that potential. This could lead to more opportunities for independent authors to benefit from the expertise and distribution channels of large publishers and increase their exposure.

Whatever happens in the publishing industry, nothing can replace creativity, imagination, and the pleasure of reading a good book. As an author, you will have to remain agile, willing to adapt, and ready to seize new opportunities, but the inspiration for your books and the quality of your writing will still come from deep within your spirit. That will never change.

# Further Reading

## Associations

American Christian Fiction Writers (**www.acfw.com**)

American Christian Writers (**http://www.jameswatkins.com/acw**)

American Crime Writers League (**www.acwl.org**)

Association of American Publishers (**www.publishers.org**)

Association of American University Presses (**www.aaupnet.org**)

Association of Author Representatives (AAR) (**http://aaronline.org**)

Chick Lit Writers (**http://chicklitwriters.com/blog/**)

Children's Book Council (**www.cbcbooks.org**)

Graphic Artists Guild (**www.graphicartistsguild.org**)

Historical Novel Society (**www.historicalnovelsociety.org**)

Horror Writers Association (**www.horror.org**)

Independent Book Publishers Association (**www.ibpa-online.org**)

International Association of Crime Writers (**www.crimewritersna.org**)

International Auto/Biography Association (**www.theiaba.org**)

International Digital Publishing Forum (IDPF) (**http://idpf.org**)

International Food, Wine, and Travel Writers Association (**www.ifwtwa.org**)

International Thriller Writers Association (**www.thrillerwriters.org**)

Mystery Writers of America (**www.mysterywriters.org**)

National Association of Memoir Writers (**www.namw.org**)

National Writers Association (**www.nationalwriters.com**)

PEN America (**www.pen.org**)

Poets & Writers, Inc. (**www.pw.org**)

Romance Writers of America* (**www.rwa.org**)

Science Fiction and Fantasy Writers of America (**www.sfwa.org**)

Sisters in Crime (**www.sistersincrime.org**)

Society of Children's Book Writers and Illustrators (**www.scbwi.org**)

The Association of Publishers for Special Sales (**www.spannet.org**)

The Authors Guild (**www.authorsguild.org**)

The National Writers Union (**www.nwu.org**)

Western Writers of America, Inc. (**www.westernwriters.org**)

Writers Guild of America, West (WGAW) labor union for screen and entertainment writers (**www.wga.org**)

# Big Five Publishers

Hachette Book Group (HBG) (**www.hachettebookgroup.com**)

HarperCollins Publishers (**www.harpercollins.com**)

Macmillan (**http://us.macmillan.com**)

Penguin Random House (**http://www.penguinrandomhouse.com**)

Simon & Schuster (**www.simonandschuster.com**)

# Blog Sites

Blogger (**www.blogger.com**)

LiveJournal (**www.livejournal.com**)

Self Publishing Review (**www.selfpublishingreview.com**)

Wordpress (**www.wordpress.com**)

# Blog tracking

Addict-o-matic (**http://addictomatic.com**)

BoardTracker (**www.boardtracker.com**)

BrandsEye (**www.brandseye.com**)

Brandwatch (**www.brandwatch.com**)

Reputation.com (**www.reputation.com/myreputationdiscovery**)

SDL (**http://www.sdl.com/products/sm2/**)

SiteMention (**http://sitemention.com**)

Social Oomph (**www.socialoomph.com**)

socialmention (**http://socialmention.com/alert**s)

Topsy (**http://topsy.com**)

Trackur (**www.trackur.com**)

Twazzup (**www.twazzup.com**)

# Book Design

EasyBib bibliography (**www.easybib.com**)

Free Tutorials Baycon Group (**www.baycongroup.com/el0.htm**)

Identifont — Online digital font directory (**www.identifont.com**)

InDesign Magazine (**www.indesignmag.com**)

Lyon, Jack M. *Typesetting in Microsoft Word*
(**www.selfpublishing.com/design/downloads/articles/typesetting.pdf**)

Microsoft (**http://office.microsoft.com/en-us/excel-help**)

Microsoft (**http://office.microsoft.com/en-us/excel-help**)

PDF Converter (**www.freepdfconvert.com**)

PDF Desk (**www.pdfdesk.com/winpdf.html**)

PrimoPDF (**www.primopdf.com/index.aspx**)

Print in PDF (**www.printinpdf.com**)

Self-Pub by Jera Publishing LLC
(**www.self-pub.net/templates.html**)

Tiny Tutorials' Adobe Classroom printable typographic ruler
(**http://tinytutorials.wordpress.com/2010/09/16/printable-pica-ruler/**)

Worldcat bibliography (**www.worldcat.org**)

# Bookkeeping

IRS Publication 583: Starting a Business and Keeping Records. IRS.gov
(**www.irs.gov/pub/irs-pdf/p583.pdf**)

Microsoft Excel templates (**http://office.microsoft.com/en-us/templates#**)

Small Business Administration free online classes
(**www.sba.gov/content/recordkeeping**)

SBA local branches (**www.sba.gov/content/find-local-sba-office**)

# Business and Taxes

IRS Publication 547: Casualties, Disasters and Thefts
(**www.irs.gov/pub/irs-pdf/p547.pdf**)

Register Your Fictitious or "Doing Business As" (DBA) Name
(**www.sba.gov/content/register-your-fictitious-or-doing-business-dba-name**)

SBA.gov's Business Licenses and Permits Search Tool
(**www.sba.gov/content/search-business-licenses-and-permits**)

# Cell Phone Novels

Cosmoblonde (**www.cosmoblonde.de**) (German language)

Figment (**http://figment.com**) (English)

Textnovel (**www.textnovel.com**) (English)

# Copyright and Public Domain

Creative Commons (**http://creativecommons.org**)

License Music Now.com (**http://licensemusicnow.com**)

"Understanding Copyright and Related Rights," World Intellectual Property Organization (WIPO) (**www.wipo.int/freepublications/en/intproperty/909/wipo_pub_909.html**)

# Data Storage

Carbonite (**www.carbonite.com**)

CrashPlan (**www.crashplan.com**)

Just Cloud (**www.justcloud.com**)

Mozy (**www.mozy.com**)

My PC Backup (**www.mypcbackup.com**)

SugarSync (**www.sugarsync.com**)

ZipCloud (**www.zipcloud.com**)

# Directories

American Booksellers Association Book Buyer's Handbook (**http://www.bookweb.org/resources/bbh**)

*Book Dealers Dropship Directory* (**http://infomarketplace.tripod.com/bookdealer.htm**)

*Book Trade in Canada* and *Canadian Publishers Directory* (**www.quillandquire.com**)

*Books in Print* (**www.bowker.com**)

*International Directory of Little Magazines and Small Presses* (**www.dustbooks.com/d.htm**)

*Small Press Record of Books in Print* (**www.dustbooks.com/sr.htm**)

# E-books

eBook Crossroads.com (**www.ebookcrossroads.com/epublishers.html**)

EBook Template Source
(**www.ebooktemplatesource.com/free-ebook-covers.html**)

Cover Factory (**www.coverfactory.com**)

My eCover Maker (**www.myecovermaker.com**) subscription-based templates

ScribD (**www.scribd.com**)

Smashwords (**www.smashwords.com**)

# Editing

Brown, Renni and David King. *Self-Editing for Fiction Writers*

Elizabeth Lyons. *Manuscript Makeover: Revision Techniques No Fiction Writer Can Afford To Ignore*

Strunk, William Jr. *The Elements of Style* (**www.bartleby.com/141/index.html**)

# Forums and Communities

Absolute Write (**http://absolutewrite.com**)

For Writers (**www.forwriters.com**)

Good Reads (**www.goodreads.com**)

Library Thing (**www.librarything.com**)

Writers Beat (**www.writersbeat.com**)

# Freelancers

Elance.com (**www.elance.com**)

Guru.com (**www.guru.com**)

Monster.com (**www.monster.com**)

# History

Black, Bruce. "Collecting Vintage Mass Market Paperbacks and Paperback Originals" (**http://www.bookscans.com/Articles/Collecting%20 American%20PBOs%20-%201.pdf**)

# Images and Graphics

BigStock (**bigstock.com**)

Creative Commons (to locate images on Creative Commons, visit **http://search.creativecommons.org**)

FotoSearch (**fotosearch.com**)

Getty Images (**www.gettyimages.com/CreativeImages/RoyaltyFree**)

Illustration Works (**www.illustrationworks.com**)

iStockphoto (**www.istockphoto.com**)

Jupiter Images (**www.jupiterimages.com**)

Katzman Stock (**http://katzmanstock.com**)

Mira (**http://library.mira.com**)

Photos.com (**www.photos.com**)

Thinkstock (**www.thinkstockphotos.com**)

Time Tunnel (**www.timetunnel.com**)

# Legal Documents and Contracts

Life story rights (**www.absolutewrite.com/screenwriting/life_rights.htm**)

# Legal Information

"Right of Publicity: an overview." Legal Information Institute (LII), Cornell University of Law (**http://topics.law.cornell.edu/wex/publicity**)

Better Business Bureau's website (**www.bbb.org**)

State attorney general (**www.attorneygeneral.gov**)

Story rights and movie rights (**http://lehmannstrobel.com/articles/acquiring-story-rights**)

The Federal Trade Commission, Bureau of Consumer (**www.ftc.gov**)

Volunteer Lawyers for the Arts (**www.vlany.org**)

# Literary Agents

AgentQuery (**www.agentquery.com**) — Agent Query offers a free searchable database of more than 900 literary agents.

Association of Author's Representatives (**www.aar-online.org**) — AAR is a professional organization for literary and dramatic agents. It was established in 1991 through the merger of the Society of Authors' Representatives, founded in 1928, and the Independent Literary Agents Association, founded in 1977. Browse its list of member agents.

*Guide to Literary Agents* (**www.guidetoliteraryagents.com**) — A Writer's Digest Book, this is a complete resource for writers who need representation.

Jeff Herman's Guide to Book Publishers, Editors, and Literary Agents (**www.jeffherman.com**)

Preditors and Editors (**http://pred-ed.com/pubagent.htm**)

*Publishers Weekly* (**www.publishersweekly.com**) — A weekly trade magazine targeting publishers, booksellers, literary agents, and libraries

*Publishers Marketplace* (**www.publishersmarketplace.com**) — A resource for publishing professionals. A $20 subscription, payable monthly, gives you access to its articles and databases.

Query Shark (**http://queryshark.blogspot.com**)

*Writer's Digest* (**www.writersdigest.com**)

Writers Net (**www.writers.net/agents.html**) — An Internet directory of writers, editors, publishers, and literary agents

# Logo Design

Guru Corporation's Logosnap.com (**www.logosnap.com**)

HP's Logomaker (**www.logomaker.com**)

# News and Blogs

Author! Author! Anne Mini's Blog (**www.annemini.com/?cat=130**)

Entertainment Weekly: Books (**www.ew.com/ew/books**)

GalleyCat. Mediabistro.com (**www.mediabistro.com/galleycat**)

*Paste Magazine* (**www.pastemagazine.com/articles/books**)

Publishing Perspectives (**http://publishingperspectives.com**)

Publishing.com (**www.pfspublishing.com**)

Silobreaker (**www.silobreaker.com**)

Teleread: News and views on e-books, libraries, publishing and related topics (**www.teleread.com**)

Writer Unboxed (**http://writerunboxed.com**)

Writing World (**www.writing-world.com**)

# POD Publishers

Amazon's CreateSpace (**www.createspace.com**)

AuthorHouse (**www.authorhouse.com**)

Infinity Publishing (**www.infinitypublishing.com**)

iUniverse (**www.iuniverse.com**)

LightningSource (**www.lightningsource.co**m)

Lulu (**www.lulu.com**)

Outskirtspress (**www.outskirtspress.com**)

# Poetry

Empty Mirror (**www.emptymirrorbooks.com/publishing**)

# Printers

Aeonix Publishing Group (**www.aeonix.com/bookprnt.htm**)

Association of Publishers for Special Sales (**www.spannet.org**)

Bookmarket.com (**www.bookmarket.com/101print.htm**)

Independent Book Publishers Association (**www.ibpa-online.org/vendors/suppliers.aspx**)

Literary Market Place (LMP) (**www.literarymarketplace.com**)

Morris Publishing (**www.morrispublishing.com**)

# Publishers

Greenleaf Book Group, LLC (**www.greenleafbookgroup.com**)

Preditors and Editors (**http://pred-ed.com/peba.htm**)

Pritchett, Farlow, & Smith Publishers (**www.pfspublishing.com**)

Publisher Lookup — AccessTextNetwork, a joint venture with the American Publishers Association (**www.publisherlookup.org**)

Scott Marlowe: Publishing's Big 6: Who are they? Big six with links to major imprints (**www.scottmarlowe.com/post/Publishinge28099s-Big-6-Who-are-they.aspx**)

# Research and Education

Authors Market/Publish America (**www.authorsmarket.net/yourbook.htm**)

Jeff Herman's Guide to Book Publishers, Editors, and Literary Agents (**www.jeffherman.com**)

Publisher's Lunch (**www.publishersmarketplace.com**)

*Publishers Weekly* magazine online (**www.publishersweekly.com**)

*The New York Times* book reviews (**www.nytimes.com/pages/books**)

Writer Beware — Science Fiction and Fantasy Writers of America's Committee on Writing Scams (**www.sfwa.org/for-authors/writer-beware**)

# Sales Tax

"Do You Have to Pay Sales Tax on Internet Purchases?" Findlaw.com (**http://smallbusiness.findlaw.com/business-operations/internet/internet-taxes.html**)

# Self-Employment Tax

If You Are Self-Employed. SSA Publication No. 05-10022. January 2011. ICN 454900. (**www.ssa.gov/pubs/10022.html**)

Topic 554 — Self-Employment Tax (**www.irs.gov/taxtopics/tc554.html**)

IRS Schedule SE (Form 1040): Self-Employment Tax (**www.irs.gov/pub/irs-pdf/f1040sse.pdf**)

# Social Media

Facebook (**www.facebook.com**)

Google+ (**google.com**)

LinkedIn (**www.linkedin.com**)

MySpace (**www.myspace.com**)

Twitter (**www.twitter.com**)

YouTube (**www.youtube.com**)

# Website

2Checkout (**www.2checkout.com**)

Adobe Web Analytics (**www.adobe.com/solutions/digital-analytics.htmls**)

Alexa (**www.alexa.com**)

ClickBank (**www.clickbank.com**)

Durango Merchant Services (**http://durangomerchantservices.com**)

FastCharge (**www.fastcharge.com**)

Flagship Merchant Services (**www.flagshipmerchantservices.com**)

GoEmerchant (**www.goemerchant.com**)

Google Analytics (**http://www.google.com/analytics/?gclid=CMryk8LijbwCF dHm7Aodwx0Aww**)

Instamerchant (**www.instamerchant.com**)

Merchant Warehouse (**http://merchantwarehouse.com**)

Pandora (**www.pandora.com**)

Paypal (**www.paypal.com**)

Playlist.com (**www.playlist.com**)

Webtrends (**www.webtrends.com**)

# Writing a Synopsis

Carmichael, Kathy. "Writing the Fiction Synopsis"
(**http://www.kathycarmichael.com/articles-and-seminars/articles-and-workshops/general-fiction-synopsis/general-fiction-synopsis-seminar**)

Charlotte Dillon's Resources for Romance Writers
(**http://charlottedillon.com/WritingRomance.html**)

# Sample Documents

## Sample Query Letter

Jane Writer
1234 Show-Don't-Tell Lane
Boston, MA 02101

January 1, 2014

Edna Editor
Best Books Ever
1234 Bindery Blvd.
New York City, NY 10010

Dear Ms. Editor,

Our era is one of constantly changing technology and lightning-speed advancements. Today's youth are in an especially exciting position to grow as leaders and innovators in an age where science and invention are some of society's top priorities. My nonfiction picture book about Thomas Edison is positioned uniquely to help young readers understand the creative processes and inventive thinking that drove one of history's greatest inventors.

*The Legacy of Thomas Edison: More than Just the Inventor of the Light Bulb* begins with a biography that highlights the dedication, drive, and creative genius that were the hallmarks of the inquisitive young Edison, a person whose insatiable love of learning and invention quite literally changed the world. The book's unique layout includes "do-it-yourself" sidebars that will get kids interacting with some of Edison's actual experiments and inventions. The book also endeavors to inspire a love of science and invention by illustrating some of Edison's thought processes and how he used his problem-solving abilities to create systems and objects that made an impact on our everyday lives.

To date, biographies of Thomas Edison focus on his life or his inventions. To my knowledge, my book is the only one that examines the workings of the inventor's mind as well as his unique creative thought processes, drive, and motivation. Young readers will gain special insight into scientific methodology and will have the opportunity to try some of Edison's experiments for themselves.

As a visual artist with a background in design and layout, I can contribute the art and graphic elements to the book. If you are interested, I can send it to you in completed form in three months. Thank you for your consideration.

Sincerely,

Jane Writer

# Sample Cover Letter — When You Are Unpublished

Jane Writer
1234 Show-Don't-Tell Lane
Boston, MA 02101

January 1, 2014

Edna Editor
Best Books Ever
1234 Bindery Blvd.
New York City, NY 10010

Dear Ms. Editor,

Congratulations on your new position at Best Books Ever. I was excited to find out about your new picture book line and am submitting my book for your consideration. *Jiminy Jumping Jacks!* is the rollicking tale of a young turtle's struggle to live up to the athletic triumphs of his best friends, Rabbit and Fox. Enclosed is my 250-word manuscript.

With an increasing focus on keeping kids healthy, parents, teachers, and librarians will appreciate the values represented in the adventures of the three friends. The book is fun for kids to read and not only shows the importance of eating right and exercise but also deals with an experience many kids can relate to. For children whose athletic abilities are not quite at the level as those of their friends, participating in sports can be disheartening. Children who are overweight often struggle with body image and feelings of social inadequacy, and turtle's interactions with his friends are taken from real-life examples.

I have taught physical education for 10 years and have seen firsthand the effects that feeling inadequate has on children's self-esteem. Not many children's books address this topic, and I hope that mine call fill a void while showing children that they can turn this difficult situation around through both perseverance *and* fun.

I appreciate your time and consideration in reviewing my manuscript. Enclosed is a SASE for a reply only. This is not a simultaneous submission.

Sincerely,

Jane Writer

# Sample Cover Letter —
# When You Are Published

Jane Writer
1234 Show-Don't-Tell Lane
Boston, MA 02101

January 1, 2014

Edna Editor
Best Books Ever
1234 Bindery Blvd.
New York City, NY 10010

Dear Ms. Editor,

*Daisy's Dash* is the humorous story of a young prankster who cannot seem to help herself. At school, at the park, at the mall, Daisy pulls pranks wherever she goes. Until one day, when she tries to pull a prank on a bigger prankster than herself.

I hope you will enjoy the unique fun and humor of Daisy's story. It shows examples of how to deal with bullies but in a way that will have young readers laughing.

I am the author of several picture books, including *Mama's Lullaby* and *The Biggest Birthday Bash*. My short stories have appeared in *American Girl* and *Highlights for Children*.

I appreciate your time and consideration in reviewing my manuscript. Enclosed is a SASE for a reply only. I am submitting my manuscript exclusively to you.

Sincerely,

Jane Writer

# Sample Proposal

### THE LEGACY OF THOMAS EDISON: MORE THAN JUST THE INVENTOR OF THE LIGHT BULB

By Jane Writer

## CHAPTER 1 — THE MIND OF THE YOUNG GENIUS

This chapter discusses the intellectual and creative development of the young Thomas Edison from the time he was rejected by his teacher to his years in home schooling. Influenced by his mother, who in his words "was the making of me," young Thomas showed an insatiable love of learning, and spent many hours training his mind and reciting poetry. Sidebars include some of the young Thomas's experiments.

## CHAPTER 2 — A WORLD OF INVENTIONS

This chapter outlines many of Edison's inventions, and how and why the inventor thought them up. Includes an exciting description of Thomas Edison and Alexander Graham Bell's working relationship, and how they competed against one another. Discusses communication science as it was then, and how Edison's inventions have developed into modern technologies. Includes descriptions of tangible ways that the inventor has influenced contemporary life, and what the world would be like without his inventions. Stresses the importance of creative and scientific thinking, and includes many detailed, full-color illustrations.

## CHAPTER 3 — APPLIED INVENTIONS AND EDISON'S METHODS

With a look at how Edison developed a system for electricity, the phonograph, and many other useful objects, kids learn about Edison's scientific methods and how he put them to practical use. With Edison's methods in mind, readers can try several experiments and inventions themselves. Sidebars are geared to encourage children in thinking scientifically and to help them generate ideas of their own.

Historic Sites

List of Inventions

Books about Thomas Edison

Index

# Sample Overview

*The Legacy of Thomas Edison: More than Just the Inventor of the Light Bulb*

During his lifetime, Thomas Edison obtained 1,093 patents for his many inventions. He is credited with inventing the light bulb, as well as the phonograph and the carbon transmitter, which made the voices through Alexander Graham Bell's invention — the telephone — audible enough to encourage the device's widespread use. Edison was a dedicated inventor who set up the first research and development laboratory in the world with the establishment of his center in West Orange, New Jersey, in 1887.

This book begins with a biography that highlights the dedication, drive, and creative genius that were that hallmarks of the inquisitive young Edison, a person whose insatiable love of learning and invention quite literally changed the world. This nonfiction picture book's unique layout includes "do-it-yourself" sidebars that will get kids interacting with some of Edison's actual experiments and inventions. Designed to educate children on the life of Thomas Edison, the book also endeavors to inspire a love of science and invention by illustrating some of Edison's thought processes and how he used his problem-solving abilities to create systems and objects that made a difference.

## Sample Author Flier

# Jane Writer

### Children's Author

> "A gifted writer...she makes reading to children fun, for adults and kids!"
>
> -Harold O'Published,
>
> Publication of the Month

When Jane is not writing picture books, you can be sure to find her giving presentations at an elementary school somewhere. The award-winning author of *This is My Bus, Jimmy's Magic Day,* and *The Dog that Wouldn't Stop Running,* she is a dedicated and talented writer for children.

Jane has published stories in *Highlights for Children, American Girl, Muse, Cricket,* and *Nick.* She loves to go horseback riding and take picnic lunches with her three children.

Jane's work has received awards from the American Library Association and SCB-WI. Visit her website at www.janewriter.com.

Jane Writer
P.O. Box 1234
Boston, MA 02101
www.janewriter.com

## Sample Book Flier

### The Legacy of Thomas Edison:

# More than Just the Inventor of the Light Bulb

By Jane Writer

During his lifetime, Thomas Edison obtained 1,093 patents for his many inventions. He is credited with inventing the light bulb, as well as the phonograph and the carbon transmitter, which made the voices through Alexander Graham Bell's invention — the telephone — audible enough to encourage the device's widespread use. Edison was a dedicated inventor who set up the first research and development laboratory in the world with the establishment of his center in West Orange, New Jersey, in 1887.

This book highlights the dedication, drive, and creative genius that were that hallmarks of the inquisitive young Edison, a person whose insatiable love of learning and invention quite literally changed the world. This nonfiction picture book's unique layout includes "do-it-yourself" sidebars that will get kids interacting with some of Edison's actual experiments and inventions. Designed to educate children on the life of Thomas Edison, the book also endeavors to inspire a love of science and invention by illustrating some of Edison's thought processes and how he used his problem-solving abilities to create systems and objects that made a difference.

*"Illuminating ... Writer shows the creative process behind Thomas Edison the thinker. Kids will love trying the same experiments Edison did as a child."*
                                                    *—Publishers Weekly, 1/1/01*

Best Books Ever, 2010, 64 pages, full-color illustrations, LC #12-34567, ISBN 1-234-56789-0, $14.95, Grades 4-8

# Sample Review Query

Jane Writer
1234 Show-Don't-Tell Lane
Boston, MA 02101

January 1, 2014

Publication of the Month
Attn: Ricky Reviewer
1234 Bowery Blvd.
New York City, NY 10010

Dear Mr. Reviewer,

My book recently was released from Best Books Ever. I am writing to ask if you would be interested in reviewing it. *Jiminy Jumping Jacks!* is the tale of a young turtle's struggle to live up to the athletic triumphs of his best friends, Rabbit and Fox.

With an increasing focus on keeping kids healthy, parents, teachers, and librarians will appreciate the values represented in the adventures of the three friends. The book is fun for kids to read and not only shows the importance of eating right and exercise, but also deals with an experience many kids can relate to. For children whose athletic abilities are not quite at the level as those of their friends, participating in sports can be disheartening. Children who are overweight often struggle with body image and feelings of social inadequacy, and turtle's interactions with his friends are taken from real-life examples.

I have taught physical education for 10 years and have seen firsthand the effects that feeling inadequate has on children's self-esteem. Not many children's books address this topic, and I hope that mine call fill a void while showing children that they can turn this difficult situation around through both perseverance *and* fun.

Please let me know if you are interested, and I will gladly send a complimentary review copy your way. Thank you for your time.

Sincerely,

Jane Writer

# Sample Review Slip

 Best Books Ever Presents for Review

**Title:** *The Legacy of Thomas Edison: More than Just the Inventor of the Light Bulb*

**Author:** Jane Writer

**Edition:** First

**Number in Print:** 100,000

**CIP/LCCN:** 1234567890

**ISBN:** 1-23456-789-0

**Pages:** 64

**Cover art:** Illustration by Jane Writer

**Price:** $14.95

**Season:** Fall 2010

**Publication date:** October 2010

**Rights:**
 a. Subsidiary: book club, paperback
 b. Syndication

Please send two copies of your review to the address below:

**Best Books Ever**
Public Relations Department
1234 Bindery Blvd.
New York City, NY 10010
Tel: (555) 555-1234; Fax: (555) 555-2345
Info@BestBooksEver.com
www.BestBooksEver.com

# Sample Press Release

FOR IMMEDIATE RELEASE

October 5, 2013

Children's Book Reveals the Importance of Team Sports

Bestselling children's author Jane Writer explores the other side of youth sports in her latest book from Best Books Ever, *Jiminy Jumping Jacks!* Released in October 2010, *Jiminy Jumping Jacks!* is available for $14.95 from Barnes & Noble Booksellers, Borders Books, Amazon.com, and fine booksellers nationwide.

Writer's picture book promises to make an impact on children everywhere who struggle with weight problems. These children often suffer from low self-esteem and feelings of inadequacy, especially when it comes to participating in team sports. While the situation may be grim for a portion of American's population, Writer makes a bleak situation fun and addresses a difficult topic effortlessly. The story of turtle and his friends exhibits a supportive situation that is sure to be a hit with parents, teachers, and children's librarians.

Writer has taught physical education to children for 10 years and has seen first-hand the positive effects of team sports on overweight children. Her program, "Fitness is Fun," has helped more than 75 children reduce their weight and see measurable health benefits. And Writer certainly has an audience — according to a recent study, one out of every three American children is overweight or obese. "Educating children about eating right and the importance of exercise is vital," said Writer. "But children do not have to know that — I hope my book makes it fun for them."

For additional information, contact Netty Networker at (555) 555-1234.

About Jane Writer: The award-winning author of *This is My Bus, Jimmy's Magic Day,* and *The Dog that Wouldn't Stop Running,* Jane Writer is a dedicated and talented writer for children. She has published stories in *Highlights for Children, American Girl, Muse, Cricket,* and *Nick.* When she is not writing or reading to kids, she loves to go horseback riding and take picnic lunches with her three children.

CONTACT INFORMATION:

Netty Networker
XYZ PR Firm, Inc.
(555) 555-1234 (voice)
(555) 555-2345 (fax)
netty@xyzpr.com
www.xyzpr.com

# Sample Author-Agent Contract

Disclaimer: Please note the author wrote this contract based on several samples, and you should seek legal advice on determining what to include in your contract. This should not serve as the exact contract you plan to use.

LITERARY SERVICES, LLC ("Agent"), and *Your Name* ("Author"), agree as follows:

GENERAL TERMS.

1.1 <u>Agent's Business.</u> Agent is in the business of representing and promoting authors and providing other literary services for authors who are working in (or aspire to work in) the professional literary world.

1.2 <u>Author's Work.</u> Agent shall have the exclusive right to negotiate for the disposition of literary rights for Author's work, *Name Of Book,* subject to this Agreement. Author is the sole owner of all of the literary rights related to Author's Work (hereinafter referred to as "Literary Rights").

For the purpose of this Agreement, the term "Literary Rights" shall mean all of the literary and other intellectual property rights of every kind and nature whatsoever related to or derived from Author's creation of Author's Work, including without limitation all publishing rights, motion picture rights, audio rights, electronic rights, and merchandising rights both within the United States and everywhere else in the world (sometimes referred to as "Foreign Rights").

1.3 <u>Engagement of Agent's Services.</u> Author hereby engages Agent (and Agent's individual literary agent), and Agent hereby accepts such engagement, as the exclusive professional literary agent of and for Author and as the promoter of Author's Work and of Author's literary career as a writer in the professional literary world ("Author's Literary Career"); provided, however, the term "Author's Literary Career" shall not include any of Author's work as a professional consultant, and Agent shall not be entitled to any compensation as a result of any income earned by Author from her work as a professional consultant.

1.4 <u>Independent Contractor Relationship.</u> Each of Agent and Author shall be deemed an independent contractor, and neither shall be deemed to be the employee of the other, i.e., nothing in this Agreement shall be deemed to create an employee/employer, partnership, or joint venture relationship between Agent and Author.

1.5 <u>Term.</u> The term of this Agreement shall commence upon the signing of this Agreement by Agent and Author and shall continue unless terminated as provided in Paragraph 6.10 below.

1.6 <u>Territory.</u> The territory governed by this Agreement shall be worldwide.

2. <u>PAYMENT TO AGENT, COMPENSATION OF AGENT, REIM-BURSEMENT OF AGENT'S EXPENSES, REMITTANCE TO AUTHOR, AND INSPECTION OF AGENT'S BOOKS.</u> Except as otherwise provided in this Agreement:

2.1 <u>Payment to Agent.</u> All gross receipts owed to Author by any third-party, including without limitation any publisher or distributor, arising out of, derived from, or related in any way to the sale or other disposition (during the term of this Agreement) of any of Author's Literary Work and/or Literary Rights ("Author's Gross Receipts") shall be paid directly to Agent; and, for this limited purpose, Author hereby appoints Agent as Author's limited attorney-in-fact;

2.2 <u>Agent's Compensation and Reimbursement of Expenses.</u> In consideration for Agent's performance of Agent's duties under this Agreement:

2.2.1 <u>Basic Agency Fee.</u> As Agent's basic agency fee, Agent shall be entitled to receive a total of fifteen percent (15%) of all of Author's Gross Receipts (net of any sales tax or gross receipts tax Author is liable for relative to such Author's Gross Receipts) ("Agent's Basic Agency Fee"); provided, however, Agent shall not be entitled to receive any commission or other sum with respect to any of Author's Gross Receipts arising out of, derived from, or related to any prior or pre-existing agreements between Author and any third-party; AND

2.2.2 <u>Additional Sub-Agency Fee.</u> Upon subsequent written agreement between Author and Agent, if Agent retains any co-agent or sub-agent with respect to the commercialization and/or exploitation of any Foreign Rights with respect to Author's Work and/or Literary Rights, Agent shall be entitled to receive an additional ten percent (10%) of all of Author's Gross Receipts derived from such Foreign Rights ("Agent's Additional Sub-Agency Fee"); provided, however, except as specifically provided in this Paragraph 2.2.2 and in Paragraph 2.2.3 (relating to Reimbursement of Agent's Expenses) below, Agent shall be solely responsible for all payments made and/or owed to any other sub-agent and/or co-agents retained by Agent; AND

2.2.3 <u>Reimbursement of Agent's Expenses.</u> When any of Author's Literary Work has been sold successfully in one or more of the markets (domestic and/or foreign) to which it has been submitted, Agent shall be entitled to reimbursement of the reasonable and customary costs, fees, and expenses incurred by Agent's with regard to Agent's representation of Author ("Agent's Reimbursable Expenses"). Agent's Reimbursable Expenses shall include international mail costs, courier service fees, photocopying, and the cost of books used for international submissions. Author's approval of any expenses not listed above shall be required. Agent's Reimbursable Expenses shall not include any of Agent's usual and customary office expenses, e.g., telephone, staff, etc., which will be Agent's sole responsibility.

2.2.4 <u>Effect of Sale of Rights after Termination of Agreement.</u> If Author sells or transfers any Literary Rights in any of Author's Literary Work to any person or other entity to which Agent submitted a proposal for the sale of those rights during the term of this Agreement, Agent shall be entitled to the same compensation, i.e., Agent's Basic Agency Fee and any applicable Agent's Additional Sub-Agency Fee, and to reimbursement of Agent's Reimbursable Expenses if such sale or transfer of Literary Rights takes place within ninety (90) days after this Agreement terminates. Once earned under this Agreement, Agent's right to be compensated for any sale or disposition of Literary Rights in any of Author's Work shall continue even after this Agreement terminates.

2.3 <u>Remittance to Author.</u> Within ten (10) business days after Agent receives any of Author's Gross Receipts, Agent shall pay Author all sums collected as Author's Gross Receipts less only: (i) Agent's Basic Agency fee; (ii) any applicable Agent's Additional Sub-Agency Fee; and (iii) Agent's Reimbursable Expenses. At that time Agent shall also provide Author with an accounting (with reasonable supporting documentation) reflecting Author's Gross Receipts actually collected by Agent and an itemization of all deductions for: (i) Agent's Basic Agency Fee; (ii) any applicable Agent's Additional Sub-Agency Fee; and (iii) Agent's Reimbursable Expenses.

Except as otherwise provided in this Agreement, all sums paid to Agent under this Agreement shall be deemed to have been paid irrevocably.

2.4 <u>Inspection of Books.</u> Upon written request, Author and/or Author's representative shall have the right to examine Agent's books and records to the extent that such books and records pertain to any matters under this Agreement. Such examinations shall occur not more frequently than quarterly in any calendar year and shall be conducted at Agent's offices during normal business hours and at a mutually agreeable time. In order to mitigate the costs of such examination, within thirty (30) days after Author's written request to Agent, Agent shall provide to Author (or to Author's representative) photocopies or electronic copies (readable by standard office software) of all relevant records which could be examined by Author (or Author's representative) at Agent's offices pursuant to this paragraph.

3. <u>DUTIES AND POWERS OF AGENT.</u> During the term of this Agreement and subject to all other terms and conditions set forth in this Agreement:

3.1 <u>Reasonable Best Efforts Performance.</u> Agent shall render and perform Agent's professional literary agency and promotional services required under this Agreement on a "reasonable best efforts" basis. For the purpose of this Agreement, the term "reasonable best efforts" shall mean: (i) in a manner reasonably consistent with the generally accepted standards of care, quality, skill, and diligence generally applicable to the nature of Agent's professional services within the field of professional literary agents; and (ii) in a manner reasonably consistent with Agent's responsibilities to Agent's other clients, i.e., to Agent's other professional writers who are working in (or aspire to work in) the professional literary world; and (iii) in a manner reasonably likely to enhance Author's opportunities (given Author's individual and specific strengths, skills, vulnerabilities, and challenges) to succeed as a professional writer in the professional literary world.

3.2 <u>Agent's Duties Relative to Literary Agency and Promotion of Author's Professional Career.</u> Contingent upon Author's compliance with the terms and conditions of this Agreement, Agent shall:

3.2.1 Attempt to find appropriate publishers for Author's Work;

3.2.2 Negotiate on Author's behalf appropriate contracts with publishers for the publication of Author's Work and/or with other third parties for the sale or other disposition of Author's Literary Rights relative to Author's Work throughout the world; provided, however, Author reserves final control over any agreement disposing of Author's Literary Rights, and no agreement disposing of any of Author's Literary Rights shall be binding without Author's signature.

3.2.3 Coach and assist Author with respect to the promotion of Author's Literary Career;

3.2.4 Consult with Author periodically as necessary or appropriate to maintain effective communication between Agent and Author with respect to Author's Literary Career;

3.2.5 Discuss with Author all enquiries from third parties related to Author's Work and with regard to Author's Literary Career;

3.2.6 Provide Author with periodic reports of Agent's work and Agent's plans for future work for and on behalf of Author's Literary Career;

3.2.7 Assist Author with Author's collection of all monies owed to Author by third parties with regard to Author's Work and with regard to Author's activities within Author's Literary Career, including without limitation all royalties due from publishers and other third parties;

3.2.8 Provide Author with regular written reports setting forth relevant details relative to Agent's Reimbursable Expenses that are related solely to Agent's activities as Author's Agent and not as Agent of other Authors;

3.2.9 Maintain an account for all funds collected by Agent on Author's behalf; provided that such account also may hold funds collected by Agent on behalf of other clients of Agent; provided further, except to the extent of funds that are then owed to Agent by Author (or, with respect to funds collected by Agent on behalf of Agent's other clients, are then owed to Agent by such other clients of Agent), such account shall not hold Agent's funds, i.e., except to the extent of funds that are then owed to Agent, at all times all funds owed to Author shall be kept separate from and shall not be commingled with Agent's own operating funds.

## 4. NOTICES.

4.1 Manner of Notice. All notices which are required to be given under this Agreement or which either party desires to give to the other relative to any matter under this Agreement shall be in writing and (i) delivered personally to the other party or to any officer, director, or other agent or representative of the other party designated by such other party as having authority to receive such notices, or (ii) transmitted to the other party by facsimile or other electronic transmission, or (iii) delivered by a recognized overnight or two-day delivery service such as DHL or FedEx, or (iv) transmitted to the other party by electronic mail; provided, however, that any notice transmitted by facsimile or other electronic transmission or by electronic mail shall be followed up by personal delivery or overnight delivery within forty-eight (48) hours after the termination.

4.2 <u>Notices to Agent.</u> Any notice to Agent shall be sent to Agent at the following address/fax number/email address, or to such other address/fax number/ email address as Agent may hereafter designate:

AGENT:        *Agent Name*
                      (Address)

4.3 <u>Notices to Author.</u> Any notice to Author shall be sent to Author at the following address/fax number/email address, or to such other address/fax number/ email address as Author may hereafter designate:

AUTHOR:       *Author Name*
                      (Address)

4.4 <u>Effective Date.</u> Except as otherwise provided herein, the effective date of any notice hereunder shall be the earlier of the date such notice is actually delivered personally, or the date such notice is transmitted by facsimile or other electronic transmission, or the third day after the date such notice is deposited with a recognized overnight delivery service with the delivery charges prepaid.

5. <u>DISPUTE RESOLUTION.</u> In the event of any dispute between the parties, the parties shall attempt to resolve such disputes through discussion. If the parties are unable to resolve the disagreement, the parties agree to submit the disagreement to binding arbitration before a single arbitrator chosen by the parties. If the parties are unable to agree on an arbitrator, each party shall appoint a representative, and the representatives shall choose a single arbitrator. The parties shall arbitrate the disagreement in accordance with and pursuant to the then existing rules of the American Arbitration Association. The parties also agree that an arbitrator may award reasonable costs and attorney fees to the winning party, and that the arbitration award may be enforced in any court with jurisdiction.

6. <u>MISCELLANEOUS PROVISIONS.</u>

6.1 <u>Binding.</u> This Agreement shall be binding up and shall inure to the benefit of the parties, their heirs, representatives, and assignees.

6.2 <u>Time Is of The Essence.</u> Time is of the essence as to all matters set forth in this Agreement. The failure of any party hereto to perform any obligation by the date required shall constitute a material and substantial breach of this Agreement.

6.3 <u>Governing Law and Jurisdiction.</u> This Agreement shall be governed in accordance with the laws of the state. The parties consent to the exclusive jurisdiction and venue of the federal and state courts in any action arising out of or relating to this Agreement. The parties waive any other venue to which either party might be entitled by domicile or otherwise. The provisions of this paragraph shall not be construed or interpreted to conflict with the provisions of Paragraph 6.4 above, i.e., except for non-arbitral matters, if any, the parties shall be obligated to arbitrate any dispute arising under this Agreement.

6.4 <u>Entire Agreement.</u> This Agreement represents the entire agreement between Agent and Author relative to the subject matter of this Agreement and supersedes all prior negotiations, representations, and agreements relative to such subject matter.

6.5 <u>Independent Provisions.</u> Each of the provisions of this Agreement is independent of every other provision. In the event that any provision of this Agreement is determined to be invalid or unenforceable for any reason, the remaining provisions shall continue to be binding, valid, and effective with the invalid or unenforceable provisions being stricken the same as if never written.

6.6 <u>Captions.</u> The captions herein are for convenience only and shall have no legal effect.

6.7 <u>No Assignment by Agent.</u> Without Author's prior written consent, Agent shall not assign any of its rights, powers, or duties under this Agreement; provided, however, Agent may assign its right to receive compensation and reimbursement of Agent's Reimbursable Expenses to any third-party; and provided further if Agent is no longer in existence or actively involved in the business of (or operating within the field of) literary agency, then, on written notice from Author to Agent (or Agent's representatives), Author may assume responsibility for collection of all sums owed to Author by any publisher or other third-party, and Author shall continue to have the obligation to pay Agent all sums owed to Agent under Paragraphs 2.2.1 through 2.2.3 above.

6.8 <u>No Waiver.</u> No term or condition of this Agreement may be waived except by a writing signed by the party entitled to the benefit thereof. No waiver shall be construed to apply to any further or future default.

6.9 <u>Warranties, Representations, and Indemnification.</u> Each party represents and warrants that he/she/it has the right to enter into this Agreement without impairing anyone else's rights, and that he/she/it shall not to make any commitment relative to Author's Work and Author's Literary Rights that would conflict with this Agreement. Each party shall defend, indemnify, and hold the other party harmless from and against every claim based on any alleged breach of the provisions of this paragraph.

6.10 <u>Early Termination.</u> Either Agent or Author may terminate this Agreement at any time upon thirty (30) days prior written notice to the other.

6.11 <u>Independent Advice and Mutual Preparation.</u> Each party acknowledges that: (i) he/she/it has been advised to seek independent legal and tax advice with regard to this Agreement; (ii) this document shall be deemed to have been drafted by both parties and that no presumptions shall be made against either party based on the actual drafting of this Agreement or any provision of this Agreement; and (iii) he/she/it is entering into this Agreement freely and voluntarily.

Author: _____

Agent: _____

Date: _____

## Sample Consent Form

<u>YOUR NAME</u> has my permission to use my case study responses, name, and any other information supplied to them inside of the book ____TITLE OF YOUR BOOK____. They may also use this case study if need be when advertising or promoting the book and for any future editions of the book if that shall occur. I understand I will receive 1 free copy of the book for my participation.

X_____
*Signature*

X_____
*Printed Name*

_____
*Date*

My Address to Ship My Free Copy(ies):

_____

_____

# Glossary

**ABI**: Advance Book Information. A service providing a directory and database listing for your book that can be accessed by booksellers, librarians, and distributors.

**ancillary materials**: Additional or supplemental materials, often packaged with educational books and textbooks. Can include maps, charts, and other teaching aids.

**back matter**: Material that appears in the back of a book. Includes production notes, author biography, and other matter to be included at the publisher's discretion.

**beta reader**: A person who reads your manuscript and gives you feedback while you are still working on it.

**bookbinder**: A company or craftsman that compiles the pages of a book and places them in a binding or cover.

**buyback rate**: The price at which an author buys his own books from the publisher.

**chapbook**: Books first made in the 16th century by folding a single sheet of paper printed with text to make a book.

**CIP**: Cataloging in Publication Record; it is a record the Library of Congress prepares in order for libraries and book dealers to process, catalog, organize, and place the book.

**color theory**: The relation, mixing, and harmony of colors, often with consideration to where they are placed on a color wheel.

**concordance**: An index linking individual words to a central theme or topic.

**copyright**: The legal right to ownership of original created material.

**critique partner**: A fellow writer who comments on your work in exchange for your feedback on his or her writing.

**desktop publishing**: A term used to describe publishing tasks that can be handled by PC computer software and a printer.

**division**: A group of imprints that form a department of a publishing house.

**dump**: Sales aids that often are included with shipment of newly released book. A display that can include cardboard stands and posters.

**editor**: A person who is in charge of and determines the final content of a text; a person who works for a publisher, commissioning or preparing material for publication.

**folio**: A series of pages created by folding a large printed sheet of paper in half.

**front matter**: The material in the beginning of the book that precedes the story, including the copyright notice, dedication, and title page.

**galley**: Prepublication book copy, usually printed in black and white. Can be bound or unbound.

**glossary**: Vocabulary list.

**graphic novel**: Illustrated fiction or nonfiction stories that differ from comics in that they tend to be of advanced complexity, like the plot of a novel.

**gross sales**: Sales calculated based on the retail price of the book.

**gutter**: The inner margins of a bound book; the white space created by two facing pages in the center of the book near the binding.

**hand selling**: Selling books directly to customers at an event or a book fair.

**honorarium**: A fee paid to a visiting author for speaking or presenting.

**hornbook**: A book made by affixing a sheet of paper to a handheld wooden paddle and covering it with a thin layer of cow's horn for protection.

**hybrid**: A book that belongs to two or more genres.

**imagesetting**: The process of setting up a page for printing as a high-resolution digital image.

**imposition**: A large sheet of paper printed with multiple pages of a book.

**imprint**: A specialized subdivision of a publishing house that focuses on a certain area and often carries a certain identity.

**ISBN (International Standard Book Number)**: A unique ID number assigned to each new book and used to catalog books and track book sales.

**layout**: An arrangement of the graphic elements of a printed book.

**LCCN**: Library of Congress Control Number; these are used for authority, bibliographic, and classification records and are currently structured according to length, elements, and position.

**leading**: The space between printed lines.

**Licensing agreement**: Allows a publisher to sell an idea to other companies, sometimes resulting in character and story offshoots.

**line**: Part of an imprint at a publishing house that sometimes includes series of books.

**list price**: Price on the cover of the book and in retail catalogs.

**manga**: Japanese comics, often for older youth and adult readers, but technically produced for young and old.

**manuscript**: A writer's original work.

**megapublisher**: A large publishing conglomerate owned by a media syndicate.

**noncompete clause**: A clause in a publishing contract that prevents the author from publishing a similar book without the publisher's permission.

**novelty books**: Books with added features beyond traditional binding, commonly issued from toy companies and mass-market publishers.

**net sales**: Sales calculated based on the net profit made from each sale (retail price minus production costs).

**octavo**: A series of pages created by folding a large printed sheet of paper in fourths.

**offset printing**: A method of printing in which plates are used for ink printing.

**oral tradition**: The passing down of stories and tales by spoken word.

**paperback**: A book with a paper cover.

**PCN**: Preassigned control number

**postpublication review**: Intended for the consumer; appears after the book's release to the public.

**prepublication review**: A review that releases before the book.

**prewriting**: Anything you do to help the writing along, such as character outlines, brainstorming, and note taking.

**print-on-demand (POD)**: A printing process in which books are printed as customers order them.

**print quantity needed (PQN)**: The printing of a specified number of commerical-quality books, which minimizes the setup overheads for those on a constricted budget

**pulp fiction magazines**: Magazines popular during the first half of the 20th century that were printed on cheap pulp paper and contained novels and short stories.

**quarto**: A series of pages created by folding a large printed sheet of paper in fourths.

**reading comprehension**: A person's understanding of what he or she read.

**recto**: The right page of a manuscript.

**remaindering:** Selling copies of a book at a discount before it goes out of print.

**SAN**: Standard Address Number

**signature**: Groups of folded pages numbering eight or 16, sewn together in a binding.

**sole proprietorship**: A type of business entity owned and operated by one individual.

**spot color**: Color generated by a single print run.

**storyboard**: A sequence of boxes containing the words and images of a story, usually a picture book or graphic novel that is similar to movie or television frames.

**surge title**: A book that experiences a temporary surge of popularity, such as celebrity biography or an event tie-in.

**tie-in**: A book that carries the theme of another form of media, such as a movie, TV show, comic book, video game or public event.

**unit break**: The number of books that must sell before an author receives a higher royalty rate.

**unsolicited/unagented**: Work that is without publisher solicitation or agent representation.

**vellum**: Treated animal skin used for copying early books.

**vellum paper**: Imitation vellum made out of cotton.

**verso**: The left page of a manuscript.

**widget**: A small software application that can be installed and run within a website.

**word lists**: Lists of curriculum-centered words teachers are required to include in classroom reading and instructional materials.

# Genre Definitions

**action thriller:** A story that incorporates a ticking-clock scenario and violent battle scenes.

**alternate history:** A novel that speculates on historical events.

**amateur detective:** A mystery story solved by someone who is not a detective.

**Arthurian fantasy:** A story that features the legend of King Arthur and the Knights of the Round Table.

**autobiography:** An account of a person's life written by the subject himself.

**Bangsian fantasy:** A novel that speculates on the afterlives of famous people.

**biopunk:** A story that blends noir, Japanese anime, and post-modern elements to create an underground, nihilistic biotech society.

**chick-lit:** Humorous romantic adventures designed for female readers in their 20s and 30s.

**child in peril:** Mystery or horror stories that involve the abduction or abuse of a child.

**children's fantasy:** A fantasy story written specifically for young readers.

**Christian romance:** Romances in which both the hero and heroine are Christians who adhere to Christian ideals.

**classic whodunit:** A story in which a detective solves the crime, with the author presenting numerous clues for the reader.

**comic horror:** Novels that spoof horror conventions or present the horror with elements of dark humor.

**comic mystery/bumbling detective:** A mystery story featuring humor in which the detective is incompetent but somehow manages to solve the crime anyway.

**comic sci-fi/fantasy:** A story that either spoofs the fantasy or science fiction genre or incorporates humorous elements.

**comic thriller:** Either includes comedic elements or spoofs the thriller/suspense genre.

**commercial fiction:** Novels that appeal to a wide audience.

**conspiracy:** A thriller in which the hero or heroine uncovers a conspiracy by a large, powerful group.

**contemporary romance:** A romance with modern characters and true-to-life settings.

**courtroom drama:** A mystery tale that centers on the justice system; usually the hero is a defense attorney who must prove his client's innocence.

**cozy:** A mystery tale that takes place in a small town or home where all the suspects are present and familiar with one another, except the detective, who is usually an outsider.

**creepy kids:** A horror story in which children are controlled by dark forces and turn against adults.

**crime thriller:** A tale that focuses on the commission of a crime, often from the point of view of the perpetrators.

**cyberpunk:** Sci-fi stories that feature tough outsiders in a high-tech, dehumanized future setting.

**dark fantasy:** Fantasy tales that focus on the darker side of magic, incorporating violence and elements of horror or a horror story that incorporates supernatural and fantasy elements.

**dark mystery/noir:** Hardboiled detective stories presented in an urban setting with morally ambiguous characters.

**disaster:** A story that presents natural elements as the antagonist, such as an earthquake or hurricane.

**dystopian:** Fantasy or sci-fi stories that present a bleak future world.

**eco-thriller:** A story in which the hero must battle an ecological catastrophe and the people who created it.

**erotica or romantica:** A romance story that depicts explicit sexual scenes.

**erotic fantasy:** Fantasy tales that focus on sexuality.

**erotic thriller:** A suspense in which sexual aspects are a major part of the story.

**erotic vampire:** Emphasizes the sexuality in a vampire story and includes graphic violence.

**espionage:** A thriller/suspense in which the hero is an international spy.

**espionage mystery:** A story that incorporates elements of the international spy novel but focuses more on the puzzle that must be solved.

**fabulist:** A horror tale where objects, animals, or forces are given human characteristics to deliver a moral message.

**fantasy:** Fiction that features elements of magic, wizardry, and the supernatural.

**forensic:** A thriller or mystery story that features forensic experts and focuses on forensic labs and detailed scientific procedures.

**game-related fantasy:** These are stories based on a specific role-playing game, such as Dungeons and Dragons.

**glitz/glamour:** A romance story that follows elite celebrity-like characters as they live a glamorous life traveling around the world.

**Gothic:** A story that combines elements of horror and romance with medieval props, such as castles, darkness, and decay.

**hard science fiction:** Tales set in the future that incorporate real-life, current-day science.

**hauntings:** A horror tale that focuses on a structure that is possessed by a ghost, demon, or poltergeist.

**heists and capers:** A crime tale that focuses on the planning and execution of a crime, told from the criminal's perspective.

**heroic fantasy:** A tale that focuses on the heroes of fantastical wars.

**high/epic fantasy:** Stories that feature a young hero battling an evil entity to save the fate of an entire race or nation.

**historical:** A novel that takes place in a true-to-life period of history, with emphases on the details of the setting. Sub-genres may include historical thriller, historical horror, and historical romance.

**horror:** A story that evokes fear and/or revulsion using supernatural or psychological elements.

**horror thriller:** A thriller/suspense in which the antagonist is a monster-villain and includes graphic violence.

**how-to:** A book that offers the reader specific instructions, information, and advice to accomplish a goal.

**inverted:** A mystery story in which the reader knows who committed the crime.

**legal thriller:** A tale in which the hero is a lawyer who uses his skills to battle the bad guys.

**locked room:** A mystery tale in which the crime is apparently committed under impossible circumstances.

**magical realism:** A horror story where dark forces or creatures exist in real-life settings.

**medical mystery:** A story that involves a medical threat or illegal use of medical technology.

**medical thriller:** Either a tale in which the hero is in the medical profession and uses his skills to battle the antagonist, or a story that features the illegal or immoral use of medical technology.

**memoir:** An author's commentary on the people and events that influenced a specific phase of his life.

**military science fiction:** Tales of war set in the future that incorporate real-life, current-day military technology.

**military thriller:** A story in which the hero is a member of the military working as part of a specialized force.

**multicultural romance:** A romance centered on non-Caucasian characters,

most often African-American or Hispanic.

**mundane science fiction:** Tales that include only scientific knowledge that is known to actually exist.

**mystery science fiction:** Either a science fiction tale with a central mystery or a classic mystery story with science fiction elements.

**mystery thriller:** A suspense mystery with an international story and lots of action.

**mythic fiction:** Fantasy stories inspired by classic myths, legends, or fairy tales.

**new age (fiction):** A fantasy novel that speculates on occult subjects, such as astrology, psychic phenomena, spiritual healing, UFOs, and mysticism.

**paranormal:** Includes supernatural elements, such as time-travel or characters with psychic abilities.

**police procedural:** A crime thriller or mystery story that focuses on the processes of real-life police procedures and is told from the perspective of the police as they work a case.

**political intrigue:** A thriller in which the hero must ensure the safety of the government.

**post-apocalyptic:** Science fiction tales that focus on the struggle to survive on Earth after an apocalypse.

**private detective:** A mystery in which the crime is solved by a private investigator.

**psychological horror:** A tale based on an insane or psychologically disturbed character that is often a human-monster.

**psychological suspense:** A mystery that focuses on the details of the crime and what motivated the perpetrator to commit the crime.

**psychological thriller:** A suspense that highlights the emotional and mental conflict between the hero and the villain.

**quiet horror:** A story that uses atmosphere and mood to elicit fear and create suspense, rather than graphic description.

**religious horror:** A story that incorporates religious icons and mythology, such as angels and demons.

**religious sci-fi/fantasy:** A science fiction or fantasy novel that centers on theological ideas and heroes who are ruled by religious beliefs.

**romance:** Novels that feature love stories.

**romance sci-fi:** A science fiction story in which romance is central to the plot.

**romantic comedy:** A romance focused on humor.

**romantic mystery:** A mystery tale in which the crime-solvers are romantically involved.

**romantic suspense:** A romance tale that includes a heroine who may have to solve a crime or mystery.

**romantic thriller:** A suspense in which the protagonists are romantically involved.

**science fantasy:** A fantasy story in which the fantastical elements are supported by scientific explanations.

**science fiction:** Novels that incorporate elements of science or pseudo-science.

**science fiction/fantasy:** A designation used by booksellers to collapse two separate genres into one for marketing purposes.

**science-fiction horror:** A tale that deals with alien invasions, mad scientists, or out-of-control experiments.

**sensual:** A romance story based on the sensual tension between the hero and heroine.

**social science fiction:** Stories that focus on how characters react to their environments.

**soft science fiction:** Stories based on softer sciences such as psychology, sociology, and anthropology.

**space opera:** A science fiction tale with traditional heroes and villains, and plenty of action scenes.

**spicy:** A romance that involves a married couple.

**splatter/splatterpunk:** A horror novel that presents extremely explicit scenes and gruesome violence.

**spy-fi:** Espionage stories with science fiction elements, such as high-tech gadgets.

**steampunk:** A sci-fi/fantasy tale that presents an alternate history in which characters in Victorian England have access to 20th century technology.

**superheroes:** Fantasy or science fiction tale featuring characters with superhuman abilities.

**supernatural menace:** A horror story featuring supernatural elements, such as ghosts, demons, vampires, and werewolves, which cause mayhem.

**supernatural thriller:** A suspense in which the hero or the antagonist (or both) have supernatural powers.

**suspense:** Novels that use elements of suspense to solve a crime or unravel a mystery.

**sweet:** A romance with a heroine who is a virgin.

**sword and sorcery:** A classic fantasy tale set in medieval period that incorporates wizardry.

**technological thriller:** A suspense in which out-of-control technology is central to the plot.

**technology horror:** A horror tale that features technology out of control.

**technothriller:** A thriller mystery that emphasizes high technology.

**thriller:** A novel that uses suspense to tell the story and incorporates a plot structure that focuses gamesmanship and centers on hunt-and-chase scenes.

**thriller science fiction:** A sci-fi novel that incorporates elements of a classic thriller story.

**time-travel:** Science fiction tales based on the concept of moving backward or forward through time and into parallel worlds.

**urban fantasy:** A story in which characters with magical powers appear in a normal modern setting (similar to magical realism.)

**vampire fantasy:** A fantasy novel that incorporates the classic vampire story, focusing on sexuality and romantic liaisons, without the horror elements.

**weird tales:** A horror tale that features strange and uncanny events.

**western:** a story set in the North American, South American, or Australian West.

**woman in jeopardy:** A mystery story in which the heroine is placed in peril by a crime and struggles to triumph over the perpetrator.

**wuxia:** Fantasy stories that incorporate martial arts and Chinese philosophies.

**young adult:** Books written specifically for teenagers, ages 12 to 17, with heroes the same age as the readers.

**young adult horror:** Horror stories that are written specifically for teenagers; they include heroes who are young adults and are less violent than traditional horror tales.

**young adult mystery:** Mystery stories that are written specifically for teenagers; they include a young adult hero detective who pursues criminals who are usually less violent than those in adult mystery novels.

**young adult romance:** A romance written specifically for teenagers; they include a hero and heroine who are young adults and contain very little sexual content.

**zombie:** Horror tales featuring dead people who come "alive" and torment the living.

# Bibliography

Barton, Stephanie. "7 most overlooked tax deductions." MSNBC. January 1, 2010. (**www.msnbc.msn.com/id/34961179/ns/business-personal_finance/t/most-overlooked-tax-deductions**)

Brewer, Robert Lee. *2010 Writer's Market.* Cincinnati, Ohio: Writer's Digest, 2010.

Crenshaw, Albert B. "Higher-Income Benefits Fade." *Washington Post.* February 26, 2006. (**www.washingtonpost.com/wp-dyn/content/article/2006/02/25/AR2006022500249.html**)

Delafuente, Charles. "Selling on eBay? Keep Eye on Gains." *New York Times.* February 10, 2008. (**www.nytimes.com/2008/02/10/business/yourtaxes/10ebay.html**)

Dun & Bradstreet. "Determining Whether to Use Cash or Accrual Accounting." (**http://smallbusiness.dnb.com/company-activities-management/financial-performance/12313771-1.html**)

Eckstut, Arielle, and David Sterry. *Putting Your Passion into Print.* New York: Workman Pub, 2005.

Fawkner, Elena. *Taxation 101: Hobby or Business?* AHBBO, 2001. (**www.ahbbo.com/hobbybusiness.html**)

Fleenor, Patrick. *Fixing the Alternative Minimum Tax: AMT Reform Requires Changes to Regular Tax Code. Special Report No. 155.* Tax Foundation. May 17, 2007. (**www.taxfoundation.org/news/show/22400.html**)

_____. *PEP and Pease: Repealed for 2010 But Preparing a Comeback.* *Special Report No. 178.* Tax Foundation. April 29, 2010. (**www.taxfoundation. org/publications/show/26260.html**)

Hamilton, April. *The Indie Author Guide: Self-Publishing Strategies Anyone Can Use.* Cincinnati, Ohio: Writer's Digest Books, 2010.

Holden, Greg. *Main Street Fairness Act May Be Taxing for Online Merchants.* AuctionBytes.com. April 28, 2009. (**www.auctionbytes.com/cab/abn/y09/m04/i28/s00**)

"If You Are Self-Employed." SSA Publication No. 05-10022, January 2011, ICN 454900. (**www.ssa.gov/pubs/10022.html**)

Internet Sales Tax Fairness. New Rules Project (**www.newrules.org/retail/rules/internet-sales-tax-fairness**)

Jopson, Barney. "Online sales tax battle looms in US." *Financial Times.* FT.com. June 12, 2011. (**www.ft.com/intl/cms/s/0/2e2cd154-9526-11e0-a648-00144feab49a.html#axzz1PM6HJ26A**)

Kopytoff, Verne G.. "Amazon Pressured on Sales Tax." *The New York Times.* March 13, 2011. (**www.nytimes.com/2011/03/14/technology/14amazon. html**)

Lupton, Ellen. *Indie Publishing: How to Design and Produce Your Own Book.* New York: Princeton Architectural Press, 2008.

Martin, Sharlene, and Anthony Flacco. *Publish Your Nonfiction Book: Strategies for Learning the Industry, Selling Your Book, and Building a Successful Career.* Cincinnati, Ohio: Writer's Digest Books, 2009.

Metz, Rachel. "EBay 4Q revenue rises, helped by holiday shoppers." Physorg. com. January 19, 2011. (**www.physorg.com/news/2011-01-ebay-4q-revenue-holiday-shoppers.html**)

Murray, Jean. "Can My Business Deduct Charitable Contributions?" About.com. (**http://biztaxlaw.about.com/od/businesstaxdeduction1/f/charitydeducts.htm**)

Poynter, Dan, and Dan Poynter. *Dan Poynter's Self-Publishing Manual: How to Write, Print and Sell Your Own Book.* Santa Barbara, Calif: Para Pub, 2007.

*Sales Tax on the Internet.* Nolo.com. (**www.nolo.com/legal-encyclopedia/sales-tax-internet-29919.html**)

"Self Publishing Platforms Compared – Kindle Direct Publishing, Smashwords, Lulu, BookTango, eBookIT!, BookBaby, Vook, PressBooks." BWM Books. (**www.bwmbooks.com/self-publishing-platforms-compared-kindle-direct-publishing-smashwords-lulu-booktango-ebookit-bookbaby-vook-pressbooks**)

Smith, Craig. "How Many People Uses 370 of the Top Social Media, Apps & Tools?" January 8, 2014. (**http://expandedramblings.com/index.php/resource-how-many-people-use-the-top-social-media**)

Springer, Steven E. "Do You Have to Pay Sales Tax on Internet Purchases?" Findlaw.com. (**http://smallbusiness.findlaw.com/business-operations/internet/internet-taxes.html**)

Sullivan, Robin. "The New Midlist: Self-published E-book Authors Who Earn a Living." Publishing Perspectives. June 27, 2011. (**http://publishingperspectives.com/2011/06/self-published-ebook-authors-earn-living**)

Tax Laws and Issues — E-Business & E-Commerce. Internal Revenue Service. (**www.irs.gov/businesses/small/industries/article/0,,id=209348,00.html**)

"Frequently asked questions regarding e-books and U.S. libraries." Transforming Libraries. October13, 2013. (**http://www.ala.org/transforminglibraries/frequently-asked-questions-e-books-us-libraries**)

Watson, Rick. "6 Things I Learned at the Amazon Annual Shareholder Meeting." Rick Watson's Blog, 2010. (**http://rickwatson.tumblr.com/2010-amazon-annual-shareholder-meeting**)

What Is The Difference Between Earned, Portfolio, And Passive Income? (**www.taxbraix.com/tax-articles/difference-between-earned-portfolio-passive-income.html**)

# Author Biography

✳

Martha Maeda is a freelancer, ghostwriter, and author of more than 20 books including *The Complete Guide to Green Building and Remodeling Your Home, Basic Guide to Investing in ETFs, How to Wipe Out Student Loans, How to Solar Power Your Home, How to Open & Operate a Financially Successful Independent Record Label,* and *101 Sunday School Activities on a Tiny Budget.* She is passionate about helping people who might not otherwise become authors to self-publish their work and discover their writing potential. She currently lives with her family in Orlando, Florida.

# Index

## A

advance  153
Advance Book Information (ABI)  185
Albatross Books  22
Amazon Advantage  182
American Publishers Association  27
Association
  of Author's Representatives  125
  Publishers for Special Sales  177
audiobooks  42, 152, 244
author
  platform  89, 132, 205
  -agent agreement  136
Author Central  214
Author's Guild  85

## B

back matter  315
Bantam Books  22
beta readers  72, 92, 315
"Big Five"  27, 28, 30, 34, 284
  Hachette Book Group (HBG)  28
  HarperCollins  28
  Macmillan  28
  Penguin Random House  29, 32
  Simon & Schuster  22, 29, 174
Bing  265
"boilerplate"  147
book
  back matter  200

cover  200
front matter  199
pricing
  bottom-up method  180
  top-down method  180
proposal  105
signings  53, 58, 91, 206, 226
templates  196
trailers  222
Books in Print  70, 185, 231, 265, 287
Bowker
  Identifier Services  180
  Link  184
  U.S. ISBN Agency  180
Bowker's Books  35, 70, 85
business
  expense  268
  or hobby
    3/5 year test  262
  buyback rate  148, 315

## C

Cataloging in Publication (CIP)  184
cell phone novels  280
chapbook  315
concordance  200, 315
copyright
  law  253
  registration  254
Createspace  174, 291

creative nonfiction 66
  adventure 67
  biography 67
  history 66
  memoir 68
  travelogues 67
  true crime 68
critique partner 73, 316

**D**
designing your book 106, 191
desktop publishing 20, 39, 191, 196, 316
developmental editor 75
digital
  books 45, 165
  printing 173, 176
dime novels 21
division 27, 316
do's and don'ts 104, 117, 134, 163, 190, 204, 212, 239, 260
dummy book 116
dump 316

**E**
e-book 15, 19, 25, 36, 45, 46, 122, 156, 167, 170, 173, 233, 241-248, 250
  readers 25
    Androids 241
    iPad 15, 241
    iPhones 15, 244
    Kindle 15, 42, 45, 241-244, 246-249, 252
    Kobo 242, 245
    Nook 42, 241
Editorial Freelancers Association 75
educational publishers 43
e-publishers 42

**F**
fact check 76, 77
"first right of refusal" 158
folio 20, 316
Frankfurt Book Fair 19

**G**
galley 96, 228, 316

genre 57, 319
  fiction
    action–adventure 61
    historical 59
    horror 59, 63, 283, 319, 321, 325
    mystery/crime 60, 63
    religious/inspirational 61, 63
    romance 59, 63, 70, 71, 73, 126, 284, 294, 319, 320, 323, 325
    science fiction/fantasy 60, 63
    thriller/suspense 60, 63
    westerns 61
    women's fiction 62, 63
    young adult 62, 63, 325
ghostwriter 44, 71, 80-82, 98, 331
Google+ 209, 293
graphic novel 316
gross sales 316
Gutenberg, Johannes 19
gutter 316

**H**
hand selling 316
hardcover book 23
home office deductions 272
"hook" 71, 99, 140, 202-203, 231, 235
hornbook 316

**I**
imagesetting 20, 316
imposition 20, 316
imprint 26-28, 180, 229, 244, 246, 316-317
Independent
  Book Publishers Association 177, 186, 189, 283, 291
indie
  authorship 251-252
  book (independent book) industry 175
International Standard Book Number (ISBN) 180
ISBN 35, 46, 70, 95, 107, 149, 168, 173, 180-183, 190, 199, 204, 230-231, 237, 245-247, 302, 304, 316

**K**

keyman clause 138

**L**

leading 317
Library of Congress Control Number 95, 168, 183
Lightning Source 169, 174
LinkedIn 210, 214, 234, 293
line 27, 317
   editors 75
linotype 20
literary
   agents 27, 51, 86, 99-100, , 121, 125, 126-128, 131-132, 290, 310
   fiction 58
   Market Place (LMP) 177, 191, 292
Little, Brown and Company 28
Lulu 168, 174, 191, 245, 291, 329

**M**

mainstream fiction 59
manga 281, 317
manuscript submission tracking 131
mass-market paperback 23
megapublisher 279, 317
Mergenthaler, Ottmar 20
modern publishing industry 19

**N**

narrative nonfiction 66
NetLibrary 24
net sales 317
noncompete clause 160, 317
nonfiction genres
   cooking and food 64
   how-to 64
   humor 66
   inspirational/religious/spiritual/meta-physical 65
   medical and science 66
   reference 64
   self-help 64
   travel guides 64

**O**

octavo 20, 317
offset printing 173, 176, 317
online booksellers
   Alibris 24
   Amazon.com 24, 42, 45, 53, 57, 85-86, 107, 173-174, 185, 189, 203, 214, 232-233, 236, 247, 305
   Barnes & Noble 42, 85, 107, 174, 227, 229, 241, 243, 305
   Powells.com 185
online submission trackers
   Duotrope's Digest 131
   Luminary 131
   QueryTracker 131
   Writer's Market 132
option clause 159

**P**

paperback business 21
Patterson, James 25
Penguin Random House 29, 32
phototypesetting 20
Pickering, William 20
pitch
   letter 141
   package 130-132
   paragraph 130
plagiarism 257
Pocket Books 22, 29
PrimoPDF 285
print-on-demand (POD) 24, 44, 317
promote your book 47, 108, 133, 206, 225-227, 234, 239
   Amazon Advantage 232
   author website 216
   blog 77, 103, 108, 128, 168, 207, 210-215, 219, 221, 227, 230, 234, 242, 246
   book reviews 227
   book signings 231, 237, 238
   book tour 238
   business cards 236
   directory listings 230
   media portfolio 226

paid advertising 236
press kit/releases 231-232
radio/television interviews 234
social networking 14, 208-09, 234
testimonials 95, 204, 232
proofreader 75
public domain 258
Weekly 35, 125, 237, 290
publishing contract 147
pulp fiction 318

**Q**
Quality Books 184
quarto 20, 318
query letters 85, 87-88, 92, 97-98, 104,
    119, 125-126, 130-132, 134-135,
    213, 226, 227

**R**
recto 20, 318
rejection letter 94
remaindering 318
RFQs (Request for Quotes) 177
rights
    audiobook 121, 156
    book club 124
    electronic 121, 156, 307
    exclusive 149
    film 121, 124, 138, 155
    foreign/ international 121, 124, 156
    merchandising 156
    performance 156
    reprint 155
    serial 124, 156
    television 124
    translation 121, 124, 138
romance
    novels 59
    Writers of America 59

**S**
seasonal publishing 55
self-employment tax 273
self-publishing 45, 165
signature 20, 318
"slush pile" 114

Standard Address Number (SAN) 184
storyboard 115-116, 318
submission trackers 131
subsidiary rights 121-122, 124, 137-138,
    146, 149, 155, 157
substantive editing 95
surge title 44, 318

**T**
tie-in 318
trade
    books 40
    paperback 23
traditional publishing 83
trim size 178

**U**
unagented books/manuscripts 41, 122,
    318
unit break 318
university presses 34

**V**
vanity
    presses 46
    publishers 46
verso 20, 318

**W**
work for hire 152
Writer
    Beware 48
writer's
    conference 129
    Digest 86
    Journal 80
    Market 27, 86